LAST COPY

ns should be returned on or before the last date
own below. Items not already requested by other
rowers may be renewed in person, in writing or by
ephone. To renew, please quote the number on the
rcode label. To renew online a PIN is required.
is can be requested at your local library.
new online @ **www.dublincitypubliclibra**
es charged for overdue items will include postage
urred in recovery. Damage to or loss c'
charged to the borrower.

eabharlanna Poiblí Cha⁺'
    Dublin City P'
    Leabharlar

aile,'
ub'

THE SHARED ORIGINS OF FOOTBALL, RUGBY, AND SOCCER

THE SHARED ORIGINS OF FOOTBALL, RUGBY, AND SOCCER

Christopher Rowley

ROWMAN & LITTLEFIELD
Lanham • Boulder • New York • London

Published by Rowman & Littlefield
A wholly owned subsidiary of The Rowman & Littlefield Publishing Group, Inc.
4501 Forbes Boulevard, Suite 200, Lanham, Maryland 20706
www.rowman.com

Unit A, Whitacre Mews, 26-34 Stannary Street, London SE11 4AB

British Library Cataloguing in Publication Information Available

Library of Congress Cataloging-in-Publication Data

Rowley, Christopher, 1948–
The shared origins of football, rugby, and soccer / Christopher Rowley.
pages cm
Includes bibliographical references and index.
ISBN 978-1-4422-4618-8 (hardcover : alk. paper) — ISBN 978-1-4422-4619-5 (ebook)
1. Ball games—History. 2. Sports—History. 3. Football. 4. Rugby football. 5. Soccer. I. Title.
GV861.R68 2015
796.309—dc23
2015011569

Printed in the United States of America

CONTENTS

ACKNOWLEDGMENTS

Much thanks must go to my wife, Anitra, and my friend Kevin Bales for their support and advice during the research and preparation of this book. The road was long and winding, but they provided vital encouragement and assistance.

INTRODUCTION

Football is a thing of passion. Anyone who's played any of the seven varieties of "football" and enjoyed it knows this. The ball—it may be round, it may be an ellipse—comes to you. It may have slid across the turf to your feet, or been thrown by a quarterback into your grasp, or been tossed back to you by the scrum half, and now it's yours for a few moments to do something with. And with it comes both opportunity—which lights a fire in your head because you have the ball—and responsibility, a crushing weight—I have the ball, don't lose it, don't drop it, don't mess up! And you proceed to dribble, pass, or get tackled and hurled to the turf, or maybe, once in a while, you break that tackle, you dribble past that central defender, you break right through their secondary, and hey, you even score! At the amateur level, that's the great reward, that's why you're out there on the field, despite the freezing wind and rain or the broiling sun, and if you're good enough, well then maybe you had a professional career, with its wide array of payoffs and rewards. But even the greatest players in any of the seven codes still dream of scoring, connecting, finding the perfect pass, making that great run, running onto that cross, and jumping high and redirecting it with your forehead past an anguished goalkeeper and into the net.

Apologies to goalkeepers, but then, you people know that you're different.

Football is possessively claimed by its code-keepers, the faithful fans of one or another of the codes. Our "football" is the true football, they all say. And for them, it is, but from a historical perspective, well, it gets much more complicated.

Today, there are the seven codes—in alphabetical order—American football, association football, Australian rules football, Canadian football, Gaelic football, rugby league football, and rugby union football. They can be grouped in various ways. One grouping, which we might call the Cladistic Set, places association football on one side, alone. In the middle lies Gaelic and Australian rules football. On the other side is the rugby group, which includes the American and Canadian games. Another more traditional way of grouping them is by the old ballhandling or nonhandling standard, where association football stands alone on one side of the divide and the remaining codes are situated on the other. Or you might group them by global spread, where again association football is by itself and the others are parceled out on different paths, from the most widely played, rugby union, to the most spectacular and heavily televised, American, to the lesser known, for example, Gaelic.

No matter which grouping is used, a basic fact remains: They are all descended from a common ancestor. The seven codes are a kind of demonstration of the power of evolution. Their remote ancestry, almost lost in the mists of time, involves developments in earlier civilizations that we barely know of or really understand. From fragmentary evidence we can put together a concept, a picture of how things came to be and progressed. We can see the beginnings of the intermediate species, followed by confusion, experiments, and bizarre outliers. And then we see the gradually solidifying central ancestor, which persisted despite outlandish threats to its existence. Quite suddenly, it began to speciate and spread throughout the continents to produce the flourishing world of football we know and love today.

It's a fascinating odyssey and one that I've enjoyed investigating and recording. This book is the result of an outlandish enthusiasm, an obsessive interest (according to my wife), and a lifetime of reading history from various epochs and areas of the world. It is not an academic work, but I think the speculations and conclusions can withstand close scrutiny. I do not attempt to give fully detailed accounts of what has occurred in each of the seven codes in recent times; doing so would require seven (or more) volumes. But after reading this book, the reader will have an understanding of where his or her favorite code or codes of football came from, how they arose and developed, and what elements they have retained from the common ancestor. I hope that this understanding helps fans enjoy their particular code even more than they currently do, and if they should, by accident (or design), come upon another code—say Australian rules, or rugby league, or Canadian football—being shown on a peripheral television channel, perhaps they might pause, study the game before them, and see the commonalities, the basics that these games share and have taken from the ancestral game of football.

I

ANCIENT GAMES

The first thought we need to grasp and keep hold of, for the purposes of this book, is that "football" is a concept that applies to a variety of sports, and today a family of different codes embody this concept, all with the word *football* somewhere in the mix—American football, Australian rules football, rugby football, Gaelic football, Canadian football, and, of course, the biggy, association football.

Association football, called "soccer" in the United States, can lay claim to being one of humanity's most widely practiced activities, commonplace on every continent, played by kids from Los Angeles to Buenos Aires, Capetown to Moscow, Hokkaido to Melbourne, and, in fact, just about everywhere. In one form or another, "football" is everywhere, on television screens in every town and the Internet throughout the world. It whips up fan frenzy and draws huge crowds to stadiums as diverse as the Bombonera in Buenos Aires, where the Boca Juniors play; Owen Field, aka the Gaylord Family Oklahoma Memorial Stadium in Norman, Oklahoma; and Patersons Stadium, in Perth, Western Australia, where both Fremantle and West Coast play football and Western Australia plays cricket.

"Football" is also about identity and fierce rivalries with other clubs, states, universities, and even countries. One of the longest-running, fiercest football rivalries in the United States is the one between the Ohio State Buckeyes and Michigan Wolverines. In Spanish football, no rivalry can match that between Sevilla in red and Real Betis in green— for the pride of Andalusia! But these characteristics are present in every football league and competition, whether it's a visit by the Roughriders to Investor's Group Field in Winnipeg for a game with the hated Blue Bombers or the Washington Redskins playing at Giants Stadium in New Jersey. Then there are those occasions when Wales plays England for the Six Nations crown in rugby or the Australian Wallabies play the New Zealand All Blacks in the same sport. When national teams take the field, identity on a different scale takes hold, as Americans discovered in the summer of 2014, when the U.S. Men's National Team played its heart out in the FIFA World Cup in Brazil. When Welsh football teams take the field, especially Wales' rugby side, to play England, ancient wrongs can be righted, lost battles almost a thousand years old won again, and ancient foes defeated. But, as we will see, ferocious rivalries have been a major part of "football" for quite some time, more than 1,000 years in some cases.

To understand how the concept of football arose and survived, we have to turn back the clock—way back. We can also see the odd road "football" traveled, to emerge from the mists and the fields and forests to become what it is today. It appears that football's continued existence in our own era is really something of a miracle. So many things could have intervened along the way to put an end to it. Indeed, other great games that persisted in various cultures for thousands of years faded away to almost nothing for one reason or another, but not football, which survived efforts to stamp it out to flourish in modern times in ways its ancestors would have found unimaginable.

To open this discussion, let's check in at 200 BC and take a look at three different games played in widely separated parts of the world during that time. These games, in one way or another, exhibited aspects of what makes football so attractive to so many people in modern times, namely the passion, skill, and physicality of the contests.

Please note that this book concentrates on the tale of football, while moving swiftly through the centuries, looking at various cultures at a glance. There are many references to the history of different places and times, and behind everything mentioned lies a wealth of detail that simply cannot be included here.

First we will drop in on a Pre-Classic Mayan site. Remember, this is 200 years before the birth of Jesus of Nazareth. We are in the present-day borderlands between the Mexican state of Chiapas and Guatemala. This is hilly terrain and an area filled with early Mayan towns and city-states. The agricultural basis for this culture is corn (maize) combined with squash, beans, and chili peppers. The culture has long since developed writing, a calendar, and a complex religion; however, this civilization remains in the Stone Age and, in fact, will not begin to exhibit examples of copper and copper-alloyed artifacts until the thirteenth century AD, during the later "Post-Classic" period. Instead of bronze, this civilization uses obsidian for sharp edges.

The culture is, however, wise to chemistry. They boil their corn with lime to release the niacin content, a vital B vitamin. Without it, people dependent on corn develop pellagra. They call this prepared corn "nixtamal" and grind the resulting porridge into unleavened dough, from which they roll out tamales and tortillas.

They also produce a variety of potent brews from native plants. Beer from fermented maize and agave is most likely the primary option. Another is a mead-like brew using honey and the bark of the blanche tree. But there are also hallucinogenic mushrooms like the xibalhaj okox, or "underworld mushroom," or the kaizalah okox, the "lost judgement mushroom." These items are likely kept for special occasions, for efforts to communicate with the gods or read the signs of the spirits.

They are also fairly sophisticated in their consumption of foods. Painted pottery vessels from the much later Mayan Classic Era show men taking enemas in ritual settings. The direct introduction of their powerful brews into the colon worked to speed the absorption of alcohol and anything else mixed in with it.

Thus, the culture had chips and all kinds of brew, so the only thing missing from the trinity of modern-day football-viewing heaven is the game. And as we will see, they certainly had a great game to play and watch.

The general culture of Mesoamerica—from Mexico to Honduras—originated with a people called the Olmecs, a name given to them by the much later Aztecs. The Olmec cultural sites, for example, La Venta, are on the coast of the Gulf of Mexico, in the southern states of Vera Cruz and Tabasco. The culture appears to have begun as early as 1500 BC and was well developed by 1200 BC. It lingered in the Olmec territory until about 100 BC.

By the time of our visit—to a site two hundred miles to the southeast—this culture, with unique contributions from the Mayan people, is shading into the "Classic" Mayan format. We enter a small city with pyramidal temples built from limestone and plaster, and arranged around a central plaza. Religion has a strong presence, as does art. Frescoes decorate the walls, and carvings are everywhere. Pottery in bright colors, with new shapes and forms, is standard. And behind the temples stands a ball court.

This is where the great game, variously called *ollama* by the Aztecs or *pizt* in the Mayan languages, is played. There are ball courts everywhere in the Mayan world, and about 1,300 have been identified throughout the region, with more than 500 in Guatemala alone.

The earliest ball courts were rectangles with earthen walls, but in time, stone walls superseded walls made from raw materials. Early courts were open ended, but the side walls were built with a slope to them. This also varied from place to place and era to era, suggesting that this game was likely a family of games, with changing tastes and styles throughout the centuries. The standard ball court had sloping walls, a narrow central aisle, and backcourts at either end, with stone walls, giving the playing area the shape of the capital letter "I." During this era, early in the Mayan culture, there were flat stone markers, arranged vertically on the top of the side walls, or in other cases, round, flat markers, inlaid at either end of the court. It is thought that the walls were painted bright colors, possibly with a symbolic significance.

It is not precisely known how the games were scored, and there may have been multiple systems, but crucial to all of them was the ball. The balls were made from rubber, which seems to have been an early discovery by the Olmecs, who found that a material with lots of bounce could be made by adding the juice of crushed morning glory vines to the raw latex sap of the rubber tree. As previously noted, this culture was wise to chemistry in many different ways.

It appears that the Mesoamerican ball game soon took advantage of this wonderful stuff. By our period, more than 1,000 years later, and indeed perhaps two thousand years after the discovery of rubber, the main game was played with a solid rubber ball about nine inches wide and weighing nine pounds.

The game being contested in the Mayan world, as we mingle with the crowd, is being played by teams of seven men to a side. They are wearing hip girdles made of wood and tapir hide, with pads on one knee and one upper arm. They can only touch the ball with their hips and elbows. Points are scored by driving the ball into one of the flat markers. In a later era, hundreds of years from this point, the flat markers will be replaced with stone rings, and the aim will be to get the ball through the ring.

The ball court is approximately 200 feet long, with a central playing area about 35 feet wide. There are steep, sloping stone walls, and these walls do more than keep the ball in play, as it picks up speed and momentum as it bounces off them. It is really moving now, and a player, wearing an elaborate costume of feathers, jaguar skin, and other items of decoration, leaps high to connect his hip with the ball, only to deflect it, sending it against the wall and caroming back. Another player goes low, dropping to one knee to get under the ball as it falls toward the ground and sending it high into the air. We can see that getting hit full on by this ball at top speed could knock a player off his feet or even cause fatal injury.

The players must avoid touching the ball with their feet, which would give a point or "goal" to the other team. As such, we can see that this is not "football" and, indeed, will never lead to modern football.

Players, their feathered headdresses making them seem like giant birds, leap, turn, pivot, and knock one another aside as they attempt to control the ball and drive it against one of the three markers on either side of the court.

The crowd is rapt, for several reasons. First, the game was a vital part of Mayan religious life. In a world where spirits inhabited everything, the gods ruled from the sky, and demon-lords inhabited the underworld, religious practices were a constant feature of daily life. The ball court was seen as a stage, lying between the mundane world of men and the realm of the gods. The players were astride the line, half in our world, half in that of the gods, and just as humans were watching from above the court, so they knew, the gods were watching from their side, invisible, beyond the court.

Of course, we know there were more casual games, and children and even women could play in those. But in serious games like this, only men took to the court. It is thought that these games were often organized by great nobles who might have even put on a hip girdle and participated themselves. There was a lot of gambling on the result, and the winning team seized the costumes of the defeated one. A great deal of prestige and money was on the line.

In addition, there were special games with predetermined outcomes, in which captives taken prisoner in battle would play, and lose, and their captain, preferably a noble chieftain, was decapitated. His skull was sometimes used as the core of a rubber ball. Such games were special, but this was a culture of competing city-states, and like other cultures of that form, there was much warfare. In addition, the culture retained an aspect of human sacrifice to the terrifying gods, something that lingered on to the very end.

The rules used by the Aztecs were recorded by the Spanish after the conquest. In that era, seventeen centuries ahead of the time we are visiting, a perfect apocalypse struck the region. The scourge of pestilence—lead by smallpox, with measles and influenza as accomplices, annihilated the native populations, killing, by some estimates, 9 out of 10 inhabitants.

Then the Christian fathers, who regarded Mesoamerican beliefs as anathema, turned to stamping out the ball game, because, as they discovered, its deep roots can be found in Mesoamerican myth and religion.

The great stone courts fell silent and became covered with weeds, just as the overgrowth encased the temples and frescoes. The Spanish herded the native peoples into new villages and subjected them to hard labor. Oppression, rebellion, and savage retribution were the flavors of the Mesoamerican world in the centuries following the conquest. The great ball games vanished, although a faint echo remained, because in Sinaloa, in northwestern Mexico, the game, now called *ullama*, was still being played, although not on a stone court but a "taste" outlined on the ground. The rules were much like those of the Aztec and Mayan game, and games were played with a big rubber ball that could only be touched with the hips.

However, when Mexicans, Guatemalans, Hondurans, and everyone else heads to a stadium these days, they go to watch soccer, a game from another tradition on another continent.

✵ ✵ ✵

We now move west, across the vast Pacific to China, at the beginning of the Han dynasty (206 BC–200 AD). This was a crucial moment for the world's largest single group of people. China had been unified by the fierce "First Emperor," Qin Shihuangdi, who, through warfare, had ended the chaotic period of the "warring states," which had spanned three centuries, and welded the former feudal states together into an empire, with Qin as the undisputed ruler. A centralized administration was created, and more than 120,000 members of the former feudal nobility had been forcibly relocated to palaces in the emperor's capital city, Xianyang.

The First Emperor's successor soon lost his title, and a provincial administrator named Liu Bang arose from a complex rebellion to become Emperor Gaozu of Han. Through frugality, clever diplomacy with the nomad Xiongnu (Huns), and a careful policy of replacing feudal rulers with his own relatives, Gaozu solidified the empire and set a dynasty to rule. The dynasty would govern for more than four hundred years and establish a pattern that would repeat, dynasty after dynasty, for the next two thousand years.

As we enter a parade ground at the rear of a military barracks in the capital city Chang'an, a game is underway. Two teams of six players are battling for control of a large ball, which can only be kicked. The field of play is a yard perhaps 50 meters long and half that wide, with small goals at either end. The ball has to be kept off the ground and is passed from player to player. Players exhibit great skill in fielding the passes and keeping the ball bouncing from foot to foot, before a shot can be attempted at the goals.

This is the game of *cuju*, or *t'su shu*. By 200 BC, it was already centuries and maybe even thousands of years old. Unlike the great ball game of the Maya, it was a lot like a kind of "football," somewhere on the soccer end of the spectrum.

This game was played with a ball, about the size of a number-four soccer ball, but it was stuffed with feathers and hair. It had many qualities of a "futsal" ball, allowing for good control, while lacking the bounce of an air-filled ball.

Rubber, by the way, does not seem to have been part of Chinese culture, which is slightly surprising given that China produced so many useful inventions, from the horse collar to paper, to block printing, to tofu. It's a long list. But during those times, rubber trees only existed in Central and South America, and Chinese traders do not appear to have crossed the Pacific Ocean.

In the teachings of scholar Liu Xin, who lived quite a few years after the time of our visit, between 50 BC and 23 AD, the game was referred to as *taju bingshi*—"football game for the power of soldiers"—and was part of exercises deemed useful for strengthening troops in body and mind. During this time, evidence suggests the teams were six to a side, which would fit with the size of the playing area and the physical properties of a feather-stuffed ball cased in leather.

Later, in the Tang dynasty (618–907 AD), balls filled with air, most likely made from an inflated pig's bladder, produced another style of play. In this version, teams were separated by the goal structure, which consisted of two poles 30 feet apart, connected by a pair of parallel beams. In the center, an "eye" was created about 10 feet off the ground with shaped bamboo. This structure was about four feet wide and two to three feet high. The object of the game was to keep the air-filled ball bouncing from foot to foot, never touching the ground, and attempt to kick it through the eye to score a goal. Shots that went wide went to the other team. It is thought that if one team lost control and the ball hit the ground, possession was given to the other team. This seems more like beach soccer volleyball than the true association game of football.

Later still, although it may have been played all along, was a version called *bai da*, which had more of an individual flavor. Rather like hackey sack or "keepie uppies," players formed a circle and endeavored to keep the ball in the air. The player who let it fall to the ground lost points.

Late Han period poet Li Yu wrote the following elegant verse in about 100 AD, to be inscribed on the goalposts of the game in his own era:

> Round ball, a square goal
> Suggest the shape of Yin and Yang
> The ball is like the full moon
> And the two teams stand opposed.

The following is part of a larger verse, one of the surviving 85 inscriptions titled "Jucheng ming," or "inscription on the ball wall":

> The ball is round, the ball-wall rectangular,
> Symbolic of Yin and Yang
> Let the twelve moons (months) guide the number of players,
> and they lay siege to one another.
> With six a side, the teams are balanced.

Referee and assistant are appointed.
Their interpretation of the rules must be constant
Without prejudice towards the team members
There shall be no favoritism nor high-handedness
With an honest heart and balanced thoughts.
No one can find fault with wrong decisions.
If the game (football) is regulated correctly like this,
How much this must mean for daily life.

After the collapse of the Han dynasty in 220 AD, the Chinese empire was torn into three feuding countries, and for the next four hundred years, conflicts between states, warlords, and bandits was ever present. On occasion, large areas descended into chaos, while at other times, "minor" imperial dynasties managed to fuse sections together. Many aspects of the universal culture established by the Han dynasty disappeared almost completely. For example, populist "folk" Taoism replaced the "Confucianism" that had provided the philosophical structure for the Han hierarchies. Kong-Zi, westernized to "Confucius," had produced his major work long before, roughly coeval with the Buddha Gautama, circa 500 BC.

Cuju, however, persisted, to become very popular in the Tang dynasty, although the game had changed, possibly as a result of the development of the air-filled ball.

The capital of the Tang dynasty, Chang'an, was not only the largest city in the world at this time, but it also featured many *cuju* pitches or ball courts. Soldiers formed *cuju* teams. Women's teams improved; a record, perhaps legendary, tells of a 17-year-old girl who defeated a team of soldiers with her skill. The great game continued into the Song dynasty (960–1279 AD), where it seems to have reached the height of its popularity, with professional players and teams, as well as a league for large cities. The league, called Qi Yun She, even organized national championships.

It is thought that *cuju* survived the Mongols, who invaded and crushed the Song emperors in a long, tragic war, but during the Ming dynasty, which ran from 1366 to 1644 AD, the game declined in popularity and slowly faded away.

Why this happened is difficult to piece together from the available evidence. The Ming dynasty began with a rebellion overturning a century of Mongol rule and consciously strove to revive ancient Chinese traditions. The ball game should have benefited and may have done so. We do have a painting of court ladies kicking a ball around dating from the Ming period.

The Ming dynasty was the last ethnically Chinese dynasty, and the Ming emperors pursued highly autocratic policies intended to end the perennial succession struggles that had riven the previous dynasties. Needless to say, succession struggles continued, as did endless conflict between the eunuchs, state officials, nobility, and families regarding mighty wives and concubines.

Under the Ming, beginning in 1405 AD, great fleets commanded by a remarkable eunuch general named Zheng He visited what is now Indonesia and later crossed the Indian Ocean to Africa, returning with the first giraffe ever seen by the Chinese. One of these fleets, 63 ships strong and carrying 27,870 men, embodied the power of China and was far beyond the capability of any other nation at that time. Indeed, the largest ships in these fleets measured 440 feet long, a size that European ships would not match for more than three hundred years.

However, the chief promoters of the fleets were the court eunuchs, a force forever at odds with the mandarins, the court officials and scholars of Confucian texts. Following the death of the Yongle Emperor, the struggle for supremacy gradually turned in favor of the mandarin scholars and bureaucrats. By the end of the Xuande Emperor's reign, in 1435, the tables had turned. When the fleet returned for the last time in 1433, it soon became clear there would be no further expeditions. The situation on the northern frontier was once again becoming perilous, and the Ming had lost their military edge over the nomads. The Zhengtong Emperor, under the thumb of his grandmother, provided capable rule in his early years, but the fleet was disbanded and Ming China turned inward. Indeed, the vengeful scholar administrators made sure of things by imposing a death sentence for the building of any ship with more than two masts. In 1525, during the Jiajing Emperor's reign, all oceangoing vessels were ordered destroyed.

While the Chinese peasantry generally prospered during this period and new crops were introduced, for instance, maize and sweet potatoes, brought from the Americas, which helped double the population, political decay continued to undermine the Ming dynasty. The disastrous reign of the Wan Li Emperor, which lasted 47 years, demonstrated the weakness of any autocracy. The emperor withdrew from his official duties at the age of 25. For the next 25 years, he did not appear in front of imperial audiences or at any official functions. Military problems accumulated, and the Mongols became troublesome once more. Grossly obese and suffering from ill health, the emperor's reign saw the loss of most of the empire's wealth to a small army of parasitic princes and nobles.

With this as the background, it was perhaps inevitable that the great old game would disappear. There is also the conjecture that in this period, the Chinese attitude toward physical sport shifted on a fundamental level. The object of Chinese athletic disciplines moved to efforts to improve individual health and mental strength through the practice of exercises that would train mind and body to achieve "harmony of purpose." Contrast, say, Western boxing and Chinese martial arts. The Eastern schools of martial arts were developed to teach self-defense and self-control in equal measure, and while the Marquis of Queensberry rules for boxing emphasize defense, as in the "sweet science," there remains a substantial difference with the martial arts schools of the East.

Our conclusion must be that while China developed and played a game with a degree of similarity to aspects of modern association football, it died out several hundred years ago. There remains the intriguing possibility that cultural influences may have moved back and forth along the Silk Road and that this may have included concepts concerning "football."

The Silk Road, a network of trading trails throughout Central Asia, began to markedly develop during the Han dynasty, as the Han emperors sought to buy good horses for their cavalry. In exchange they sold silk, a luxury product that made summer heat waves much more bearable. Chinese silk made its way to the Roman Empire, where it was very expensive and became a source of anxiety for the imperial treasury because so much gold and silver was spent on it.

Did the idea of "*cuju*" travel the Silk Road, too? Conversely, did the technology of an inflated pig's bladder, cased in leather, travel the other way, in the ninth century AD?

✿ ✿ ✿

Our third stop during this quick visit to 200 BC is in a much wilder place. There are no cities, no ball courts, no grand emperors, not even any temples. This is the territory of a loose collection of Celtic clans, grouped together in the Dumnonii tribe. Today the area would be Devon and Cornwall, the most southwesterly parts of England.

We descend on a clearing, and as we draw closer we can see that it is a farm field, one of several here, cleared from the forest. A crowd has gathered in the field. There is a village not far off, a collection of small buildings made with wooden post and beam construction, wattle daub walls, and thatched roofs. Pigs root around in the muddy streets.

It is mid-winter; in fact, it is the day after the solstice. The druids, who guide this society, have taken note. The sun is at its weakest and remains above the horizon for the fewest hours of any day in the year.

The people wear clothing of fur, hides, and homespun wool. Some garments show considerable decoration, in classic Celtic patterns. But on the field, most of the men are stripped down to their breeches. Their skin is oiled with lard.

A ball is produced by the village cobbler, a special ball that he has labored on for weeks. Smooth to the touch, it is made of a heavy wood, from a tree with religious significance, perhaps an apple tree. The ball is slippery, soaked in tallow, and about the size of a cricket ball or a baseball.

There are two teams, although only the locals know who's on which side. Team selection is simple, brutally so. Everyone in the village that we can see, past the fields, is on one team. This village is named for the stream that flows close by—we'll translate that to Streamville. The opposition, which looks exactly the same, is from the next village, which lies half a mile away, through the intervening woods, and is named for the beech trees common in those woods, thus, the "place of Beeches."

Important points to remember here: The Celtic world was extremely varied, with different tribes and clans holding to their own rituals, even their own versions of the common deities. We are a long way away from the kind of universal society developed by the imperial dynasties of China. Because they had no writing, the Celtic culture was transmitted by word of mouth. Thus, we are always groping in the dark when considering them. What we do know, however, with some confidence, is that in the southern part of the island, which was to become Roman Britannia and later England, religious life and social ceremonies were governed by the druids. The druids were roughly equivalent to a priest-hood, although one that stood closer to the shaman than the church. The druids celebrated their rituals outdoors, beneath the trees. They left very little for us to understand them by, and what we do know was largely recorded by their enemies, the Romans.

But from the evidence of what can be called "fossil games"—and from descriptions in relatively recent times—we can surmise that they played (the word *play* is probably inadequate, but it's what we've got!) special ball games on certain days of the year. Our evidence can be drawn from Cornish hurling, still played today, or the fierce Welsh *cnapan*, recorded in the seventeenth century, and again from the tradi-tional game *"la soule,"* played by the Celts of Brittany.

The ball is readied and will be thrown by a village elder. Does he wait for a signal from a druid in the nearby trees? Are there druids close by, observing and guiding the ceremony? We do not know and most likely never will. The game, however, was rich with symbolism derived from the religion of the area and the times, down to the use of that particular kind of wood for the ball. And it is believed that the druids were involved in most aspects of the local religious life, so it is quite possible that they signaled the start of the contest.

The object of the game? Very simple: Get the ball and somehow convey it back to the center of your own village. There might be a special "goal" there, and it could be anything from the stump of a tree to the front door of a noble's house.

The ball is thrown high into the air and comes down into a wild, livid scrum as everyone goes for it. The scrum may have lasted anywhere from a few seconds to an hour or more, depending on who got the ball and what they did with it before being buried beneath dozens of other players. The ball is thrown hand to hand, out of the central scrum, by members of one side, while members of the other village scramble to intercept it and tackle the carriers.

The ball symbolized the sun, and at some point in the development of this folk tradition, it may have been coated with tin, which would have made it shine in the sunlight.

Again and again, well-oiled youths escape the mob, making a break either toward the beech woods or to the stream. Again and again they are tackled by equally greasy youths determined to stop them. The ball was imbued with a magical power connected to the changing of the seasons, starting with the strengthening of the feeble winter sun. Taking the ball back to your home village was regarded as a crucial step in having good weather during the planting season and good crops and full bellies the following winter. Beyond that, any young man who succeeded in grabbing the ball and getting it back to his home village and into the goal was the toast of the village, with undying fame that would last the rest of his lifetime.

Hence, few things were more important in this part of the world at this time, and accordingly, the fight for the ball was fierce. Almost anything went, although we obviously don't know if there were any actual rules for the game. About eighteen hundred years later, a game very similar to this was recorded, and it was said that the use of clubs or cudgels, as well as knives and edged weapons, was forbidden.

The wild scrimmages head off into the woods and continue there for hours before one of the quickest young men in Streamville comes shooting out of the trees, running as hard as he can with the ball in his hand. Perhaps he goes right by a pair of druids, who are monitoring the game as keenly as any other spectators. Do they comment on his speed? Do they remark that the game is going well? Or do they mutter that things were better when they were young? Druids may have been as close to wizards as anyone has ever been, but they were still human, so we can imagine their reactions to the sight of this youth, somewhat scratched and a bit bruised, running like a madman for Streamville.

The young man has good reason to run hard now, for right behind him are two lads from the "Beeches" village, and behind them a rabble from both sides erupts from the woods. The boy from Streamville almost makes it out of the field, but at the last moment, one of his pursuers brings him down with a flying tackle. Within moments there's a mound of young men wrestling for the ball. It comes loose, rolling across the ground. A big youth from the Beeches has it, and he's heading back the other way, but then a Streamville youngster is there, and the one with the ball is wrapped up in another tackle and delayed long enough for the mob to bury him. And now the rest of the pack comes out of the woods, and things are pretty much back to where they started.

As we lift up and away, we can see the druids sharing a joke. They've seen many games during their lifetimes and quite possibly participated in a few when they were young. This one may go all the way to nightfall and have to be renewed tomorrow.

While all of this is speculation, it is based on an indisputable set of facts. A game similar to this is still played in Cornwall. Called Cornish hurling, the annual game at St. Colomb Major celebrates an ancient tradition. At St. Colomb, the ball is plated with silver so that it shines and catches the winter sunlight. The game is now played on Shrove Tuesday, or Mardi Gras, a convention adopted for many of the fossil games still played in Britain.

Cornish hurling, which is unrelated to the Irish sport of "hurling," was much more common until the early decades of the nineteenth century. While the game at St. Colomb is played between two halves of one village, many games pitted one village against another or the folks on one side of a stream against those on the other.

Further buttressing this speculation are two other game traditions, the *cnapan* of Wales, for which we have eyewitness accounts from the sixteenth century, and *la soule*, in Brittany, northern France. The Welsh, Bretons, and Cornish are descendants of the Celtic tribes that once occupied England. Their languages—Welsh, Cornish, and Breton—are classed as the Brythonic Celtic languages, with several clear differences with the Irish and Scots Gaelic.

❀ ❀ ❀

There have been grand traditions for ball games in different cultures, but ill chance or cultural change can destroy them. The great rubber ball game of Mesoamerica was almost eliminated by the invasion from Spain and the catastrophic social breakdown that followed. The Chinese tradition of *cuju* survived the rise and fall of many dynasties but then surprisingly faded away for poorly understood reasons.

Meanwhile, another tradition, which began in the wild woods on the edge of European civilization, would eventually lead to another game and a tradition that underlies our modern codes of football.

2

FROM GREECE TO THE CRADLE

Welcome to the playing field in Athens, around 500 BC. Okay, it isn't much to look at, just a space near the Agora—the marketplace—but this is an important patch of ground for the history of football. This is where it begins. To one side is a small temple; a walled enclosure stands on the other. On the wall is a bronze hoop perhaps a foot wide, set vertically about eight feet from the ground.

In the National Museum of Archaeology in Athens, they have a "Ball Player Relief" that shows players engaged in a ball game. The relief is one side of a base that originally supported a nude male statue. Other details of the game come from ancient writers like Antiphanes.

Two teams of youths are formed, old rivals. To our eyes they seem the same, wearing just loin cloths and sandals, but a few of them are also sporting small vests. An older fellow has the ball in his hand, because he's the acting judge of the contest. This ball is about the size of a cricket ball or baseball, made of tightly stitched leather and stuffed with sawdust and sand. It weighs approximately five ounces and is firm, even hard, to the touch.

A few dozen spectators are present. More are drifting in from the tavernas and market. This is a grudge match. The local crew has been itching for a rematch with the other group since losing to them two months prior. The newcomers are from the south side, across the Acropolis in Koele, and are regarded as upstarts in the hierarchy of the city's youth. The leader of the locals, a tall, clean youth, hails from the street of Old Vines, near the Acharnian Gate. His team consists of old friends from that neighborhood with high social status. Everyone knows this will be a hard-fought game.

The teams square off, lining up on either side of the older fellow with the ball. He hurls it into the air, and they go for it.

The first objective is to get possession. Without the ball you cannot score. Everyone is relatively short—this is ancient Greece, after all—but they are fit and enthusiastic, and a jam of bodies goes up with hands outreached for the ball.

A tall, skinny youth from the local team comes down with the ball safely cradled to his belly. The burly leader from the south instantly rams into him, wrapping his arms around him and seeking to pull him down before he can pass the ball. But the kid is too quick, and the ball has already gone to another youth. He slips it behind his back to the team's leader, perhaps he's even a "captain," who runs three steps and throws it over the outstretched hands of several opponents to a barrel-chested local youth known for his ability to withstand tackling. Nonetheless, a scrum has already formed around him, and the ball pops loose. For a moment it's visible, spinning slowly in the air, and then the leader of the south side grabs it one-handed, tucks it close to his body, shoves one of the locals out of the way, knocking him onto his ass, and sprints for the wall with the hoop. Everyone is after him, but before they can lay a hand on him, he jumps up and gracefully lobs the ball through the bronze hoop.

One point to the south side team. Groans and boos arise from the onlookers, overwhelmingly drawn from north side neighborhoods. The local guys stare at one another, hot-eyed and angry. The guy that gave up the ball curses steadily under his breath, vowing to level the south side leader the next time they clash.

The ball is once again hurled into the air, and players from both sides come crashing together. A heavyset carpenter's son from Koele, near the Piraian Gate, has the ball for the south side team. He's tackled at once but cleverly dishes the ball off to the side. The south side team is good at quick, short passing. The ball flies from one hand to the next, sometimes even being handed on as the carrier is being dragged to the ground.

Nothing can stop them as they close in on the hoop. The crowd is getting desperate. Everyone in North Athens wants the upstarts to lose. Can the drive be stopped?

The ball is slipped to the south side captain once more, who spins around and starts to throw it into the hoop. It looks as if it will be 2–0 in another second, but another player gets there just in time to deflect the ball.

Restrained cheers break out from around the field of play. Maybe, just maybe, the north side crew can handle these upstarts.

Grounding the ball gives possession to the south siders, but they must start from the prescribed distance from the hoop. They make a run for the hoop, slipping the ball back and forth at a great pace, keeping it away from the north side boys, working their way through them, pushing them aside when they have to, getting in range of the hoop. Twice they charge in and almost get close enough for a shot, but both times the north siders halt the charge.

And then, out of nowhere, the tall, skinny kid plucks the ball right out of the south side captain's hands and passes it to his own captain, who takes two steps and throws it through the hoop. The crowd, which is now swelling with people who have gotten off of work from building sites across the Panathenaic way, gives off a roar of relief.

It's 1–1, and things are just getting started.

This is my reconstruction of the ancient game of *pheninda*, a ball game that was played in most Greek cities beginning in the early days of the eighth century BC, throughout Roman times, until the fourth century AD, and probably long after that. And while this description may contain a few incorrect details, I believe it's correct overall.

Pheninda is important for our story, not only as a game in and of itself, but because it begat another game, called *harpastum*, developed by the Romans, who took it up in a big way in the first century BC and made it part of their military training. This, I argue, had a vital and far-reaching effect on the history of football.

By all accounts, *pheninda*, which was very popular in Athens, resembled a cross between handball and rugby. There was constant passing of the ball and tackling to try and prevent those passes. The ball was small enough to hold in the hand and made of leather, packed tightly with sawdust. The game was rough, fast, and, above all, fun. It spread throughout the Greek-speaking world, which after the conquests of Alexander the Great (356–323 BC) came to include Syria, Judea, and even parts of Egypt.

This was not the only ball game played by the ancient Greeks, although it seems to have been the most popular. Another game, *episkyros*, is also of considerable interest, because it featured a larger ball that was kicked for distance. Two teams lined up on a field and tried to kick the ball over the heads of the opposition and an end line behind them. The ball was made from an inflated pig's bladder, cased in leather. This is the earliest known example of this kind of ball.

Although there's little in the way of written records concerning ball games in ancient Greece, some evidence supports their presence.

Today, in the West, we look back on the civilization of ancient Greece with a definite sense of affection. It comes down to a sense that this was where our world began. These were people we could kind of understand. Their philosophical output was prodigious, and we still teach it in our schools and universities. Their dramas and comedies are still performed in our own theaters, and their theaters were the first to be built. Their architectural style remains a favorite, and bleached out copies of it abound in our cities and universities. We feel a sense of kinship with them that we don't with Ashurbanipal or the Pharaohs, let alone Emperor Wudi of China or the gorgeously attired Sky Jaguar King of the Classical Maya.

And beyond Plato, Socrates, Sophocles, and Euripides, beyond Athens and Sparta, there's the historic fact that the Greeks fought off the mighty Persian Empire in the fifth century BC. Had they failed, had Athens become a satrapy of the older eastern world, it is quite possible that much of European history would have taken a very different track. There might well be no English language, or French, and probably no football of any kind, anywhere.

The Greeks, however, never accorded ball games the kind of respect they gave to the individual sporting events celebrated at the Olympics or other great games. And unlike the Olympics, they left us with little in the way of dates or even origin myths concerning *pheninda* and *episkyros*. Still, we can make an educated guess about where the Greeks picked up the idea of ball games.

Let's travel back to about 1800 BC. We are deep in the Bronze Age, when the first Greek tribes arrived in the Eastern Mediterranean. These were the Achaean Greeks, and after conquering the earlier inhabitants of Greece, they developed the Mycenaean culture. They grew wheat, barley, figs, grapes, and olives, and depended on fish for much of their protein. Instead of the porridge-like beer consumed in Egypt and Mesopotamia, they drank wine, usually mixed with water. They built fortress citadels, surrounded by farming communities.

The metal of the day was bronze, an alloy of one part tin to nine parts copper, which produced a revolution in daily life. Although it remained expensive, it was used to fashion metal tools, knives in particular, with a sharp edge. As soon as it appeared in any cultural area, the older stone tools seemed primitive.

For these early Greeks, the big cultural glow was on the southern horizon, in Egypt. They knew about Egypt from the visits by the two trading peoples of the Eastern Mediterranean, the Cretans of the "Minoan" civilization and the Phoenicians, who hailed from ports in what is now Lebanon. Their small, single-masted ships brought such Egyptian manufactures as jewelry, bronze weapons, textiles, and figurines north, where they were exchanged for raw materials like amber and silver, as well as wine and slaves.

In Egypt, the Cretans were called the Keftia and were well liked. Their ships visited the Egyptian ports along the Nile Delta. They were even granted the unique privilege of being allowed to take cats out of the country, something that would earn anyone else a death sentence.

It is important to note that it seems that this was the moment when cats got their big break and set out to take over the world. Long before this, the Egyptians had domesticated the small North African wild cat, Felis Silvestris Libyacus, which, uniquely among small wild cats, is truly tamable. In 2007, studies published in the *Science Journal* on feline mitochondria demonstrated that five female ancestors from Egypt gave rise to today's domestic cats. In ancient times, cats proved invaluable in reducing the number of the mice and rats living around the granaries. An early image of a domesticated cat has been dated to approximately 1950 BC, but through succeeding dynasties, the love of cats, as seen in the cult of the goddess Bast, later Bastet, became a notable feature of the culture. The cult of Bast grew much larger. Egyptians mummified both real and fake cats by the millions and entombed them in the temples of the cat-headed goddess. Cat images and statuettes proliferated, as did cats themselves. The Cretans took cats with them to Crete and, inevitably, everywhere else their small ships sailed. Cats have never looked back.

We know that a certain culture of ball play was alive in Egypt. There was *seker hamat*, a game that appears to have been something like baseball practice. A player with a club, or bat, knocked a small ball long and far, and others ran to catch it. Pharaoh was recorded as playing this one. At the well-known tomb of Beni Hassan, there was found a painting dating from about 2000 BC, showing girls playing a game of ball. The girls are riding on one another's backs, tossing colored balls back and forth. It is assumed that if a rider dropped a ball, she became a horsey, but alas, we have never found the rule book or any description of the game. And the Egyptians played some kind of proto-hockey, as well as other games involving small balls of painted wood or leather. The Cretan traders couldn't have been immune to these things. At some point those brightly painted balls must have gone north, as gifts for children back home or trade goods to be taken to Mycenae, where their novelty value could have helped clinch a deal for wine, a nice price for a piece of amber, or a handsome slave from Thrace.

So did the Bronze Age Greeks play ball games? Unfortunately there's no direct evidence, but we do have one clue that comes from Homer, who composed *The Odyssey* in about 750 BC. The Greeks of Homer's *Iliad* and *Odyssey* are Achaeans, seen as great heroes from the perspective of Homer's time, approximately 500 years after the fall of Troy.

Shipwrecked at one point, Odysseus is saved from drowning by a friendly goddess and manages to reach the isle of Scheria, where the Phaeacians dwell. Exhausted, he crawls up the beach and hides under a bush. He is awakened by Princess Nausicca and her maidens happily playing ball on the beach, most likely a game of catch. The ball falls in the water and the girls let out a shriek, which awakens the comatose mariner. He crawls out of hiding and seeks assistance from the princess. A little later, after being welcomed by Nausicca's dad, King Alcyon, Odysseus witnesses after-dinner entertainment that features a pair of skilled ballplayers, who may even be jugglers and keep a selection of colorful balls in the air with various tricks of hand and foot to delight and amuse the king and his guests.

The Odyssey is set in the years immediately after the Trojan War or sometime around 1200 BC. The ball play of the Phaeacians is introduced as a normal activity that Homer's listeners in 750 BC would have no trouble understanding. This suggests that by Homer's time, ball games were indeed commonplace. It is also possible that Homer was not being anachronistic here and that he knew whereof he spoke, and that games of ball were part of Greek culture in the era of the Trojan War.

That conflict appears to have been the last hurrah of the early Achaean Greeks. Soon thereafter, another set of Greek tribes, the Dorians, invaded Greece from the north, and the Mycenaean citadels were burned. Within a century, a dark age had fallen on the region, and literacy died out among the Greeks.

At about the same time, iron began to replace bronze. Iron had been an expensive curiosity first worked by the Hittites, until it was discovered how to reliably smelt iron and hammer some carbon into it to create "wrought iron," which was harder than bronze and kept a sharper edge. Wrought iron, hammered on an anvil, contained 0.02 to 0.08 percent carbon content, absorbed from the charcoal used to melt the iron ore. Iron tools and weapons were now cheaper to make than those of bronze, and the new technology quickly spread.

Meanwhile, into the cultural void of the Dark Ages stepped the Phoenicians, who maintained the Mediterranean trade routes from Spain to Egypt (the Cretans had been overrun by Greek invaders long before). In about 800 BC, close to Homer's time, the Phoenicians began a settlement on the coast of Africa, in present-day Tunisia, which they called "Qart Hadasht," or New City. To the Romans it would become Carthage, and their greatest foe in the time of the Republic.

Rome itself was founded in approximately 750 BC, under the influence of the Etruscans, who dominated central Italy during this period. Thus, both of the powers that would contend for mastery in the Western Mediterranean five hundred years later were founded within a few decades of one another.

The Phoenician legacy includes their written script, which became the basis of the new Greek alphabet. Sadly, we have little in the way of Phoenician documents themselves, and what we know of this active and enterprising people comes from Greek and Roman sources, neither of which were well disposed toward them.

Another Phoenician legacy may have been the concept of a purpose-built arena or stadium for watching sporting events. At Amrit, in modern-day Lebanon, which was once Phoenicia, there is a large stadium, first uncovered by French archeologists in the nineteenth century. It is thought that this structure dates back to the Bronze Age and thus is the earliest such stadium known anywhere, although the Olmec ball courts built of earth possibly predated it.

The Greeks emerged from the Dark Age in the eighth century BC, and their civilization soon began its impressive rise. Along with literacy, the Greeks developed the earliest democracy, and they centered their cities on the Agora. This set them apart from the Egyptian and Mesopotamian models of civilization, where the center of society was the temple or palace, with their granaries. In Babylon and Memphis, everyone in the town was on the dole, given beer and bread every day, according to their social station. The Greeks went shopping instead and used coins, an idea they adopted from the Lydians and their famous King Croesus.

At this point, the Greeks already had a lot of ball games, which they called *sphaeromachia*—ball fighting. Many of these games were localized, played in a single small city or even just a neighborhood. From this activity four main games were developed that were played on a wider basis.

Episkyros: A kind of soccer, although the ball could be thrown, as well as kicked. The ball was large, with an inflated pig's bladder inside a sewn leather casing. Outside modern technology, nothing beats this for the combination of weight and bounce when it comes to kicking a ball for distance and power. The field of play had two end lines and a center line, and two teams competed. This was a game for a large number of players. The object of the game was to drive the ball over the opposition's end line. There were no goals. This game was apparently especially popular in Sparta, where it played a part in the hard, physical education of Spartan youth.

Pheninda: Another team game, played with a small ball that fit into the hand. It was something like modern-day handball crossed with rugby. One team endeavored to keep the ball away from the opposing team, passing it from hand to hand across the field of play and then tossing it through a metal hoop arranged vertically, as opposed to the horizontal arrangement of a basketball hoop. Tackling was rough, and there may have been games with two hoops. This game was popular in Athens.

Ourania: A game of catch played with a large ball. This was a game for individuals. A player with the ball stood in the center of a circle formed by the other players. He or she threw the ball high into the air and called out the name of another player. That player then had to move to the center and catch the ball. The process was repeated. If a player dropped the ball, he or she had to leave the game. There may have been a much rougher version of the game, played by boys, in which the player throwing the ball into the air would try to block the player designated to catch it and prevent him from getting into the center.

Arpaston (later *harpastum* in Latin): Related to *pheninda*, but rougher and simpler. This was the "grab away" game of ball. The field of play could be square or circular. A line was drawn through the middle of the field of play and each team assigned a side. The object was for a player to grab the ball, which was small and made of leather stuffed with sawdust, and take it back to their own end line for a score. As with *pheninda*, the ball was thrown high into the air in the middle of the playing area to start things off. Players with possession of the ball could be tackled. Passes could be blocked or intercepted. If the ball fell to the ground, possession went to the other team.

These four games spread throughout the Greek-influenced world for hundreds of years.

From second-century AD author Athenaeus, who wrote the "Deipnosophists," or "Banquet of the Learned," we have the following passage: "*Harpastum*, which used to be called *pheninda*, is the game I like most of all. Great are the exertion and fatigue attendant upon contests of ball playing, and violent twisting and turning of the neck, too. Hence, Antiphanes, 'Damn it what a pain in the neck I've got.'"

Athenaeus describes the game as follows: "He seized the ball and passed it to a teammate while dodging another and laughing. He pushed it out of the way of another. Another fellow player he raised to his feet. All the while the crowd resounded with shouts of 'Out of Bounds! Too far, Right beside him, Over his head, On the ground, Up in the air, Too short, Pass it back in the scrum.'"

Now, Antiphanes was a playwright active in Athens during the third century BC. He is known for a large number of comic plays and frag-ments of plays. From this quote it seems that *pheninda* was a common part of social life, much like pickup soccer and basketball games today. Athenaeus, who resided in Egypt, was writing 500 years later, when both Greece and Egypt were part of the Roman Empire.

The process that began with those brightly colored balls of wood or leather from ancient Egypt had passed through the Greek culture and emerged with these four popular games, which spread widely throughout the Mediterranean world. The games were simple and only required a ball and perhaps some chalk to mark out the field of play.

Another intriguing point is the Greek urge to plant colonies up and down the Mediterranean coast. Greek cities flourished on the coasts of Sicily and Southern Italy. The Greek city of Phocaea, on the coast of what is now Turkey (modern-day Foça, Turkey), was a leader in both long-range trade voyages and founding distant settlements. According to the historian Herodotus, the Phocaeans were the first Greeks to make long voyages, exploring the Western Mediterranean on the heels of the Phoenicians.

The Phocaeans founded several colonies, including Emporion in Catalonia and Elea in Italy, but most important for our story was the earlier founding of Massalia on the coast of southern France, which today is the French city Marseilles.

The Phocaeans later abandoned their home city rather than submit to the rule of the Persians, who conquered Lydia and their city in 546 BC, sending another wave of colonists to Massalia.

Massalia was well placed to take part in a crucial area of trade. To make bronze, which was still an important material in the culture, tin was needed. The best resource for tin lay in the far north, in the Tin Islands, or Cassiterides. These islands had been famous for tin for some time, and tin mining had begun there as early as 2000 BC. Today, of course, we know them as the British Isles, and the source of the tin was the most southerly and western county of England—Cornwall.

Artifacts found in Cornwall demonstrate linkage with the Mycenaean Greek world, which, of course, crashed with the invasions and the Dark Age, but trade probably continued at a lower level and recovered as Greek culture revived from 800 BC onward. Trade revived because without tin you could not make bronze, and bronze remained in demand even as iron became more popular.

In about 500 BC, Hecataeus wrote of the islands beyond "Gaul," where tin could be obtained. And in approximately 325 BC, Pytheus of

Massalia traveled to Britain, most likely to Cornwall itself, where he found the trade in tin flourishing.

At some point the trade in tin from Cornwall came under the control of a Celtic tribe, the Veneti, who lived on the southern coast of Brittany. The Veneti—no relation to the Veneti of the Adriatic from whom came Venice—were mariners who built stout oak ships, single masted with a large sail made of leather capable of withstanding the Atlantic waves and weather.

The ships of the Greeks and Phoenicians always struggled with the rougher waters of the Atlantic, so the Veneti had a great advantage. Their control of the tin trade provides us with a visible route between Massalia and Cornwall.

From southern Brittany, tin would have been taken by ship to the estuary of the Dordogne, where the city of Bordeaux sits today. From there river boats would have carried it to higher ground, where Montauban lies. Then it would have gone in portage and on other boats through the valley, to Toulouse, then Carcassonne, then Narbonne, and then across the gulf to Massalia.

Going the other way were Greek trade goods, metal implements, kraters and cups for serving wine, amphorae of wine and olive oil, and cloth and jewelry. And considering the Greek culture of the time, it seems likely that a few of those handmade leather balls, for *pheninda* and even *episkyros*, would have made the trip, too.

Alas, the Veneti were a proud people, and in 56 BC, they fell into war with Julius Caesar, who was busy solidifying Roman control of Gaul. At first the Veneti had the advantage, because although the Romans had built ships to challenge them, the Veneti sailing ships were too stoutly made and sat too high in the water for the Romans to attack them. They resisted ramming, and from their decks the Veneti could rain arrows and rocks on the Roman galleys.

However, it was never wise to bet against Julius Caesar, or Roman ingenuity. The Romans equipped their galleys with long billhooks and used them to slash the halyards controlling the sails on the Veneti ships. Immobilized, the Veneti vessels could be boarded, and once you were boarded by Roman legionaries in this era, you were in trouble.

Their fleet defeated at last, the Veneti fortresses were reduced one by one, and Caesar slaughtered or enslaved the entire population as an example to the rest of the Celtic tribes of Gaul.

Caesar went on to make his famous visit to southern Britain a couple of years later.

Interestingly enough, not only does Cornwall have Cornish hurling and an ancient tradition of rustic ball games, but Morbihan and Brittany in general are also the heartland of another game of similar scope to hurling—*la soule*.

As described by revivalists in recent times, *la soule* was played with a leather bag, something like a tote bag, filled with sawdust and sealed tight. As with many of these kinds of "fossil games" played in the region from Brittany to the North of England, the object of the game was to get possession of the bag, break away from the opposition, and take the bag back to your own village. The obvious difference between *la soule* and Cornish hurling is the size of the "ball," i.e., the tote bag, and the removal of the "hurling" aspect, i.e., the ability to throw the ball in long passes or just gain ground; therefore, *la soule* would seem to be even more about struggles in field and thicket, and then frantic running and pursuit across hill and dale.

The origin of the *soule*, or bag, is a mystery. It was a unique style of "ball"; however, as we shall see, other old games have evolved using local materials and concepts, and equally strange ideas regarding the "ball."

So, the evidence is there, albeit circumstantial, to envisage a link between the Greek ball games and the games that developed among the Celts of Brittany and Cornwall. For certain, the Greeks had their games, and equally certain, the Celts had theirs. A trade in tin connected the ball-playing area of the Celts with the Greek colonies of the Mediterranean, and the possibility that Greek traders took well-made *pheninda* and *episkyros* balls to Brittany, and thence to Cornwall, cannot be dismissed. Unfortunately, leather balls rarely survive the test of time, and all we are left with are "fossils" in the form of games with long pedigrees stretching back into antiquity.

As a general note, this is pretty much how it is in the realm of paleontology, too, where fossils of some species are common and others have never been found, nor will be, due to the extremes of fortune required for something to fossilize, survive eons in the rock, and then be exposed to our eyes. Nevertheless, paleontologists have pieced together a compelling view of the ancient world, progressing from the early creatures of the seas in the Cambrian era 540 million years ago, through the triumphs of the dinosaurs, to the more modern world of mammals, the ice ages, and man. Thus, it must be for our history of a game of the people, unheralded by kings and queens, played with balls prone to decay.

There remain some questions concerning the Greeks.

The Olympics are one example. The Greeks considered themselves superior to other peoples, and one reason for their self-belief was their devotion to athletics. In this regard they had a point, as no one before them, and few since, had fetishized the athlete to quite the same extent. The Olympics began with just a single foot race, the "stade," held in 776 BC. But within a couple hundred years other events had been added to fill out the schedule with many of the kinds of competitions that developed from hunting and warfare, for instance, throwing the javelin or racing in chariots.

The Olympics had been joined by other similar games. These included the Pythian, held every two years after the Olympics; the Nemean Games, held on the third year after the Olympics; and the Isthmian Games, held the year after the Olympics. Together they made up the Panhellenic Games. Thus, there were important athletic events each summer.

Greek concepts of gender and a cultural misogyny forbade women from participating. The athletes also competed naked, slicked down with oil, to ensure that the participants were male. Married women were banned as spectators due to the nudity, on pain of being hurled to their deaths from a nearby cliff top. Unmarried females, however, even young girls, were allowed to watch. Here, I suppose, we can see how different Greek culture was from our own.

Moreover, only Greeks were allowed to take part in the games. Everyone else was seen as *barbaroi*—barbarians—incapable of appreciating the finer qualities of these events. This prohibition was eventually lifted, pretty much by force, first by Alexander the Great, who conquered Greece and demanded that his Macedonian, Greek-speaking men be allowed to partake. A few hundred years later, the Romans arrived, and what the Romans wanted, the Romans tended to get, so Romans participated as well after that.

What also seems odd, in our modern world filled with all kinds of sports, including a large number of team games, is that no team games and no ball sports were ever included in the Panhellenic Games. This was due to the Greek pursuit of individual *kleos*, or glory. A team sport, no matter how rough and difficult, inevitably offered a more complicated, nuanced kind of victory. On the winning team, some players might have performed well and some not, so why should they share in the glory?

And glory there certainly was. To the victors went the spoils. From public adulation to having taxes forgiven for the rest of their lives in their home cities, winners were treated quite well. Statues were erected in their honor and their names attached to the year in which they won, at least in their home cities.

But there is another thought regarding the lack of team games in the Olympics. Their ball games, what we know of them, lacked definite positions. They had no quarterbacks, no star strikers. Anyone on the team could kick the ball over the other team's end line in *episkyros*. The games were simple, the absolute opposite from American football and even modern rugby or soccer, which have evolved to have an extensive list of rules, as well as complex tactical schemes. In the Greek ball games, there probably wasn't enough positional emphasis to create true star players, no goalkeepers to stave off the opposition, no quarterbacks to drive their teams to victory, no superstar forwards exhibiting astonishing skills that would make them the toast of the town or the entire country.

There remains a lot of truth in the idea that Greece is where our own world really began. Greek culture rested on the labor of an army of slaves, and it was profoundly misogynistic, closer to Saudi Arabia than California when it came to women's rights. Male homosexuality was widely accepted, especially in militaristic Sparta, where every youth was coupled with an older one, who was his guide and lover. But these same Spartans were the most feared soldiers the world had ever seen to that point.

And yet, wildly different as they were from us, we still celebrate their achievements, which were extraordinary. One can hardly name an area of modern life and not find an ancient Greek fingerprint on its origins. In the case of football, I believe those prints are everywhere. As we might expect from their colonies in the Mediterranean, Greek culture left a large footprint. Nowhere is this more visible than in Italy, where the Romans took up so much that was Greek, from Homer to the

Olympian gods themselves. And once adopted, these things were last-ing.

And so we have this final glimpse of the ancient game of *pheninda*, this time from the early twentieth century, in rural Southern Italy, from a time when people gathered for long lunches and took siestas after-ward, while the children played games. By this time, from about 1900 to 1910, *pheninda* had evolved into a game for kids, and there had been some changes. The field of play was marked out into a row of separate squares, all the same size. At each end of the row of squares, set up on a tree or pole, was a vertically aligned hoop. Another variation, with a single hoop, had the squares arranged in a circle. The players were each assigned a square, with the teams interspersed, so a red player would have blue players on either side. The ball had to be passed along the row of squares and then thrown through the hoop, while the other team did its best to knock it down or intercept it. The isolation of the players removed the inherent violence of the old scrum, as well as some of the trickery, but the essence of the game remained. Perhaps it is still being played in some remote corner of La Campagna, where people still take picnics in the fields with their families and friends. If so, it's an example of cultural conservation and a fossil game that has survived long after its time passed away, preserving a living memory of ancient Greece.

3

THE CRADLE OF FOOTBALL

Our best data sets regarding the development of the games that eventually gave rise to "footeballe" come from the "fossil games" that still survive, primarily in parts of England and Scotland. One of the best-known events is the Ashbourne Game. It's played twice a year, on Shrove Tuesday, aka Mardi Gras (Fat Tuesday), and the following day, Ash Wednesday. Ashbourne is a prosperous market town in Derbyshire, located at the southern end of the Peak District—a range of low, rounded mountains. The surrounding countryside is beautiful. Just to the west lies Dovedale, the haunt of Izaak Walton, author of the original text for the sport of fishing, *The Compleat Angler*, completed in 1653.

Ashbourne is, in fact, almost in the geographical center of England, and it has seen its share of history. And as we swoop in to visit, we will witness a little slice of that history, an ongoing tradition that harks back at least a thousand years, and probably even farther than that.

As we drop in on the town on this cool, typically gray-skies day in February, it's immediately obvious that something is going on. There are hundreds of people in the streets, even with a sharp little wind out of the west. The shops and banks, and even the pubs in the center of town, have their windows boarded up as if expecting a hurricane. There are no parked cars in sight. If you look closely you will even notice that anything breakable has been removed. It looks as if the place is ready for war, which it is in a way, because as they say here in Derbyshire:

> Shrove Tuesday and Ash Wednesday,
> These days are always set

To play a game of football
Through sunshine, snow, and wet.

Indeed, this ancient game is now the Royal Shrovetide Football Game, since it's been blessed a couple of times by visiting princes of Wales, most recently in 2003, when Prince Charles showed up and was warmly greeted and carried shoulder high through town by three burly fellows to perform the duty known as "turning up the ball."

This will be a "football" game that doesn't involve the ball getting kicked. It's more a game of "townball" in a style that derives from the Middle Ages. The teams are the Uppards, traditionally drawn from those born on the north side of Henmore Brook, which runs through the town, versus the Downards, who hail from the south side. Tradition has been superseded in the modern era, however, and outsiders can join in, too. Indeed, the game today will involve teams of several hundred on either side—two large, unwieldy mobs, most of whom will never touch the ball and may hardly even see it.

This is not a game with referees, umpires, whistles, or flags. The rules are few indeed, and just about anything short of murder goes.

The game is played with a special ball, about twice the size of a soccer ball and much heavier. For years they have been made by a local artist, John Harrison. Each ball is hand sewn of leather, stuffed with cork chips, and then finished off with an elaborate paint job that takes weeks to complete. There's usually a Union Jack on there and suitable decoration, plus a handsome inscription, with the date in large letters at the top and bottom. Depending on whether someone scores a goal, or, in Ashbourne terminology, "goals the ball," the handsome ball will go home with the goal scorer, and if no goal is scored, it will go to whoever "turned up the ball" at the beginning of the event.

Experienced players tend to wear thick shin pads and steel toe boots, because they know that, at the very least, their feet are going to be stepped on. Some will wear the bottom half of a wet suit as well, because they know the game can move into chilly Henmore Brook, which can be anywhere from ankle to knee deep in February.

Just before 2 p.m., the pubs empty out and shut their doors, and the final boards go up on windows throughout the town. The crowd moves down to the Shaw Croft car park, behind the local supermarket. The mayor, or some visiting dignitary, gets up on the raised steps there, called the "Plinth," and makes the usual short speech, asking everyone not to damage gardens and private property, as the survival of the game depends on the willingness of the people of the town to endure it twice a year. He also reminds everyone of the rules: Motor vehicles may not be used to transport the ball, and murder is against the law.

Well, that's a relief, right? But as we look around at the competition, we may have some second thoughts about taking part in the festivities. Nearby stand the pubs and the world of warm, comfortable British pubdom—comfy seats, a roaring fire, a pint of fresh ale.

A group of large men saunters past, obviously rugby players judging by their size and demeanor. There are several other clumps of similarly massive fellows, some wearing rugby kits. On occasion, American, Canadian, Australian, and New Zealander accents can also be heard. This game draws people from throughout the world.

The crowd thickened considerably during the mayor's speech; there seems to be a couple thousand people on hand now. Someone hands the mayor the big, brightly painted ball, and he holds it over his head, garnering a roar from the crowd. There's something truly primal about this noise, enough to send a shiver down your spine. Everyone's ready to go, but first tradition demands that everyone sing a verse of "Auld Lang Syne," followed by "God Save the Queen."

Once the echoes of the crowd have died down, the mayor "turns up the ball," hurling it two-handed into the waiting crowd. The group gives out a tremendous roar as the big ball sails across the car park and falls into one thousand outstretched arms.

At first it's just chaos. We're at the back of the crowd, it seems, with a lot of kids and older people, who mostly appear to be in attendance just to enjoy the excitement. But toward the middle of the car park, there are violent motions, cries of rage or pain that break through the wall of roaring sound. The large guys we noticed earlier are forcing their way through the lesser fry to form what is called the "hug." You can always tell where the hug is, they say, because rising from it are plumes of steam.

As the hug forms, the mass takes on some degree of organization. On one side of the hug are about a hundred determined Uppards, and on the other side a roughly equal number of Downards. Surrounding them are hundreds of somewhat less-determined folks of all sorts.

It is important to note that to win the game, one side must take the ball a mile or two out of town, to either the site of the old Sturton Mill to the east, where the Uppards can score, or the site of the Clifton Mill, which lies southwest, where the Downards can score. Both are on the brook, of course, and to score the ball must be taken to the monuments that long ago replaced the mills. Once it's there, it must be handed to the designated goal scorer, and he must tap it against the board fastened to the monument three times. As previously mentioned, this is "goaling the ball." There's no way to score without getting wet, either, and this is February.

The hug begins lurching about in a crazy way, a few steps this way and then a few steps back, like a vast, drunken animal. In the center, the ball is in the grip of about a dozen arms, and everyone surrounding it is heaving and shoving with all their might. The paint job is already taking a beating.

Suddenly something breaks the lock. We can't tell exactly what happened, but the ball flies 50 feet down the street, away from the hard-armed heart of the hug. The Downards have apparently ripped it free and thrown it where they want to go.

Now comes a moment of crowd dynamic, which is a bit scary really, because the mob is turning and moving in the direction of the ball. We must go with the flow in this situation, as there is basically no other choice.

There's a lot of struggling up ahead. The ball is thrown again, flying even farther down the street. The large men are pushing hard to get through the crowd and back into the action.

The ball makes it to the corner and stops, and a new hug forms around it. Now we're jammed up somewhere on the outer edge of the formation. At least three hundred guys are packing in tighter and tighter leading into the event horizon and the ball itself. But this hug is different, because it's in motion. The Downards have momentum, and the mob keeps moving, step by step, like a gigantic rugby maul. We can suddenly see the value in having steel toe boots, as everyone is stepping on everyone else's feet, a lot, and in a very un-English way, and no one is saying "sorry."

Every so often the hug sways across the street and runs up against a building. The windows are boarded up, of course, but shouts of "Glass!" ring out, and everyone eases up a bit and the hug moves back into the street.

It already feels like we've been in some kind of battle, even though the game's barely half an hour old, and we've come nowhere close to the ball. There's this wild, insane sense of exhilaration, poured over ice cubes of fear, shaken, not stirred, and downed with a gulp. It's the closest thing to old-fashioned war without actual bloodshed.

The Downards have once again broken loose with the ball and are running it down the street, while the Uppards pursue them furiously. Someone nearby has been knocked off their feet, and we hear a shriek that cuts through the general roar. The crowd pulls up around the fallen, someone helps him up, as others push past, and everyone begins moving again, but even farther back from the ball.

This time the run goes on for maybe half a mile and is well out of the town center, passing by modest English midlands houses of gray stone, some with windows boarded up, just in case.

We have finally caught up with the hug as it moves over a low stone wall and gets stuck in the woods. This happens, they say, and it can stay there for a while. We can see the steam rising up through the bare branches of the trees. We ask people by the wall if they know what's happening, but they don't. Welcome to the fog of war.

About an hour later, many guys in the woods pull back to the road. Loads of kids gather around them. We go in to take a look. The ground is thoroughly trampled, and fragments of clothing can be seen here and there. It's slightly reminiscent of the aftermath of a rock festival.

Suddenly, with what seems an indecent lack of warning, the mob ahead, in the trees, begins parting like magic, and four big guys appear with the ball, running right at us. It's impossible to tell if they're Uppards or Downards, and by this point we can't remember whether we joined the Uppards or Downards. Other guys crash into them. We dodge a young tree, squeeze past a fat guy in a Manchester United shirt, and there it is, the ball, the fabulous beast at the heart of all this madness.

Six or seven big guys wearing rugby shirts and wet suits are wrestling for the ball in tight quarters between the trees. One of them slips, and the others swing our way. The guy in the Man United shirt mutters, "Oh, blimey," as he gets crushed against a tree, and we're now shoulder to shoulder with some giant who I think is Australian and actually has the ball. Pushing against him to avoid being crushed against the tree, my hand brushes against the ball. We just touched the ball!

The ball is wet and warm, almost hot, probably due to the energy expended on it during the past couple of hours. It's amazing it's still in one piece. Hats off to John Harrison—he really knows how to make 'em. The paint job is still magnificent, and I'd love to take this baby home and put it somewhere in the house. It's much more impressive than some poor animal's head.

More big guys have run up, and we're leaving the woods. The hug is thickening again. The pressure from all sides is terrifying. We can't move, we can barely breathe. All that can be heard is a brutal kind of grunting, like a rugby scrum, come to think of it, and constant cries of "Push It!" from the back, or maybe it's the front. Who knows at this point.

We are peeled out of the action as the hug spins and more and more guys push in from all sides. The ball is gone, and the hug turns like some monstrous, 30-ton animal with several hundred legs and heaves itself back over the low stone wall and into the road. Guys in the middle are screaming as they are crushed against the wall, but the hug doesn't hear them, it just keeps going. Then we're back at the wall ourselves, and we jump it, thankful that there's room to do so.

And now things are moving quickly again. The Uppards have the ball and are running it back into the town center, hotly pursued by the Downards. We only know this from rumor, because we're way behind and out of the action. Everyone is jogging along now, heading back into town.

We're sweating. It feels as if we've played a full half of a hard-fought soccer or rugby game. And there's a weird sense of triumph, because we actually touched the ball for about a second. On the other hand, our feet are telling us they're going to be extremely sore the next day, having been stepped on way too many times.

The game goes into town, then stops, hugs again, and circles there for more than an hour. It then reverses again and comes roaring back at us. This time the Downards take the ball all the way to Watery Lane, and soon there are about two hundred of them in Henmore Brook, up to their knees in cold, muddy water. Hundreds more are watching and yelling, peering down and trying to see what the hell is happening. Joining this particular hug would mean taking a bath in freezing cold water, which is steadily turning into liquid mud. A glance at the watch shows that it's close to six o'clock. If no one scores a goal by six, the game will go on until darkness falls, which won't be long afterward. At that point it will be called and end in a goalless draw (tie).

But now comes another breakthrough, as the Downards force a way through the Uppards' defenses and reach the six-foot stone monument that marks where the old Clifton Mill used to grind local wheat. While a group of Downards holds off the exhausted Uppards, the designated scorer lifts the muddy, wet ball and smacks it three times against the board to "goal the ball."

The score is 1–0, Downards, and a few minutes later the bell tolls back into town for six o'clock, and the game is over. The Uppards will have to wait until the next day, Ash Wednesday, for their chance at revenge, when the entire, strange, wonderfully crazy event will be repeated.

Later, in a crowded pub, pints and sandwiches in tow, we reflect on the excitement and occasional stark terror of mob football. Part of it is just being in a large, active crowd. Being in a crowd can be exciting. Of course it depends on the crowd. Waiting on platform six for the 6:15 to Romford, White Plains, or Paramatta is one thing, but being on the fringes of a violent riot is quite another. In today's buttoned-down, air-conditioned world, most crowds in the United States and Europe are corralled, policed, and funneled to their seats in a stadium or concert hall. There's still an element of excitement from seeing all those people who've come for the game or music, but the focus is on the event, not the crowd. Another sort of crowd with excitement to it is one that gathers at a rock festival. Once upon a time, festivals were pretty chaotic affairs, teetering on the edge of collapse. This edginess made them peculiarly memorable, even when they slid into disaster. Today, they're run on commercial lines, and so they're much safer and, consequently, much less notable.

Far more exciting, and dangerous, is the crowd at a demonstration that turns violent or, beyond that, a straight-out urban riot. If you've ever been caught up in either of these two scenarios, you know the strange edge to the experience. Running through the streets with thousands of people, bottles flying overhead and police charging into action with truncheons and tear gas, is scary, but it's also undeniably exciting. If you make it out of the immediate danger zone unhurt, there's a powerful urge to see what the hell is happening, where the smoke is rising and the cops are thicker than bees on honey. People will circle around, peering down the road and heading off to one side to try to get a better view. Some will even head right back into the fray. Conclusion: We're human, we crave excitement.

Getting whacked on the head with a bottle or billy club is the downside, of course, but some people really love danger—check out the guys who run with the bulls at Pamplona, jump off buildings with a small parachute, or go surfing during hurricanes.

Mob football has some of that edge, that weird, feral feeling of things being out of control, of the everyday rules having been tossed aside, and yet it's combined with some of the pleasures of modern-day codes of football. There's a ball, there's a purpose to the whole thing, involving goals and scoring.

Of course, a real battle with edged weapons, spears, and shields would be the ultimate entry into the danger zone, but that type of conflict has such a heavy downside that no one can quite call it "fun." Even historical reenactment can't go far in the direction of reality there, because, well, war with edged weapons isn't at all like our modern technological warfare. No, it's savage stuff involving blood and guts, and stink and horror, and as a species we've been there and done that, and we don't want to do it again. The days when young men grew up knowing, and fearing, that they would one day stand in the "shield wall" with sword or axe in hand, as the Danes or English, or Irish or Scots, or French, or, well, just about anyone, advanced toward them, shields lowered and spears out, are over, although, alas, war continues.

But unlike a riot or battle, the Ashbourne game is just a game, and so it's both exciting and a little dangerous, and yet ultimately safe. There is no danger of being shot or stabbed, although you need to keep your wits about you when the hug bears down and threatens to trap you against a wall.

Big-crowd excitement also presses on the walls of our evolutionary heritage. Before agriculture, which began only eleven or twelve thousand years ago, a blink in the eye of our evolutionary history, humans lived in small groups. A clan of one hundred people coming together in one place would have felt like a rock festival.

Today, most of us live in large, bustling cities, although it sometimes seems as if everyone in a city wishes he or she were living somewhere peaceful and rural. This desire led to the suburbs, which is why we get stuck in traffic twice a day commuting. Urban crowding—platform six, waiting for the 4:15—is boring and mundane, while mob football, like a riot, is not, and if you get sucked into the hug, the memory will stay with you for the rest of your days. Finally, the Ashbourne game and other fossils like it are time machines of a sort. This is a trip back to an earlier world, to the Middle Ages, or even older times, to the days of the cradle of football. And that's where we must head for now, to the small region of northern Europe that, by a series of flukes, served as the birth place and incubator for football in all its modern forms.

By the time Roman rule had solidified over Gaul and southern Britain, circa 80 AD, ball games of various kinds had taken root in both places. From the survival of fossil games, we know that Cornwall, Wales, and Brittany shared in the Celtic passion for games like Cornish hurling, described in chapter 1. Whether that game's tradition was inspired by Greek games via traders from the south or came from an older indigenous root is unknown. Either is possible, and so it is a blend of both, although the lack of such games among the Gaelic-speaking Scots and Irish inclines this writer to believe the Greeks had something to do with it. Not that those groups did not have ball games. *Camanachd*, a form of field hockey originally played in the West of Scotland, was also widely played in Ireland. More recently, the Irish have played their own style of hurling, a unique sport in which a hard ball is struck with a bat or carried with repetitive touches to the bat and then fired at a goal, hockey style. In addition, there is the modern Irish style of football, called Gaelic football, which is described later in this book. But of fossils, like those of Cornwall, Wales, the border region of Scotland, and towns like Ashbourne in central England, there are no survivors. They were either stamped out long ago or never existed.

As mentioned earlier, the Romans took up the Greek ball games, especially the simple, rough game of *harpastum*. This game became a favorite in the Legions, and wherever the Legions were stationed, the Legions played *harpastum*.

The Roman Empire in the west fell to pieces shortly after 400 AD. When the region reemerged from the Dark Ages that followed, folk "football" in various forms was part of the culture from northern France through England and Wales to southern Scotland. It was not visible on the Rhine, nor anywhere else in the former Roman dominions. The cradle of football, in other words, was rocking on either side of the English Channel, or to be French about it, La Manche.

How did this happen?

Roll back to Roman times. Having occupied Gaul and Britannia, the Romans' first job was to neutralize the druids. Julius Caesar had identified them as the core of the resistance to Roman rule. In Gaul, the Romans basically bought off the Gallic aristocracy by incorporating them into the Roman system. Rebels went to the slave market. As many as 1 million Gauls became slaves courtesy of Caesar's conquests. New schools were founded to replace those of the druids, breaking their grip on Gallic society. In Britannia, always at the heart of the druidic system, the struggle lasted longer and was less conclusive. The Romans destroyed the more obvious nodes of druid power, but Romanization of Britannia was concentrated in the southeast of the island, leaving the far west and the north to the spirit worship of earlier times, which continued even into the Christian era.

To be clear, the process of leavening the native culture with aspects of that of Rome (and with it, Greece) did not occur overnight, nor was it complete. "Romanization" is a broad description of the process; however, a distinct Romano-Brythonic culture appeared, along with urban centers and villas, leaving a variety of archaeological remains and finds. Britannia was rarely mentioned by Roman historians once the region of modern-day England and Wales had been subdued. Scotland, then Caledonia, remained beyond Roman control, being too poor, wild, and expensive to conquer. The Emperor Hadrian built a wall across the northland to delimit the end of the Imperial writ in about 128 AD. Emperor Antoninus Pius pushed it north 50 years later, but only temporarily. Roman control began to disintegrate in the latter part of the fourth century and ended with the withdrawal of the last Legion in 410 AD. For the Romans, this chilly island of fogs and rain was a peripheral concern and a province that hardly paid for itself.

The present-day fossil games of clear Celtic origin, for instance, "hurling" in Cornwall, clearly survived the Roman presence. Similar games survived in Wales and much farther north, in what became the Scottish "Borders." The reasons for this stubborn survival probably include thumbing the nose at the Latin-speaking conquerors in their forts, as well as satisfying the old druids, still hiding out in the hills and deeper forests. But more than that, these people really enjoyed the games. They satisfied a spiritual sense, welcoming the spring, blessing the fields in a symbolic manner, and, by the by, giving the men who were fit an opportunity to run like madmen through the woods and fields in pursuit of the hard, slippery wooden ball.

Ball games weren't the only aspects of the older Celtic culture that survived Romanization. When Britannia was abandoned by Rome in the fifth century AD, there was a revival of the old Celtic style of pottery. Bowls and cups bearing the ancient nonrepresentational designs reappeared after a gap of four hundred years. This is hard evidence for the persistence of cultural memory.

For football, the other key development was the spread of *harpastum*. Wherever there was a Roman fort, the natives would see *harpastum* being played on a regular basis. Local children would have been one of the first audiences, and it can't have been too long before old *harpastum* balls, no longer good enough for the Legionaries, would have begun to pass into the hands of the town kids living around the military base camps. Those kids would've played their own games, perhaps straight *harpastum*, perhaps with a twist or two of their own devising.

In a decade or so, those kids would be the young men in the town, and they'd be completely familiar with *harpastum* and its local derivatives. Ten years further on and they'd be the tradesmen, carpenters, and local chieftains, and their own kids would be hanging around the Legion, playing ground, begging an old ball, and learning the tricks of the game.

These town-dwelling Celts had relatives in the countryside, of course, and when they went to visit them, they took gifts, Roman textiles, beads, and housewares. Their kids likely would have shown off the Roman game. We can imagine the heated debates about that, probably with some fights over fouls, long arguments about the rules, and much sulking afterward. And when the town kids returned home, maybe they left behind an old Roman ball. And no sooner were they out of sight than the village kids were playing the new game, helped by the fact that *harpastum* was always very simple.

And let us spare a moment's thought for the old man in the village, who patiently crafted the hard wooden balls used for summer and winter games of *cnapan*. He might well have been the *crydd*, or cobbler, or perhaps a carpenter. But in his hands the old skills lived on and with them the memory of the druids. Then one day some youngster would show him a Roman-made *harpastum* ball. One can imagine him poring over this alien thing, studying the double-lapped seams and excellent, tight stitching, while musing about the weight of the sawdust with which it was stuffed. Behind that ball lay the vast weight of Roman civilization and the traditions inherited from Greece, and thereby from the true antiquity of Egypt by the Nile. How many old *crydds*, confronted with such a ball, might then have sat down to make their own? These were men of skill, remember, who worked with leather and thread their entire lives. That Roman ball would have been a challenge and one that, I imagine, they would've been happy to meet.

The end result, during a period of 50 to 100 years, would have been the slow drift of elements of *harpastum* into less organized village games. Not all at once, but drip by drip, the elements that made *harpastum* exciting would be borrowed for other games, played outside the limits of Roman observation.

Still, it's a long way from *harpastum*, with its small ball and simple but careful rules, to the wild ball of mediaeval England and Normandy. Alas, the critical centuries are known as the Dark Ages for good reason. Little written information has survived from the period 400 to 800 AD.

However, while the Roman-built towns slowly decayed, even being abandoned entirely in places, and Latin fell out of use, the ball games remained and, indeed, would be passed on to the future.

Here we need to draw a quick picture of how Gaul and Britannia turned into Frankia and Angle-lond.

By the third century AD, the Roman Empire was in desperate straits. The Germanic tribes throughout the Rhine had experienced population growth and were hungry for land. They had formed federations, like that of the Alemanni, or "All Men," and the Franks, or "Free Men."

Further east, other tribes had coalesced into the Saxon nation, and some of them had moved to the German coasts, where they began to seek their fortune from piracy. This soon made life difficult on the shores of Britannia.

To save the empire, Diocletian doubled the size of the army in 286 AD, but the taxes to pay for this slowly sucked the life out of Roman society. To escape taxes they could not pay, people fled the cities and towns. The economy began a long slide back to subsistence agriculture, and small farmers became serfs.

After 360 AD, the western half of the empire rapidly deteriorated. The Franks crossed the Rhine, occupied Belgium, and became "Foederati," or allies of Rome. After the Visigoths sacked Rome in 410, the Franks took over northeastern Gaul. At the same time, Britannia, now stripped of Roman troops, proclaimed a shaky independence.

By this time, many German tribes were on the move, driven by land hunger and a new terror out of the east, the nomadic horde of the Huns. This culminated in the bloody battle of Chalons in 451 AD, when the "Last of the Romans," Flavius Aetius, pulled together an alliance of Visigoths, Franks, Burgundians, Alans, and a modest Roman army to match and defeat the Huns, with their allies the Ostrogoths and Gepids. The defeat of Attila, the self-proclaimed "Dread of the World," at Chalons spared Gaul and Western Europe from complete conquest by the Huns, with possible extreme consequences. Attila hated Christianity and had sworn to extirpate the entire religion.

The Huns withdrew, and Gaul was saved from devastation. As a side effect, the empire of the Huns never extended into the region of the cradle of football. Indeed, although Attila invaded Italy the following year, he died in the winter of 452–453, and his sons' squabbling over his empire tore it to pieces.

Flavius Aetius's success made him a target of the Roman emperor's paranoia, and he was murdered at the imperial court in Ravenna. In anger at this treachery, the Franks, who had fought for Rome under him, threw off their status as "foederati" and proclaimed independence.

At about this point, a plague swept through Europe, leaving in its wake a brief peace of exhaustion over lands devastated by economic decline, war, and endless armed raiding by one horde or another out of the east.

In these chaotic times, the Franks produced their first great ruler, Clovis (Louis, 481–511), and, under his leadership, took control of northern Gaul. They defeated the Visigoths and extended Frankish rule southwest to the Pyrenees.

Clovis also made the wise decision to convert to the Roman Catholic form of Christianity, which put the Franks into the same church as the Romanized Gauls they ruled. Another vital component of Frankish success lay in their openness to letting talented local rulers rise into their ranks. And, most important of all, the Franks did away with the harsh Roman taxes and replaced them with much milder taxes in kind and services, a forerunner of the feudal system that was beginning to evolve throughout the bankrupt lands of the former Roman Empire in Western Europe, providing Frankish kings with something like a real state, with real revenues. Thus, Frankia quickly outpaced its competitors to become the leading state of the new Europe, springing up amid the ruins of Rome.

Meanwhile, across the channel, Britannia had fallen to pieces. The last Roman Legion had withdrawn in 407, and small-scale wars, along with famine, followed. When the British prince Vortigern achieved a semblance of national rule in 445, he appealed to Flavius Aetius for help in fending off the Picts, who were raiding deep into northern Britain. Aetius, however, had his eyes on the Huns, so Vortigern invited some Saxons in as foederati. The Saxons quickly dealt with the Picts but then quarreled with their hosts about compensation. The Saxon foederati soon rose up against the Romanized British aristocracy. The fighting swung this way and that, but by 460, a full-scale migration of the Romanized British was underway to Brittany, "Little Britain" across the channel.

Bands of Saxons, joined by Angles, a related people from southern Denmark, began to land on the eastern and southern coastline of Britain. Now, instead of simply raiding, they came to stay. In some cases they rowed their 30-oar "keelboats" up the broad rivers to establish themselves inland.

This was also the time of the legendary Artorius, or King Arthur, as he would later be mythologized. Under Artorius, an army of Britons is thought to have waged a bigger campaign throughout the north and into the west to stem the Anglo-Saxon invasion. Sometime between 500 and 517 AD, a Saxon force was defeated at Mount Badon, and for about 50 years, the Saxon advance was halted. Indeed, the Britons appear to have won back territory in the southern and central region of the island.

This period of relative calm was to bring tremendous consequences for the future nation of England, for during these decades the first wave of Angles and Saxons settled in among the native Britons. Inevitably, there was a commingling of cultures. Fire and sword was the story in some places, and in others, villages of Saxons were set up in uncultivated areas next to older villages of Britons. Saxon warriors were known to show up in a British district, defeat the Romano-British aristocrats, and take over the village. The bulk of the population remained the same

Celtic-tinged peasantry as before. Some were enslaved, but because the invaders in this era were predominantly young men, there was strong pressure to interbreed with the Britons, quickly producing a new generation with one foot in either camp. The result was a crazy quilt of culture, which can be seen today in the names of villages, towns, and rivers. While rivers have retained their Celtic names, most English villages have Anglo-Saxon names, but among them are places with "Wal" or "Bret" prefixes, indicating that the invaders saw them as places populated by Britons.

Beginning in about 550 came a second, larger wave of invaders. The Angles had already taken Norfolk and Northumbria, and they began to spread in the north, while the West Saxons built up the Kingdom of Wessex in the southwest. Toward the end of the century, the Angle kingdoms of the north were united under the mighty warrior Ethelfrith and the remaining British realms east of Wales conquered. By 613, the boundaries of Angle-Lond, the future England, had begun to take shape.

And what of ball games in all this upheaval?

Crucially, in both England and northern France, the process of conquest had been tempered to one degree or another. The Franks took the Gallic upper class into their ranks. They entered the Roman church and became assimilated into the culture of Gaul.

Across the channel, in more thinly populated Britannia, the process of acculturation was much patchier. The Angles and Saxons did not resurrect the Roman towns, but built their own villages, often far from Roman roads. Nor did they welcome the Romanized British aristocrats, who either fought them to the death or fled to the west or even to Brittany. They did not embrace Christianity at this time, either.

Here and there throughout the landscape of both Frankia and Angle-lond, the old tradition of a spring ball game survived. We know this because we have surviving fossil games that date back to the Celts and druids, and we also know that when the veil lifted on the Dark Ages, folk football games were being played throughout the cradle region, from the Scottish Borders to Wales, Brittany, and Normandy.

Of course, any effort to trace the origins of football through the Dark Ages runs up against the complete lack of written records from the time. Apart from Gildas in the sixth century, the Venerable Bede in the eighth, and the *Anglo Saxon Chronicles*, there is only Beowulf and a handful of Welsh and Saxon poems to describe the lives of people in this era. None of them mention football.

We do have those fossil games, however, and from those we can tease out some interesting threads.

Charlotte Sophia Burne, author of the well-known nineteenth-century compendium of folk tales, songs, and legends *Shropshire Folk Lore*, also wrote about the survival of a fierce tradition of folk football in the Welsh county of Dyfyd. This is to the west of Wales, where the low Cambrian Mountains curve around the wide sweep of Cardigan Bay. Pembrokeshire, where George Owen described *cnapan* in the sixteenth century, is only a few miles farther west.

Miss Burne, writing in 1887, interviewed an elderly man in the Lampeter Workhouse, who recalled the *bwl troed* game in the parish of Llanwenog, which lay across the Teifi River to the south and east.

Here the game was played between the "Blaenus," which roughly translates to "natives," i.e., Welsh-speaking Celts, and the "Paddy Brothers," or "Bros," as they were called, from a traditional belief that they were descendants of Irish invaders who had settled in the hills long before. (An Irish invasion of Pembrokeshire occurred in the sixth century.) The Blaenus farmed the lowlands along the river, while the Bros herded sheep in the hills above. Thus it had been for about twelve hundred years.

This game was always held on Christmas Day, which, although unusual, was not unique. The morning was given over to religious observances and the game held at midday, at which point the entire population of the parish would assemble along the road dividing the highlands from the lowlands.

The ball, the *bwl troed*, literally, "ball of foot," or sometimes the *bwl ddu*, "black ball," was round and made of leather, and it contained an inflated pig's bladder. The rules were simple and similar to those of *cnapan*, described almost three hundred years earlier.

The ball was thrown up on the road and scrambled for by the assembled Blaenus and Bros. It could be thrown, kicked, or carried, and the object of the game was to fetch the ball back to either the Blaenus stronghold at New Court or up the hillside to the Bros hamlet of Rhyddian. Tackling was rough, and many kicks were exchanged. Rough play would occasionally lead to an outbreak of more direct combat with fists, but this never halted the game, which rolled on to leave the combatants behind until they finished their fight or came to their senses.

The field of play covered the entire parish, an area of many square miles, and the game lasted until one side got the ball back to their stronghold. It might well be pitch dark by that time.

Victory was celebrated in time-honored fashion, with long, loud cheering and the discharge of every gun in the village.

Winning this game was so important, according to Burne's informant, that a Bros or Blaenu would rather lose a milk cow than see the football go to the other side of the parish.

Other than the fierceness of the competition, what can we deduce from this old folk game?

First, this was the west of Wales, as far from the Saxons the Celts could go without taking to their boats. The Brythonic language and traditions remained strong. Among the traditions was the Celtic way of scoring, by simply taking the ball home with you—just as we've seen with Cornish hurling and *la soule* in Brittany.

Second, the game had made a transition to newer technology at some point. The hard wooden ball of hurling and *cnapan* had been exchanged for a round leather ball, encasing an inflated pig's bladder. The result was not unlike a Roman follis type ball or the kind of ball that became widely popular in the fifteenth century in England for "Kicking Camp." (Or, earlier, in Tang China, for the aerial form of *cuju*.) The advantage of the leather ball was that it could be kicked for distance, which considerably changed the dynamic of the game. In Cornish hurling or other "small ball" games played with wooden balls, the ball could be thrown, but rarely as far as a football can be kicked; moreover, once an inflated ball is moving, it can be kicked along in a way that can quickly cover a lot of ground, if that ground is open enough, as in a field or meadow. The larger leather ball is also harder to lose in the bushes, rushes, or vegetation.

Finally, and most important, this is a clear example of how a ball game could channel an ancient animosity between two distinct communities into a relatively safe form of conflict. Rather than outright warfare or blood feuds, they could fight each over something as trivial as a football.

Well, clearly it wasn't so trivial to them!

So, here's the social mechanism by which the ancient games of the Celts and Romans could be passed on to the Saxons and Franks. The process could take many paths, but let's imagine an area where an old Celtic village survived between new Frank or Saxon villages. Some intermarriage would inevitably have taken place, and with it would have come other kinds of mixing, usually concerning heated protests of bitter-minded elders and hard-hearted zealots on both sides.

But on a certain day of the year, perhaps in the spring or midwinter, the Celts produced a ball, maybe even a leather-covered one in the Greco-Roman style, and across the fields and open heath they went, whooping and hollering as they kicked the ball and one another, or carrying it under the arm as they charged through the opposing ranks.

The first time this happened, the Saxons probably ran for their swords and shields, convinced the Wales, the Britons, were about to attack them. But then, as they watched their crazy neighbors, they likely saw that it was just a big, wild game of some sort.

The Germanic newcomers were also fond of play—and fighting— and this kind of rough play was obviously fun and bound to appeal to them.

Sooner, rather than later, perhaps a challenge was sent from the Saxons to the Celts on the hilltop. How about a game?

Surely this would have set off arguments among the Celts. The wounds were too deep, too recent, the hatred too strong. But here was an opportunity to rub the Saxons' noses in their athletic inferiority to the superior, natural Celts.

And in time, a game was set up.

As is usually the way with things football, I expect it took many years for the Saxons to master the tricks of the game and break a seemingly unshakeable Celtic grip on victory, which, of course, would have served to further sharpen the edges of the competition. That is, until that day when, at last, an Edward or an Alfred got away from the trapping, tackling Celts to run the ball all the way back to Saxton, bringing hard-earned victory to the newcomers at last.

With that victory, the game of football took small step forward, edging away from extinction and toward a new, rough, burly sort of life in the coming Middle Ages.

But before that there would come further tests, and both Angle-Lond and Frankia would be hammered hard on the forge of war and social evolution. Wielding the hammers would be a variety of characters, from the great Arab general Abderrahman Ibn Abdillah Alghefeki to such Viking killers as Eric Bloodaxe and Ubbar the Boneless. The most important blacksmiths in this work would ultimately be offspring of the Vikings. Of them, the Norman, William the Bastard would deal the most telling blows, and with them would come huge consequences for football as well.

4

THE MIDDLE AGES

Games ancestral to modern football existed before the Dark Ages, which came after the fall of the western half of the Roman Empire, and we know that similar games were being played when literacy returned and drove back the shadows.

What happened in between?

We can only make conjectures from the existing evidence, for example, the "fossil games" and the tales from the likes of Charlotte Sophia Burne's interviewee in the Lampeter Workhouse.

One interesting fossil is particularly fossilized, in that it's been dead for almost five hundred years. But in a description of this long-dead game, we can get a glimpse at another aspect of the pattern of cultural mixing that took place on the island that was Britannia and became England, Wales, and Scotland, and the way that an ancient game shifted to a more modern one.

This game was played in Chester, chief town of Cheshire, which lies on the border with Wales, in North West England. Chester began as a "castrum," a Roman fort. Indeed, wherever you see a "chester" or "caster" suffix in an English place name, it usually refers to a Roman fort. To them it was Deva Victrix, built in 70 AD, in the heart of the lands of the Cornovii tribe. The name "Deva" may have been taken from the river Dee or the Celtic goddess of the same name. The Victrix stood for the XXth Legion, Valeria Victrix, who were based there. Settlement grew up around the fort, and interactions between local Celts and Roman soldiers and administrators became commonplace. The Legion was withdrawn in the late fourth century, after three hundred or so years of Roman rule. An amphitheater, built shortly after the fort, could seat as many as 10,000 and was the largest military amphitheater built in Britannia by the Romans.

After the Roman withdrawal the area became a scene of warfare between the Romano-Brythons and Angles and Saxons. There are no records, but the legendary Artorius, King Arthur, is supposed to have fought a great battle in the city. Two hundred years later, the great Angle warlord Ethelfrith of Northumbria finally routed the Brythons (or Welsh) in the Battle of Chester, and from then onward the area remained in Anglo-Saxon hands, except for a brief period when it was occupied by the Danes. The Anglo-Saxons called the city Ceaster.

After the Norman conquest in 1066, Chester became the center for an Earldom and an important base of defense against the threat of raids by the Welsh from their fastness in North Wales.

The Anglo-Saxon period remains shadowy because of the lack of written records. In our hypertexted, 24-hour news cycle world, it's hard to imagine a time when virtually no one knew how to read or write. The Anglo-Saxon kingdoms, Mercia, Northumberland, Essex, Wessex, and Sussex, were established during the Dark Ages, so we have mere bits and pieces relating to this process and just a handful of written records.

The Angles and Saxons converted to Christianity in the seventh century, and their own buildings slowly grew up around Roman ruins. Where the Romans built with stone, paved their streets, put in sewers and water supplies, the Saxons built with wood, wattle, and withe, with dried mud walls, and their streets were unpaved, mostly muddy, and stinking of raw sewage.

The last pagan king, the Jute, Arwald of the Isle of Wight, was slain in battle in 686. Three years later, King Aethelred of Mercia began building the Minster of St. John the Baptist in Chester.

Churches, cathedrals, and multigenerational projects built with stone were one side of things, and on another were guilds. The name comes from the Saxon term *gilden*, meaning to pay or make payment. Each member of a guild contributed a small sum at regular intervals to the guild, in a form of benevolent association. Guilds took care of their members when they fell sick or became too old to work. There was a significant religious component, too, even to the extent of subsidies for members' all-important pilgrimages to holy sites like Canterbury, the leading cathedral in the land.

In any craft guild, organized to protect the men of a particular craft, there were the masters, who had full membership, the journeymen, who were on their way to such membership, and the apprentices, youngsters learning the trade. The rules for advancement were always strict.

Among the early guilds in the city of Chester were the weavers, tanners, saddlers, shoemakers, carpenters, and ironmongers. After the Norman conquest some of the Saxon craft guilds became the basis for merchant guilds, with official charters granted by the king or municipal authorities, be they mayors, abbots, or barons. Armed with a charter, such guilds controlled their craft or area of trade within the town, keeping out competition in the manner of a cartel.

The guilds were also a vital part of any medieval town's social life. In Chester, they organized the mystery plays and the midsummer show.

And then there was the ball game. The Chester game was famous throughout the land during the Middle Ages for its violence, which apparently outdid that of the other similar games that raged on Shrove Tuesday (Mardi Gras) and Ash Wednesday, as previously described in Ashbourne and St. Colomb Major.

The Chester game involved interesting aspects of the way things worked in a medieval town. Daniel and Samuel Lysons's *Magna Britannia* includes a description dated from the sixteenth century that states, "Upon Goteddsday, at the Crosse upon the Rood Dee, before the mayor of the cittie did offer unto the company of the Drapers an homage, a ball of leather, called a footeballe, of the value of three shillings and four pence, which was played for by the shoemakers and saddlers, to bring it to the house of the Mayor, or either of the Sherriffs."

The Drapers were a superior guild of merchants, with nationwide connections and a Royal Charter. Under their auspices, the apprentice "boys"—many of whom were in their 20s or 30s—from the lesser craft guilds of the saddlers and shoemakers would do battle for the footeballe. An item like a footeballe, priced at three shillings and four pence in say 1300 AD, would, in modern money, be anywhere from £200 to £400 ($300 to $600), primarily from the cost of the skilled leatherwork going into it.

The ball, an expensive artifact for the times, was thrown out to the two "teams," although "small armies" or "mobs" might be better descriptions, and all hell would break loose. Daniel and Samuel Lysons elucidate, "Much harm was done, some having their bodies bruised and crushed, some their armes, heads, legges broken, some otherwise maimed and in peril of their life."

This was a hug with even fewer rules than that of Ashbourne. And clearly there was some kind of fizz going on between the shoemakers and saddlers, the kind of enmity we still see today in the soccer world between fans of some clubs, like those of the Boca Juniors and River Plate in Buenos Aires, or West Ham and Chelsea in London. Maybe it had something to do with the price of leather and who got the best hides to work with. More likely it had no obvious origin and was just one of those things; perhaps apprentice saddlers looked down on shoemakers, who resented that and took any opportunity to take saddler boys down a peg.

It's also interesting to note that the goals were the houses of the mayor or the two sheriffs. That the city had two sheriffs is an interesting side topic, and that the goals were their houses must have been mightily inconvenient.

But there was another aspect of this rough game that is of singular interest for this history, because in another ceremony, the saddlers—who may well have been the oldest craft guild in the city—would present a "ball of wood painted with flowers to be fought for by the mob," as described by Daniel and Samuel Lysons in *Magna Britannia*.

Balls of wood, whether covered in tin or painted with flowers, were surely the products of an older culture, the Celtic world that preceded the Roman conquest, the coming of the Saxons, and the rebuilding of the land into the Kingdom of England.

Here are two aspects of the early history of football side by side: a ball with great symbolic value and a cultural legacy of times far in the past thrown to the "mob" on the one hand, and a game of "town ball" with a leather ball and a designated contest between apprentices of two guilds on the other.

But the fate of the Chester game is equally important, for it was a signpost to the future. After flourishing in its barbaric glory for centuries, the game was suppressed in 1533. By then, in the days of Henry VIII, old medieval England was caught up in the transformations that would lead to our modern era. Having a large, heaving mob raging through the streets on Mardi Gras in pursuit of a footeballe was seen as both dangerous and retrograde.

The mayor of the time, Henry Gee, was smart enough to know that banning the old game would not be enough on its own, and so he substituted a horse race, held on Shrove Tuesday in 1539. In 1609, the day was changed to St. George's Day. The race became cemented into the social round of the city, and the old game was forgotten. The race, originally run on the Roodee, a band of flat ground in the heart of the city, was then held outside the city in the Forest of Gaitres and then moved to its present site, Knavesmire, in 1731. The Roodee is now called the Chester Racecourse, and it may be the oldest still-running horserace in the world.

While wild, unruly games of football evolved from the village level to games between apprentices in the new towns and cities of the early Middle Ages, grander events on wider stages were threatening the very existence of the cradle of football region.

As mentioned earlier, the Frankish kings had made a sensible decision in matters of religion, converting to the Roman Church. This made them part of the same congregation as the Gallo-Roman aristocracy and eased their way to creating a functioning state. The other German tribes either remained pagans or were converted by priests of the Arian, Christian heresy. This was a fatal weakness for the various Goths, Suebi, Vandals, and others because they stubbornly clung to Arianism, in which God the Father is seen as utterly distinct from God the Son. But throughout these dark centuries, from the fall of Rome to the return of literacy in the tenth century, Christianity spread to much of Western Europe, forming the central pillar of the new culture arising in the place of Rome; however, actors from the periphery were to threaten the new Christian lands, including the cradle of football area.

Let us turn away from the cradle for a moment and take a quick peek at the other centers where great ball games had developed.

By the seventh century, when Angle-Lond was ruled by seven petty kings and Frankia's Merovingian dynasty was growing weak, in faraway China, events were underway on a far grander scale. First, the "lesser" dynasty of the Sui had managed to reestablish the imperial idea, ending three centuries of chaos and warfare. They had rebuilt civil administration, regained sound finances, and imposed bearable levels of taxation.

Buddhism had been adopted as the official spiritual force. In 618, the Sui gave way to the Tang, as Li Yuan, a northern aristocrat, usurped the throne and proclaimed himself Emperor Gaozu. The Tang were the next major dynasty. They would fully restore China's Imperial glory, and as previously noted, this would be a time of great popularity for athletic contests, including the *cuju* form of football.

Cuju courts would become commonplace throughout Tang China's cities, and the game itself underwent a shift, as an inflated ball replaced one stuffed with feathers. One intriguing possibility is that the inflated ball, similar to the Greco-Roman *follis*, had traveled east on the Silk Road until it reached China. The Greeks had developed the basic concept of an inflated pig's bladder set inside a casing of stoutly sewn leather some time during the late Bronze Age, at least a thousand years before. Balls of this kind were used for *episkyros*. This was long before the beginning of the Silk Road and the start of trade between China, via many intermediaries, and the Mediterranean world. Of course, there are no known records, and we are unlikely to ever know for sure. Indeed, the Chinese civilization was highly inventive—everything from paper to gunpowder had been invented there—so it is quite possible that they had also discovered for themselves the football-friendly use of a pig's bladder. Once it had been heated carefully using a flame to make it round, it was blown up like a balloon and encased in leather to make a ball with some bounce and enough weight to be driven for distance with a good kick.

Moving across the vast Pacific Ocean to Mesoamerica, this was the Classic Period of the Mayan civilization. Calakmul had replaced Tikal as the dominant Mayan city. Farther north, in Mexico, the great city of Teotihuacan had already fallen, being burned and sacked in about 550 AD, possibly as a result of internal unrest due to prolonged droughts and famine. Throughout Mesoamerica, from the cities of central Mexico to the classic Mayan cities in the Yucatan, the great ball game with the rubber ball was one of the strong motifs of the culture, along with warfare and human sacrifice. It would continue, jumping from the Mayans to the Toltecs to the Aztecs, until the Spanish arrived and their priests set about suppressing it.

Swinging back to Europe and the Mediterranean, we see the former Eastern Roman Empire, now known as the Byzantine Empire, holding on to both the light of Roman civilization and the cross of Christianity.

While the popes in Rome suffered from the oppression of the Lombards, yet another German tribe that had migrated south, the Visigoths, held Spain, but the Byzantines had regained North Africa and parts of Italy, and they were also holding onto Egypt and the Levant.

However, while the Byzantines had weathered the assaults of the Avars in the Balkans and the Sassanian Persians in the east, a minor event far to the south would soon change everything. In 622, a camel trader and sometime prophet named Mohammed, of the tribe Quraish, was expelled from Mecca, a relatively obscure Arabian town best known for its possession of the Kaaba, or Cube, a holy site ascribed to Abraham and Ishmael two thousand years earlier. Mohammed had argued that the collection of Arab idols kept in the Kaaba amounted to nothing more than superstition and were offensive to Allah, the Arab name for God. He reported visions of the angel Gabriel and direction from the one God in a series of chapters that became a book called the Koran (Revelation).

Mohammed found a new following in nearby Medina and returned in triumph to Mecca in 630. He died in 632, and almost immediately, new Arab armies, imbued with the fires of Islam, swept to the north, west, and east. From early raids to later major campaigns, the Arab armies were generally victorious, spreading Islam and the Koran as they went.

While the prophet is recorded in hadith (teachings) as having urged children to practice archery and learn to swim and ride a horse, ball games were never high on the list of preferred activities in the Muslim world, although in Egypt they still played their own form of hockey. Again, it is important to mention that pigs did not prosper in the conditions of Arabia and were absent from Muslim menus. Without pigs or the rubber tree of Central America, a bouncing ball would have been hard to achieve. So, football-type games were absent from this region. This has changed today, with the pursuit of soccer from Morocco to Iran and Malaysia to Sudan; however, there is no evidence that the Muslims played ball games, in particular football-style games, in the premodern period.

The Arab armies were primarily cavalry, on good-sized horses, and they employed stirrups, giving them strength in the saddle for fighting hand to hand. In this era, heavy cavalry were deemed close to unstoppable, and when deployed, it usually frightened the infantry into panicky flight and disaster. For the next seven hundred years or so, the heavy cavalry, in the form of massively armored knights, would be the dominant force on European battlefields. Only the advent of first the longbow, and then the firearm, would end that dominance.

A pair of crucial battles with important implications for our story of football illustrates this dynamic. In both, an army of infantry faced an army heavy with cavalry. On both occasions, the infantry force had the advantage of standing on higher ground.

Following the 711 defeat of the Visigoths, the forces of Islam had overrun most of Spain, setting up the first of these decisive events, the Battle of Tours, in 732. The battle matched Charles Martel and an army of trained, experienced Frankish infantry against an army of Moorish cavalry rolling north from Spain into the heart of the Frankish kingdom.

The Arab–Moorish force was intent on looting the fabled monastery of St. Martin in the city of Tours. Against such a move, Charles Martel—nicknamed "the Hammer" for his ability to hammer money out of the wealthy Frankish church—placed his army on an area of high ground near the city of Poitiers. The Franks stood their ground, holding a "shield wall," with their axes, spears, and swords at the ready.

Historians are divided as to the importance of this battle. Some maintain that since no other force in Northern Europe would have been capable of standing against an army like that of Arab general Abderrahman Ibn Abdillah Alghefeki, defeat here for the Franks could have marked the beginning of the end of both Frankia and, indeed, western Christendom. Others dismiss this idea and believe that the tide of Islam had already reached its high point and would inevitably recede.

The Muslim army has been estimated at between 30,000 and 80,000 strong. Charles Martel had about 20,000 to 30,000 Franks and Burgundians, plus local militias, who were much less willing to stand in a shield wall.

Modern historians note that both armies lacked supplies and had to live off the country. Thus, they were likely smaller than most records indicate.

This was to be the first great test of the Frankish realm, as well as of Charles Martel's generalship. Accounts of the battle are few and vague; its location is barely known, other than it lay between Tours and Poitiers in Western France.

It is worth noting that at this date, the long decline in population that had begun in about 400 AD had started to bottom out. The former Roman Empire had contracted by about one-third in terms of population, except where German tribes had pushed in and intermarried with the locals. The population collapse explains, in part, the weakness of European regimes at this time.

Martel kept his battle-hardened, veteran infantry on high ground, perhaps a hillside. The approaches were broken up by trees and gullies. For a week the armies faced one another, and Martel used the local militias to scout the Arab army, raid when possible, and gather food from the local farms. Abderrahman had promised his men riches from looting the fabled abbey in the city of Tours, but to get there he had to push through the army of Franks. Finally he could wait no longer, and Abderrahman ordered an attack—it was late in the season, and the Arabs feared the cold of approaching winter. Repeated cavalry assaults failed to break the Franks, who held their shield wall while both sides suffered casualties. The Arabs eventually wavered, as defections, fear of the loss of booty already taken, and a sense of futility in the face of stubborn defense by the Franks led to a withdrawal. The Franks had won a significant victory, with disciplined infantry withstanding heavy cavalry. Tours, the Abbey of St. Martin, and the rest of Frankia and Christendom were saved from the Muslim threat.

Fighting continued with Moorish expeditions in the south of France, but the Battle of Tours was a high-tide mark, and never again did Islam threaten to obliterate Christendom in the west.

Then, in 750, the faraway caliphate in Baghdad fell into open civil war, and the threat of invasion by Muslim armies faded away. The end result for the cradle of football was further protection from devastating raids and conversion to Islam.

But another threat was soon to materialize, this time emerging from the northern mists, borne on swift ships. The Norse, or the Vikings, as they are popularly known, began raiding the coasts of Northern England and Scotland in the late eighth century, about 50 years after Charles Martel had stopped the Islamic threat in the south.

The Vikings would prove much more troublesome and difficult to cope with than the Moors from Spain. They would also leave their mark on the development of games of folk football.

The "Norse" were from Norway, but the greatest challenge to the Anglo-Saxons came from the Danes. The first dramatic event in this tale came with the raid on the rich monastery of the Island of Lindisfarne, off the coast of Northumberland, in 793 AD. Monks were slaughtered, buildings burned, and treasures looted, while the Norse bandits again disappeared into the sea.

This pattern repeated itself ad infinitum during the next two hundred years. The small realms of England, Scotland, Ireland, and Wales could not cope. No local king could afford to watch the coasts and mobilize sufficient forces to catch or defeat a couple of boatloads of heavily armed Norse "Vikings." By the time a local lord could get to a burning village with his horsemen, the Vikings were long gone.

Viking war bands soon took to landing and roaming inland, seeking rich churches and towns with loot. As the Danes became the primary source of Viking raids and invasions, their numbers grew. In the ninth century came the first crisis for the Saxons. The Danes conquered much of the eastern part of the country, named the "Danelaw." Danish place names, for instance, town names that end in "by," are common there, from Whitby to Derby.

Alfred the Great, King of Wessex and then of England, rose up to smite the Danes after 871. After a decade or more of inconclusive fighting, Alfred realized that to stop the threat he needed to reorganize the Kingdom of Wessex in a fundamental way. He established *burhs* (boroughs) in the towns, with a standing military force in each. He also built a fleet. With new tactics he had better success, and the first crisis passed.

But the Danes would come again one hundred years later, and under Sveyn Forkbead and his son Cnut, they would conquer England in 1015. Cnut became another "the Great" and ruled England, Denmark, and part of Sweden in a small empire for almost two decades.

The Norse raids had devastated Ireland and Scotland. The Norse colonized the Orkneys and Shetland islands, and in Northern France, the Viking chief Rollo (Rolf), having seized control of the province of what became Normandy, converted to Christianity and pledged feudal allegiance to the Frankish king Charles. There continues to be a fierce debate about Rollo's origins, with Norwegian and Danish historians at odds so furious at times you can almost imagine them taking up their own shield walls and fighting one another for the right to claim Rollo as their own.

But it was Rollo's great-great-great-grandson, born a century after his death, who would become the most famous Norman of them all. This was William the Bastard, who became William the Conqueror, King of England.

Following Cnut, the Saxons regained the kingship of England, but only for the reign of Edward the Confessor, who died without an heir. That left three claimants to the throne, Harold Godwin, crowned as Harold II, his brother Tostig, allied with Norse King Harald Hardrada, and William of Normandy, "the Bastard."

In 1066 came the second of the important battles for the future of football. Now, more than three hundred years after Charles Martel's Franks had withstood the Moorish cavalry at Tours, the darkness of the Dark Ages was peeling back as literacy returned and with it record keeping. As a consequence, we have far more established detail about the Battle of Hastings than the Battle of Tours.

In the three-way contest for the throne of England, William of Normandy ended up in a direct battle with Harold Godwin, on a hill a few miles inland from the town of Hastings.

William landed a small army, perhaps 10,000 strong, on the coast of Southern England. He had 5,000 cavalry, the rest foot soldiers and archers. Harold Godwin, meanwhile, had defeated and slain his brother Tostig and the Norwegian king at Stamford Bridge in Yorkshire. Now he hastened south to confront William.

Harold arrived with a typical Saxon army, 7,000 men, all infantry, but much of it relatively inexperienced, men of the *fyrd*, or local levy. On the top of a hillside they formed a shield wall.

The battle, on October 14, 1066, lasted all day. The Norman cavalry tried several times to break the Saxon shield wall but failed. Next the Normans used a difficult, dangerous tactic of attacking and then pretending to retreat in disorder, hoping to lure the Saxons out of their shield wall. The trick worked. The less experienced men of the Saxon *fyrd* set off in pursuit. Discipline was lost, and the Norman horsemen turned around and cut them down. King Harold died, it is said with an arrow in the eye, and the Saxon army disintegrated with as many as 4,000 casualties.

William and his Normans rode on to London, and he assumed the title of William I, King of England, ending the line of Saxon kings and introducing, among other things, the use of the French language at the court of England.

In Europe as a whole, this battle was not seen as very important. Events in the east, where the Byzantines were now hard pressed by the Turks following the Battle of Manzikert in 1071, were of much greater concern. This led the pope to call for a Crusade to free the Holy Land, especially Jerusalem, from the grip of Islam.

Thus, while William and his Norman barons were establishing an iron-fisted rule over the English, the rebounding economy and population of Western Europe was projecting force, with an army of mailed knights, into the Middle East. The Crusade even succeeded in capturing the cities of Antioch and Jerusalem and establishing small Christian states. The contrast with the situation three centuries earlier is dramatic.

In the cradle region, feudalism and the two- or three-field system of agriculture were firmly in place. The family dynasty of William the Conqueror ran out of heirs within a century, and following a civil war, the throne passed to Henry of Anjou, the first of the Plantagenet Kings of England in 1189. Henry was already the Count of Anjou, Count of Maine, and Duke of Aquitaine, and now he added Duke of Normandy and King of England to his titles. England and France were thus interwoven, and warfare would result for much of the next three hundred years.

The Catholic Church was deeply woven in to the fabric of life, with feast days and festivals, many of them borrowed from older pagan feasts and celebrations. For our story, it is Shrove Tide, or Mardi Gras ("Fat Tuesday"), that takes on unique importance. While traditional "folk" football games are known from other days of the year, the festival of Shrove Tuesday was the day chosen for most.

This made sense, because Shrove Tuesday is the feast day before the beginning of Lent on Ash Wednesday. The name comes from "to shrive" or confess, as in one's sins, on the day before the solemn beginning of Lent. So, naturally, it became the day when people tried to eat all the things they were going to do without during Lent, like pancakes and other richer, fatty foods.

About the same time, perhaps in 1190, one William Fitzstephen, a cleric in the administration of Thomas Becket, the Archbishop of Canterbury, provided us with the first surviving description of Shrove Tuesday activities, including games of ball outside the walls of London:

> On Shrove Tuesday, boys from the schools bring fighting cocks to their master, and the whole forenoon is given up to boyish sport; for they have a holiday in the schools that they may watch their cocks do battle. After dinner all the youth of the city goes out into the fields to a much-frequented game of ball. The scholars of each school have their own ball, and almost all the workers of each trade have theirs also in their hands. Elder men, and fathers, and rich citizens come on horseback to watch the contests of their juniors, and after their fashion are young again with the young.

It's not much of a match report, but it is our first scrap of information derived from something other than a fossil game. This scrap is part of Fitzstephen's account of life in London at the time, which appears as a preface in Becket's biography. Becket was murdered by overeager knights, possibly on Henry's orders, which occasioned a crisis in the state and caused Henry to accept some serious "shrivening" with birch rods and much prayer in penance.

What we can establish from this piece of information is that, quite simply, as conjectured before, games of ball were now established among the youth, whether they be scholars or workers.

A century later, in 1287, the Synod of Exeter saw the Bishops ban "unseemly sports" from churchyards. Here we have our first known effort at banning football. That it was football that m'lords wanted to ban is pretty certain, because from this point onward there grew a continuing tension between the authorities—civil, religious, and even military—and the passion for wild games of ball that disturbed the peace and set mobs loose in the streets.

Sovereigns inveighed against football again and again. During the long, intermittent warfare known as the "Hundred Years War," in which English kings vied to become kings of France, Edward III, Richard II, Henry IV, and Henry V invoked laws to ban football and punish anyone for playing it, for fear it would turn youths away from practicing with the longbow, the weapon that gave the English an edge over French cavalry armies.

However, in this era, the state had limited power to do much about an issue such as this. Laws were passed, but there was no enforcement capability. There were no police, for instance, only sheriffs and a few constables, usually temporarily appointed for a particular emergency. Hence, again and again throughout the years came these almost plaintive-sounding, stern demands that, for example, "Na man play at the fute-ball," as a decree from Scotland's parliament demanded in 1424. The people who liked rough football ignored their rulers and continued playing. The lamentations about football continued, too. In 1555, football was banned at Oxford University, after one too many violent incidents in the town. In 1571, Queen Elizabeth I demanded that "No football play [was] to be used or suffered within the City of London."

Did this stop the game? The short answer is no.

While footeballe was arousing the ire of sovereigns and bishops—and this occurred in Northern France, as well as in England and Scotland—a couple of innovations had taken place.

At some point, impossible to accurately date, games of early, rough mob footeballe had become customary at some of the great fairs. These games were often called "camp ball," roughly meaning "battle ball." Camp ball was not restricted to Shrove Tuesday and seems to have been more impromptu, organized via a challenge between villages or at the fairgrounds. The number of players was smaller, generally 10 to 15 a side, going by accounts from the eighteenth century, in East Anglia, where this game persisted as a folk tradition. Except for occasions when someone was killed, they don't seem to have produced the angry outcry caused by the regular games played in urban areas, which is understandable—50 men fighting over a ball in a field near a great fair would be just another fun aspect of the festivities and something to watch. The same battle on Cheapside or any market town's Broadway would involve damage to property and a general upset to normal life.

In the first English–Latin dictionary, published in 1440, and attributed to a friar in Norfolk, East Anglia, camp ball was defined as follows: "Campan or playar at foot balle, pediluson; campyon, or champion."

The next development, and again, there are no records and almost nothing to go by to date this, but at some point, in about 1400, the term *kicking camp* began to be used. If the game now involved kicking the ball, then it was not using the heavy, sawdust-stuffed balls known from town ball. Instead, it was most likely using a ball of leather, encasing an inflated pig's bladder.

There is an intriguing reference in a verse praising St. Hugh, the Bishop of Lincoln, who died in 1200: "Four and twenty bonny boys, were playing at the ball . . . he kicked the ball with his right foot."

In a collection of manuscripts of the "miracles" of Henry VI dated from between 1481 and 1500, thus at the end of the Wars of the Roses and beginning of the Tudor era, there is a description of a game played at Cawston, Nottinghamshire: "[C]alled by some the foot-ball game. It is one in which young men, in country sport, propel a huge ball, not by throwing it into the air, but by striking it and rolling along the ground, and that not with their hands, but with their feet." The game was also described as being rough, "abominable enough" indeed.

Once again we're left to wonder how this technology, which originated with the ancient Greeks, had reached the market towns of medieval England. Is it possible that this kind of ball technology had been lost and was rediscovered from some obscure locality? Or, an even more entertaining thought, had it traveled to Tang China, been popularized, and then traveled back on the Silk Road to Western Europe?

In Italy, beginning in the same century, in the cities of the north, particularly Florence, but also Venice—a trading hub with links to the Silk Road via the Middle East—another violent style of football had developed: *calcio fiorentino* or *calcio storico* (historic football). This was a game played by young aristocrats, not the mobs of England and Northern France, and it had few rules. Teams were limited to 27 a side, and goals were scored in the style of *episkyros*, by being driven over the end line into netting. Violence was acceptable, but only by the tackler to he being tackled, and fists and feet were part of tackling; however, punching someone who didn't have the ball was out. Players wore expensive clothing, too, perhaps to emphasize how different they were from the common mob.

Today there is a revival of *calcio storico* in Italy. They use soccer balls, and that style of ball seems to have always been the one in use, which again raises the question, Was this follis-type of ball simply revived from ancient Italian tradition? Or did it reappear in the hands of some trader who had bought it in a market in the Levant? And again, to tease out a possible route of transmission just a little bit more, merchants from Northern Italy, including Florence, regularly made the trip to England during the summer for the great fairs, where they sold cloth and other highly prized Italian manufactures. Was this how inflated footballs came to late medieval England? However it came to be, this crucial change for the games being played in the English countryside had taken place by the middle of the fifteenth century, circa 1450. And as it did, a form of "footeballe" began to solidify there, with customary rules and agreed forms of play.

5

THE END OF THE MIDDLE AGES

The tide of the long, on-and-off war between the kings of England and the kings of France had turned, even as the 19-year-old Maid of Orleans, Joan of Arc, was burned at the stake on May 30, 1431. Four years later, Burgundy switched sides to back the French Valois family's grip on the throne. The French continued to gain victories; the English king, Henry VI, lost his possessions in France; and at the final battle, Castillion, near Bordeaux, in 1453, the English defeat was marked by the use of three hundred guns, dug into an artillery "park" on the battlefield, which were used to slaughter the English as they advanced.

Although English kings and queens continued to claim the throne of France until 1800, by which point it was pretty moot, since Napoleon Bonaparte was about to crown himself emperor, the quest for that throne was finished after Castillion. For England, the next few decades were the time of the Wars of the Roses, a bloody struggle for the English throne between the houses of Lancaster and York. For France, other struggles loomed, but for Europe as a whole, the French victory and the use of artillery was underlined by the fall of Constantinople to the Ottoman Turks, who battered the walls to rubble with siege guns.

The Middle Ages were coming to an end.

And now, as the Tudors inherited the throne of England, European sailors were beginning the voyages that would take them to the Americas, around Africa, and on to the rest of the world.

As previously noted, the enormous irony that underlies this is that Ming China, in the years before Joan of Arc's rise to fame, had also begun exploring the world, with huge fleets of enormous ships. But all that had ended abruptly, and Ming China had turned inward, leaving the world's oceans open to the Europeans.

The discovery of the Americas led to conquests by the Spanish of both the Aztecs and the Incas. The great Mesoamerican ball game was one casualty of this process. Enormous amounts of precious metals flowed from both Peru and Mexico to Spain, first as loot, and then, after the mountain of silver ore at Potosi was discovered, as the fruit of the slave labor of tens of thousands of Andean natives. That silver flooded Europe and ruined the Spanish economy because most of it was spent on goods and armaments, and most of the goods were manufactured in the Dutch Netherlands. The flow of silver sparked a steady, remorseless inflation in Europe at large that ran through the latter part of the sixteenth century into the seventeenth century and played havoc with many customary systems of payment for goods and services. It also elevated trade and boosted industry, simply by virtue of there now being more money in the economy.

As outlined in the previous chapter, the authorities at the city and state levels had decided that town ball, or mob football, was generally a bad thing, and they had inveighed against it for centuries. They would continue to demand that it cease, with little effect, for centuries to come—although, as also mentioned, there were occasional successes, and terrifying old games were suppressed. There were, however, countercurrents. King James I, who followed Elizabeth I on the throne, had a *Book of Sports* published, in which he called on good Christian men and youths to play football on Sunday afternoons, after attending church services in the morning. This may be seen as a piece of propaganda directed at the crusading Puritans, who were out to ban activities of any kind, other than religious observance, on the Sabbath.

Nonetheless, in the countryside of England, Wales, Scotland, and Brittany, curious customs and truly odd variants on the "mob football" theme continued, and some continue today.

One of the best examples comes from the village of Haxey, in northern Lincolnshire. The village is just south of Epworth, home of John Wesley, founder of the Christian Methodists. It lies about halfway between the cities of Sheffield and Kingston-upon-Hull.

Legend has it that in the fourteenth century, Lady de Mowbray, whose husband was the local lord of the manor, was out riding on a windy day toward the next village, Westwoodside. As she rode, her hood was blown off by the wind. Thirteen peasants working in the field chased it about in the wind. The one who finally caught it was too bashful to hand it back to Lady de Mowbray and gave it to a bolder lad, who did the deed. As she thanked him for it, she remarked that he had acted like a lord, while the one who'd caught it first had acted like a fool.

To commemorate this moment of feudal chivalry, she donated 13 "half-acres" of land on condition that the chase for the hood be performed every year. This mysterious formulation was presumably to allow the rents on those "half-acres" to help pay for the festivities. Only one half-acre remains, it seems, and all the deeds related to this have been lost.

The most likely Lady de Mowbray would have been wed to the Third Baron Mowbray of Axholme, John De Mowbray, 1310–1361. A deed granting land to commoners was enacted by that baron in 1359, which appears to cement the legend in a degree of historical fact.

It is also important to highlight that Axholme and that entire district was a center for flax growing, the essential fiber for fine linen and canvas, a fabric in various weights used for everything from coats to sails. Just a decade prior, in 1347–1349, the land had been devastated by the Black Death, the terrifying Bubonic plague, which by some estimates killed about a third of the population of England and France, producing a shortage of labor and increasing the power of peasants in the economic balance.

The traditional celebration of the rescue of Lady de Mowbray's hood turned into a variant on mob football at some undetermined point. Today the "hood"—a leather tube filled with thick rope—is fought for by a large crowd on the 12th night after Christmas, everyone seeking to take it to one of four local pubs. Once inside the doors, it remains there for the rest of the year. In the Haxey hood game, the "hug" is called the "sway," which nicely captures the kind of organic, uncontrollable movement of several hundred people pushing this way and that.

In many ways it's the trimmings of this tradition that are the most remarkable aspects of it. First a "Fool" is nominated, and with him the 12 "Boggins" on St. John's Eve, June 23. Then near Christmas, Fool and Boggins tour nearby villages seeking funds for the festivities and inspiring everyone to come out and join the "sway."

On the big day, the Fool dons a special hat, old trousers with red patches, a red shirt or coat, and red flowers in the band of his hat. His face is smeared with red ochre and soot. He is equipped with a little whip with a sock filled with bran at the tip, with which he strikes passersby who come within reach.

The 12 Boggins must wear red shirts, coats, or sweaters, with top hats decorated with flowers, and the King Boggin, their leader, carries a wand made of 13 twigs of willow bound together with withe. Twelve of the wands, representing the 12 apostles of Christ, are laid one way, and the 13th, representing Judas Escariot, is placed upside down.

The Boggins are the traditional players of the game, who have a special role in the early part of the game, involving the lesser hoods.

Meanwhile, activity in the parish has ceased at noon, and everyone heads to Haxey village. The officials (and many others) tour the pubs, taking free drinks proffered by the landlords, who are hoping the hood will come their way, a singular honor in this village.

The Fool leads the procession along the main street of Haxey to the church green. The Fool may kiss any woman he meets on his march to the church, and when he reaches his destination he first attempts to escape his fate by running away, but he is quickly captured and made to stand on the "Mowbray Stone," a horse-mounting stone outside the church. There he gives the traditional speech of welcome. Part of this speech is mysterious: By tradition he announces that "two and a half bullocks" have been killed, and the remaining half is still running in the field and can be brought in if needed. He ends with the following little rhyme:

> Hoose agen Hoose
> Toon agen Toon
> If tho' meet a man, knock him doon
> But don't 'urt 'im!

While he is speaking, damp straw is set on fire behind him to send up a cloud of smoke. This is called "Smoking the Fool" and harks back to an ancient ritual that used to take place the morning after the game.

Prior to the twenty-first century, the Fool was not only smoked, but he was also hung from a tree over the fire and only cut down when he was about to become asphyxiated and then left to roll about in the burning straw. In 1956, he apparently caught fire and had to be assisted by the crowd.

The "Toons" in the rhyme are Haxey and Westwoodside, and the "Hooses" are the four pubs, the Carpenters Arms in Westwoodside, the Duke William Hotel, the Loco, and the Kings Arms, all in Haxey.

Following the "Smoking of the Fool" the crowd, which includes those who plan to wrestle for the hood, as well as those who just plan to watch, sets off to the traditional field on Upperthorpe Hill between Haxey and Westwoodside, where it is thought the legendary event involving milady De Mowbray occurred in 1359. Here the Boggins form a ring around the Lord of the Hood.

The games begin at three o'clock, as one by one 12 "hoods" made of hessian sack, rolled up tightly, are thrown into the crowd. Youngsters grab them and try to get through the ring of Boggins. If they make it, they keep the hood. If not, the hood is returned to the Lord of the Hood, who throws it up again. After a while the Boggins stop actively pursuing the youngsters, and the lesser hoods are taken off the field.

Now the real business begins, and the "sway hood"—the leather tube filled with heavy rope—is thrown up and the mob fights for it. The object is to get hold of it and bear it away to one of the four pubs. Unlike at Ashbourne, where Uppards and Downards are, to some extent, organized, things here are more chaotic, although the Lord of the Hood is the referee and exercises a slight degree of control. The sway goes this way and that; sometimes it collapses, and a break is called while people are helped to their feet and things are sorted out. The sway can last anywhere from an hour to 12 hours, but in recent times the game has rarely gone more than four hours. The Boggins are tasked with trying to protect homes and property from the fury of the sway as it blunders about. The game continues until the hood is brought to one of the pubs, touched by the landlord, and brought inside. The landlord pours beer over the hood and hangs it behind the bar on the two special hooks put there for this purpose. Once upon a time, the hood was roasted over an open fire and then soaked in ale, which would be drunk by everyone present. The hood remains in place until the next New Year's Eve, when it is collected by the Boggins for the next game.

Needless to say a lot of ale and lager (plus wine, whiskey, gin, and vodka) are consumed during the celebrations.

In recent years the Kings Arms, which is the easternmost of the four pubs, has retained the hood far more often than its rivals. The Duke William got the hood in 2012, for the first time in a decade, and the

Carpenters Arms had it in 2011, but the Loco bar hasn't received it since 2005, when a side door was ripped off the building by the sway.

The Haxey Hood is truly a wonderful example of how weird and splendid an ancient tradition can become. It is also a well-set feast for scholars of medieval custom and history. Modern-day folklorist scholar Venetia Newell ties the event to Plow Monday celebrations, which were common in Lincolnshire and held after the Christmas holiday, before work resumed on the fields. The Plow Monday plays always featured a bashful Fool and a Lady, and were followed by boisterous games of the local boys, who were called "Plow Bullocks." This possibly accounts for the reference to "two and a half bullocks" in the Fool's speech.

One easy guess is that the rope originally bound inside the leather hood was made from flax fiber, for as mentioned earlier, this was flax country and was prosperous as a result. The fiber gathered here, woven into sailcloth, would take English ships throughout the world.

For another old traditional game with some mysterious aspects to it, let us move about 50 miles southwest, from Haxey to the village of Hallaton, just east of Leicester city. Here, on Easter Mondays, they hold the Hare Pie Scramble and Bottle Kicking. As might be expected from a title like that, there are legends attached to this one.

One school of thought says this is an ancient affair, that the Hare Pie is part of Saxon (or older) Easter celebrations, when the first young shoots of green would appear in the forests and fields. Christina Hole (English Custom and Usage 1941) thought the event was a survival of an ancient ceremony celebrating the chasing away of winter by the spring. It links to the Saxon goddess of spring, Ostara, and the myths concerning Easter rabbits and eggs. In the primary version of this myth, the goddess found a goose dying of the winter cold. She turned it into a rabbit, or a hare, and it rewarded her by laying gloriously colored eggs. Ostara was depicted with a hare's ears, sometimes even a hare's head. Ostara appears identical to the Greek goddess Eos or the Roman Aurora. Easter was related to the cycles of the moon, and hunting of hares was a common Easter activity in parts of England.

Slightly similar traditions involving hares are known from other parts of the English Midlands. In Colcshill, Warwickshire, a live hare would be given to the parson early on Easter Sunday. In return, he would give a hundred eggs, a calf's head, and a groat (a coin worth 4.5 old pence). Another tradition had the mayor and corporation (aldermen) of the city of Leicester, in their full official uniform and regalia, traipsing out to the Dane Hills on Easter Monday to "hunt the hare."

Hares, it should be noted, have a long relationship with sacred rituals, going back to Celtic times.

More prosaic by far is the local legend that this all began when two local ladies were saved from a raging bull by a startled hare that ran out and distracted the animal before it could charge the women. They thanked God for their deliverance by setting up a fund with the Vicar, who would provide 1 hare pie, 12 penny loaves, and 2 barrels of beer for the poor on Easter Monday each year. It was understood that the villagers would battle for the loaves and the beer.

Another legend has it that neighbors from the village of Medbourne snuck in and stole the beer, leading the Hallaton folk to charge down the road to retrieve it, igniting the rivalry between the villages that continues to this day.

Today the hare pie is actually made from beef.

The "bottles" are small barrels holding a gallon, and there are three involved in the "kicking." Two are filled with beer, and the third is solid wood, painted red, white, and blue, and called the "dummy." These little barrels were originally used by plowmen, taken to the fields filled with weak beer or cider to give them something to drink during long days at work. When the bottle kicking side of things began is unknown, but it appears to be several hundred years old.

The festivities begin with a parade through the village of Medbourne. Then everyone heads to Hallaton for the church service. After church the Hare Pie Parade is held, led by the "Warrener," carrying his staff with a metal hare on top. With him goes a lady in medieval dress, carrying a big basket of bread. Then come two young ladies carrying the pie, followed by three men each carrying one of the small kegs. They leave from the Fox Inn in Hallaton and walk to the gates of the church. The vicar then blesses the pie, which is cut up and passed out to the crowd. It was once thrown to the crowd, who "scrambled" for it, but today the distribution is rather more decorous and pieces are handed out. The crowd then marches back to the Buttercross in the middle of the village, where the loaves of bread are handed out, and everyone returns to the Fox Inn for refreshments. Soon, however, everyone goes back to the street and sets off for Hare Pie Bank, a long, green slope where the game begins.

The "bottles" are tossed in the air three times, to start the "kicking." The object of the game is to seize the bottles and move them across two different streams about a mile apart. Because there are three bottles, the winning village is the one that moves at least two bottles across the streams.

The Hallaton team is restricted to Hallaton residents, but Medbourne's team is open to outsiders. Both sides are usually at least a hundred strong.

There are a few rules. No weapons are allowed, and certain extremes of violence are forbidden, for example, gouging eyes, strangling, and trampling fallen opponents.

The "field of play" contains many obstacles, including ditches, hedges, and even barbed wire fences. Injuries are common, and ambulances are on hand to take seriously hurt people away for medical care.

As with any of these traditional games, there's no real time limit, and play can go on well into the night.

As with the Haxey Hood game, the Hallaton–Medbourne one leaves us with many questions, many of them unanswerable. Why the little barrels? Was this an accident of history? Did it come down to either the lack of a good cobbler in the village or a cobbler who refused to make a ball? Or did the idea of using the "bottles" trump any concern about a ball right from the start? Or, again, if this is one of the truly ancient game traditions, was it once played with a wooden ball?

In the North East of England, in Durham and Northumberland, and across the border in Berwickshire, now part of Scotland, there are a number of traditional "ba' games"—most involving a small ball that fits the hand, but also one or two that use a soccer ball. They traditionally used a ball with a pig's bladder encased in leather.

As with Haxey and Hallaton, these old-time traditional games come with lots of mysterious elements.

For example, in Duns, Berwickshire, there is one of the region's specialties, a game between married men of the village and the bachelors. It is now played in midsummer on the Friday night of "Reivers Week," not Shrove Tuesday, as in the past.

Three balls were carried in the pregame procession. One was gilt, gleaming with gold, the second was silvered, and the third was spotted with red and blue.

At noon the privilege of throwing up the ball was auctioned off and usually won by the Hays family from Duns castle. At 1 p.m., the ball was thrown up in the market square, with the usual chaos and mayhem breaking out. The bachelors had to take the ball to the hopper of the nearest grain mill, about a mile distant from the square. For the married men the goal was much closer, at the pulpit of the church.

Today three ba's are thrown up. The ba's are flattish-round affairs that fit the hand and are not exactly balls. They are thrown up by someone from the Hays family, who are the lords of the castle. Then the Reiver's Lass, elected for the festival from the female population at large, throws one up. Finally, the Wynsome Mayde, elected from the local school, throws the last one. The teams remain the same as of old, but the goals are now the Post Office and the White Swan pub.

The games are rough and short, usually lasting half a hour to a hour.

The term *Reivers* refers to cattle thieves, raiders, and rustlers coming from both England and Scotland who raided along the border region for centuries prior to the union of Scotland and England in 1707. In fact, the reivin' continued long after the union, too.

A similar game pitting married men against bachelors was played at Scone, in Perthshire, farther north and properly in Scotland.

Another ba' game is known from Jedburgh, also in Berwickshire and even closer to the Scotland–England border. Indeed, ba' games were once common throughout this area in almost every small town and village. It is said that these games may have originated in Jedburgh and featured the use of an English soldier's head in the early days. The Jedburgh game is played between the Uppies, from the higher part of the town, and the Doonies, from the lower half. The ball is a small one, stuffed with straw and decorated with ribbons. This game is played on Fastern E'en, which is Shrove Tuesday. The ball can be thrown or carried, and the aim is to take it or "hail" it either to the upper town or lower town.

These games with the small "ba" that fits the hand are in some ways reminiscent of ancient *pheninda* and *harpastum*. Once again, we have to wonder if there isn't some line of descent between Celtic villagers watching Romans play the game. That it would more likely be the Roman influence is emphasized by the lack of football-type games among the Highland Scots. In the Highlands and the Hebridean Islands, before soccer arrived in the nineteenth century, the primary sport was *camanachd*, a violent but skillful form of field hockey also known as shinty; however, any such link has been lost in the mists of time.

Another game recorded with a small ball that would fit the hand was the camp ball of East Anglia. In this case "camp" meant battle, and this was just as violent a game as any of the other *harpastum*-style sports. The field of play was as much as two hundred yards long, with goals at either end. The teams were 10 to 15 a side. The ball would be thrown up in the center, and the two teams, lined up to receive it, would hurl themselves in to retrieve it. This game apparently did not allow *pheninda*-style handoffs of the ball; it always had to be thrown to pass it. Taking the ball through the opposition's goal was the object and was called a "snotch." The first team to gain seven or nine snotches won. This game was popular in Norfolk, Suffolk, and Essex, but it seems to have died out in the early nineteenth century.

There are many other examples of "fossil games," many that today simply use a soccer ball. At Alnwick, in Northumberland, also in the "borders" region of reivin' and war, there is the annual "Scoring the Hales" game on Shrove Tuesday. This game was once held in the town, on the streets, but it was moved to a field donated by the Duke of Northumberland to keep the tradition alive. The tradition also mentions that the earliest game was played with a Scotsman's head. Many are the references to games of this type being played with someone's head in the distant past. While this seems unlikely, heads being heavy and messy things once removed from a body, there does remain that tradition among the Maya of casting a great new rubber ball about a decapitated prisoner's skull. Some basic human warlike instinct may be involved.

The field here is two hundred yards long; the goals, called the "hales," are decorated with branches and leaves. The teams come from the rival parishes of St. Michael and St. Paul, and the game today usually lasts about two hours, or however long it takes to score the best of three hales.

A bit farther south, in Chester-le-Street, in County Durham, there was another similar game, played between the "Downstreeters" from the southern side of town and the "Upstreeters" from the north. There was an interesting and rather unique way of winning this game. The game ran from 1 p.m. to 6 p.m., and whoever had the ball on their side of the dividing line between Upstreet and Downstreet at 6 p.m. were the victors.

It seems that this game was once played with the town ball type of ball—big, heavy, stuffed with peas and sawdust—but at some point in more recent times that ball was replaced with the leather around a pig's bladder type of ball. The game was banned in 1932, by the police, and died out—exactly the fate that the Duke of Northumberland avoided at Alnwick.

The point of this short tour of fossil games is to show how different and various these games could be. And please note, there are many other examples. Now most Shrove Tuesday games were closer to the Ashbourne model. They used a big leather ball, and the rules and aims of the games were similar. But everywhere local traditions intruded, often with charming complexity, as with the Haxey Hood and Hallaton games.

Of course, to the west of Angle-Lond, in Wales and Cornwall, another tradition continued. As briefly mentioned in chapter 1, in Cornwall a traditional game called "hurling" continues today, with roots in antiquity.

In the western part of Wales, in Pembrokeshire, in the sixteenth century, a local historian, George Owen of Henlyss, recorded a game of *cnapan*, which has many similarities with the hurling at St. Colomb Major. Owen wrote in considerable detail about the game:

> The game is thought to be of great antiquity and is as followeth. The ancient Britons being naturally a warlike nation did no doubt for the exercise of their youth in time of peace and to avoid idleness devise games of activity where each man might show his natural prowess and agility, as some for strength of the body by wrestling, lifting of heavy burdens, others for the arm as in casting the bar, sledge, stone, or hurling the bawl or ball, others that excelled in swiftness of foot, to win the praise therein by running, and surely for the exercise of the parts aforesaid this *cnapan* was prudently invented, had the same continued without abuse thereof. For in it, beside the exercise of the bodily strength, it is not without resemblance of warlike providence, as shall be hereafter declared.

There were five fixed, or standing, *cnapan* days in Pembrokeshire.

[T]he first at Bury sands between the parishes of Nevern and Newport upon Shrove Tuesday yearly; the second at Portheinon, on Easter Monday, between the parishes of Meline and Eglwyswrw; the third on low Easterday at Pwll-du in Penbedw between the parishes Penrhydd and Penbedw; the fourth and fifth were wont to be at St. Meigans in Cemais between Cemais men of the one party, and Emlyn men, and the men of Cardiganshire with them of the other party, the first upon Ascension Day, the other upon Corpus Christi day, and these two last were the great and main places, far exceeding any of the former in multitude of people for at these places there have often times been esteemed two thousand foot beside horsemen.

Owen goes on to describe one of these grand games, with a couple of thousand participants:

About one or two of the clock afternoon begins the play, in this sort, after a cry made both parties draw to into some plain, all first stripped bare saving a light pair of breeches, bare-headed, bare-bodied, bare legs and feet; for if he leave but his shirt on his back in the fury of the game, it is most commonly torn to pieces and I have also seen some long-lock gallants, trimly trimmed at this game not by clipping but by pulling their hair and beards.

The foot company thus meeting, there is a round ball prepared of a reasonable quantity so as a man may hold it in his hand and no more, this ball is of some massy wood as box, yew, crab or holly tree and should be boiled in tallow for to make it slippery and hard to hold. This ball is called *cnapan* and is by one of the company hurling bolt upright into the air, and at the fall he that catches it hurls it towards the country he plays for, for goal or appointed place there is none neither needs any, for the play is not given over until the *cnapan* be so far carried that there is no hope to return it back that night, for the carrying of it a mile or two miles from the first place is no losing of the honour so it be still followed by the company and the play still maintained, it is often times seen the chase to follow two miles and more. . . . It is a strange sight to see a thousand or fifteen hundred naked men to concur together in a cluster in following the ball as the same is hurled backward and forward. . . . The gamesters return home from the play with broken heads, black faces, bruised bodies and lame legs. . . . Yet they laugh and joke and tell stories about how they broke their heads . . . without grudge or hatred.

This comes from Owen's *Description of Pembrokeshire*, published in 1603, the same year Queen Elizabeth I died. Owen was well born, educated at the Inns of Court in London, and he collected information about his native Wales, from heraldry to historical buildings. He also studied the landscape and made a number of observations of the geology. For this he is regarded as a forerunner of the modern schools of geology, which began a couple of centuries later. There is a ridge, the Dorsum Owen, named for him on the moon.

Cnapan, as recounted by Owen, had existed since early times and was exclusively played in the western counties of Wales, Carmarthen, Cardiganshire, and Pembrokeshire. The games continued in full fury until the later decades of the nineteenth century, when rugby football replaced them. Wales remains a stronghold of rugby today.

George Owen died in 1613, during the reign of James I (James VI of Scotland). His contemporary, just to the south, across the Severn estuary in Cornwall, was Richard Carew. Carew writes about the hurling, or *hyrlian*, in his native county in his *Survey of Cornwall*, published in 1602.

Traditional hurling can still be seen at St. Columb Major, where the ball, made of apple wood, is covered in silver. It fits in the hand but weighs about 20 ounces. The silvering of the ball was also seen in a now-discontinued game held in Truro, the county capital, located about 10 miles southwest of St. Columb Major. The Truro game was set between married men and bachelors, as seen far to the north in the borders games of duns and the Scottish game of scone.

There is a hurling ball dated from 1704 in the museum of Penzance, near the toe of Cornwall. As with many silvered hurling balls, it bears an inscription, which reads, "Paul tuz whek Gwaro Tek heb ate buz Henwis," which translates to, "Ball holders—fair play is good play."

Similar inscriptions can be found on many silvered hurling balls. The tradition in St. Columb is that whoever retains the ball at the end of the game has "won" it and may retain possession but must produce a new one for the next game. This is not a casual undertaking, since the balls are thought to cost as much as one thousand pounds ($1,600).

In St. Columb they play twice a year, on Shrove Tuesday and 10 days later, on the second Saturday after that date. The teams are drawn from the Countrymen, who live outside the village but in the parish, and the Townsmen. Before World War II, the Countrymen outnumbered the

Townsmen. Today the situation is reversed. The goals are about two miles apart. The Country goal is a stone trough once used for watering horses, while the Town goal is at the base of a stone cross. It is also possible to win by simply taking the ball far enough to cross the parish boundary. Thus, the entire parish, which measures about 20 square miles, is the field of play. The game begins with a large scrum in the middle of town around 4:30 p.m. At this point, the game is somewhat ceremonial, with pauses to allow youngsters (and others) to touch the ball, which is regarded as lucky. A "break" is eventually made by one of the two groups, and the serious action begins on the roads or fields outside the village. When the game has been won, the victor is returned to the village on the shoulders of his teammates. The ball is later produced again and taken to the village pubs, where it is dunked in jugs of beer. This becomes "silver beer" and is shared among the throng.

This form of hurling was common throughout Cornwall until the latter decades of the nineteenth century. Today it has dwindled to just a few remaining examples, St. Columb and St. Ives, and also as part of the "beating the bounds" ceremony held every five years at Bodmin. In this version there are no teams, and the silver ball is thrown into the Salting Pool to start things off. The ball is then carried on a prescribed route to finish at the Turret Clock on Fore Street. Whoever is carrying the ball at the finish wins £10.

The St. Columb game is a fossil and one that I think recalls an old tradition. When Richard Carew was surveying the county at the end of the sixteenth century, he found that "Hurling to Country," the game set between parishes or involving an entire parish, was found in western Cornwall, where the Celtic traditions were strongest. This accords with the findings of George Owen in Wales, where *cnapan* flourished in the western counties.

However, Carew also recorded another game, "Hurling to Goles," which was played in the eastern part of the county. This game was played on a field similar in size to a modern rugby or soccer pitch between teams of 15, 20, or 30 players. The ball was not silvered, and the goals are described by Carew as follows: "[T]hey pitch two bushes in the ground, some 8 or 10 foote asunder; and directly against them, 10 or 12 score off (200–240 feet), other twayne (another pair) in like distance, which they terme their Goales."

Carew also mentions goalkeepers and players passing the ball back and forth. This was a regional variant on the game that had begun centuries before and been refined into a standard, with a handful of real rules.

This had begun back in the fourteenth century with "camp ball," which evolved into "kicking camp." At some point in the fifteenth century, the term *footeballe* was used for the first time, and with that the game moved away from the chaotic mobs, bizarre traditions, symbolic silver, and other medieval devices and colors of ball.

And the cultural references to camp ball and football were beginning to multiply. In William Shakespeare's early play *A Comedy of Errors*, probably written in about 1590, Act II, Scene 1 includes the following:

> Am I so round with you as you with me,
> That like a football you do spurn me thus?
> You spurn me hence and he will spurn me hither:
> If I last in this service, you must case me in leather.

To spurn in this case is to kick or drive away, as with a ball.

In the play *The Blind Beggar of Bethnal Green*, by John Day, first performed in approximately 1600—although not published for another 60 years—there is this: "I'll play a gole at camp-ball." In 1605, Shakespeare wrote *King Lear* (published 1608), and Act I, Scene 4, reads, "Nor tripped neither, you base football player."

Meanwhile the imprecations against mob football continued.

This might come in a gentle verse, as from Barclay in 1598:

> The sturdie plowman,
> Overcometh the winter with driving the foote-ball,
> Forgetting labor and many a grievous fall.

But Sir Thomas Elyot, in his *The Book Named the Governour* (1531), was harsh. Indeed, Sir Thomas belonged to that section of the populace that disliked almost any form of exertion or exercise. Thus, "boulynge" came in for scorn, along with skittles and quoits. "Footeballe" was "nothing but beastlie furie and exstreme violence, whereof procedeth hurted, and consequently rancour and malice do remain with them that be wounded, wherfore it is to be put in perpetual silence," i.e., banned.

"Beastlie furie" or not, the game remained somewhat dangerous. A game in Elizabeth's years on the throne, in 1581, produced a well-recorded fatality. Montague Shearman, in his *Athletics and Football*, published in 1887, notes that the coroner's inquisition read,

[P]ost-mortem taken at Sowthemyms, Co. Middlesex., in view of the body of Roger Ludforde, yoman there lying dead with verdict of jurors that Nicholas Martyn and Richard Turvey, both late of South-emyms, yomen, were on the 3rd instant between 3 and 4 P.M. playing with other persons at foote-ball in the field called Evanses field at Southmyms, when the said Roger Ludforde and a certain Simon Maltus, of the sd parish, yomen, came to the ground, and that Roger Ludforde cried out, "Cast hym over the hedge," indicating that he meant Nicholas Martyn, who replied, "Come thou and do yt." That thereupon Roger Ludforde ran towards the ball with the intention to kick it, whereupon Nicholas Martyn with the fore-part of his right arm and Richard Turvey with the fore-part of his left arm struck Roger Ludforde on the fore-part of the body under the breast, giving him a mortal blow and concussion of which he died within a quarter of an hour, and that Nicholas and Richard in this manner feloniously slew the said Roger.

Elizabeth I had demanded an end to these games in and around London on several occasions. That did not prevent them, of course. Alas, for Sir Thomas Elyot and those like him, "beastlie furie" or not, foote-balle was in the blood of Englishmen (and Welsh, Scots, and some Irish, too) by this time, and it wasn't going away. Writing about football and athletics in 1887, Shearman recorded that in 1608, from the town of Manchester's "Lete roll" (a record of court proceedings) came the following complaint: "With the footebale, hath been greate disorder in our towne of Manchester, we are told, and glasse windows broken yearlye and spoyled by a companie of lewd and disordered persons."

As another note of the changes in daily life, "glasse windows" were becoming common in English towns. These were windows made from a great number of small, diamond-shaped panes, held together with lead. They can still be seen on Tudor houses in old English town centers. Glasse windows let in more light, allowing for more reading; by this time, books other than Bibles were being printed and read in ever larger numbers.

Some of this progress may have stemmed from the work of Richard Mulcaster, who attended Eton College in the 1540s and became the first headmaster of Merchant Taylors' School in London in 1561. The Merchant Taylors were a livery company, a merchant guild, with a Royal Charter dating to 1327. This was the largest school in England at that time. Mulcaster produced several important works, the best known of which is the *Elementaire*, published in 1582. In this work he strove to standardize English spellings and included a list of 8,000 "hard words." At the time English was still a young language, loaded with loan words from French and Latin on top of an Anglo-Saxon base. It was not respected among scholars or even at court. Latin was used for documents and official statements. Mulcaster noted that English would soon displace Latin in these aspects of use, and he campaigned to develop rules for spelling English words.

His other great work was in promoting football, or "footeballe," as it was called in the sixteenth century. He found many benefits in footeballe and wrote of them in his 1581 work *Positions Wherein Those Primitive Circumstances Be Examined, Which Are Necessarie for the Training Up of Children*. He claimed health benefits from playing footeballe, as well as an overall positive educational value. Mulcaster also wrote of the need for referees, or some official, to oversee games. In addition, he referred to coaches, or "trayning master," and to both teams—"sides"—and player positions, "standings."

Mulcaster offers our first evidence that there was now a game with teams that were not massive mobs, with both rules and someone to adjudicate those rules. "Some smaller number with such overlooking, sorted into sides and standings, not meeting with their bodies so boisterously to trie their strength: nor shouldring or shuffling one another so barbarously . . . may use footeball as much good to the body, by the chiefe use of the legges."

Here we see a clear split in the evolutionary line of "footeballe." On the one hand, barbarous mobs, whether in the streets of Tudor- and Stuart-era cities or in the countryside, were frowned upon. Pure expressions of native joy and fury, they were dangerous from the point of view of property owners and the custodians of what law and order existed. On the other hand, beginning in the great schools was a sense that "footeballe," once given rules and placed under the command of an official, could be a great tool in the education of the young. And please note, the young in question were the young men of the upper classes, not those of the unruly mobs in Cheapside.

Another small signpost along the way comes from a teacher in Aberdeen, Scotland, named David Wedderburn, who wrote a Latin textbook called *Vocabula* in 1633. In this slim volume, Wedderburn refers to "keeping goal"—perhaps the first reference to this construction and an interesting one that clearly has a long provenance. After all, why isn't it "blocking goal" or "defending goal"? Wedderburn also alludes to holding the ball and "driving" other players, i.e., tackling them physically.

A couple of years later, in 1635, Francis Willughby was born at Middleton Hall in Warwickshire. Willughby studied at Bishop Vesey's Grammar School and Trinity College, Cambridge. He traveled with the naturalist John Ray, whose student he was, and after a tour of Europe began preparing his master work, *Ornithologiae libri tres*. Willughby died of pleurisy in 1672, before it was finished, and Ray completed it. This work is regarded as the beginning of scientific ornithology in Europe.

Willughby also wrote a scientific study of games, which was left unfinished at his untimely death, at the young age of 36. It has been published as *Francis Willughby's Book of Games*. In it he describes a number of popular games of the seventeenth century. For us, the vein of gold here is his description of "football."

The game he describes is simple and pretty rough, but less so than the riotous mob games of the cities. It takes place in a cleared field, "a close that has a gate at either end. The gates are called goals." The ball is well described. Willughby writes, "They blow a strong bladder and tie the neck of it as fast as they can, and then put it into the skin of a bull's cod and sew it fast in." Two teams of equal number are selected. Some players are positioned to "guard the goals," while others are attackers who move to the front as forwards.

There are some important rules. If the ball goes out of the field or over the boundary line, it is kicked back in from where it left the field of play. It is not lawful to simply kick another player in the shins; "[T]hey must not strike higher than the ball." Another rule with considerable import is that which allows for the calling of a "mark" when a player catches the ball "on the full," that is, without it bouncing first. After calling a mark, he may not be tackled, and he marks the ground with his heel and may take a free kick from that point. This rule, by the way, except for the marking the ground with the heel, lives on in Australian rules football. Variants also survive in American and Canadian football: the "fair catch" rule.

Willughby's life spanned the tumultuous era of the last part of Charles I's reign, the English Civil War (1642–1651). This was a series of conflicts, first between Charles I and Parliament, which ended in 1649, with Charles's execution at the block. The final struggles were between Charles II's supporters and Parliament, which ended at the Battle of Worcester in 1651 and left the younger Charles in exile at the French court.

Oliver Cromwell, who had marshaled the New Model Army and led it to victories over the Royalists, then became the protector of the nation from 1653 to 1659. He led that army to Ireland, which had rebelled in 1641 and been more or less independent for a decade but had allied itself with Charles II, triggering an invasion by the Parliamentary army. Cromwell proceeded to crush the Irish–Royalist forces, and the usual seventeenth-century resort to atrocities, including the massacre of Roman Catholic priests, blackened his name forever in Irish hearts and minds.

The English Civil War had the effect of ending the rule by "divine right" of kings and queens in England, and later Britain. The power of the purse, of taxation, had passed bit by bit to Parliament. This was ultimately inevitable; the medieval kingdom had mostly been financed by levies on the royal lands and occasional—and much resented—levies on the nobility and church. Medieval kings were always desperate for money, primarily because they were continually fighting, and war was expensive. Charles I spent most of his reign struggling to squeeze tax money out of Parliament. His Catholicism, respect for French ways, and expensive habits—paintings and luxury at the Royal Court—set him on a lethal collision course with Parliament and much of the population. In the end, he paid with his life.

This period also saw the first mass emigration from England to the New World, the exodus of the Puritans from an area of East Anglia, North Essex—South Cambridge and Suffolk. Twenty thousand of these folk left the England of Charles I, whose Roman Catholicism they feared and despised, and settled in Massachusetts.

Within 20 years, they were followed by waves of defeated Royalists who either feared Cromwell's new order or hated it so much they quit

England and headed for Virginia. The Royalists were predominantly from the West County, the South West, and they took with them a view of the world very different from that held by the Puritans.

Another, lesser known side of Oliver Cromwell is that he was a keen player of footeballe, at least if we accept the description in James Heath's *Flagellum*, a slanderous biography of Cromwell published in 1663, after the man was safely dead and out of the way. His days as an undergraduate at Cambridge University were said to have been spent in games of "football, cudgels (cricket), or any other boisterous sport or game."

As lord protector of the realm, Cromwell set in motion the enforcement of the Puritan ideology. That meant bans on bear baiting (Queen Elizabeth had been a big fan), cock fighting, horse racing, wrestling, and football.

However, we also have a record of Cromwell being an enthusiastic spectator of a game of Cornish hurling that was staged in Hyde Park, London, in 1654. The game featured two teams of 50 apiece, Cornishmen versus "Others."

Right there, it seems, we have the endless conundrum of football. It has to be violent, to a degree, to have that edge that provides excitement, but in this there is an ever-present threat, detected by those like Sir Thomas Elyot, who fear that "beastlie furie" we love so much.

6

THE AGE OF RULES
Part I

So when and where did the modern world begin? This hoary question has spurred many to opine, some to rage, and others to weep, no doubt. After Galileo peered through his telescope at the moons of Jupiter in 1609, it was once and for all understood that the Earth does not stand at the center of the universe. What about the epic meeting of Edmund Halley and Isaac Newton in Cambridge in 1684, from which would come the "Philosophiae Naturalis Principia Mathematica" and the opening of the doors of perception regarding physical laws and our world? Another, earthier school of thought scoffs at all this and points to the fields and the three-field system of crop rotation, which replaced the two-field system and increased yields. Or how about new crops, for instance, the spread of the humble turnip, which not only fed people but also animals and is rich in Vitamin C? Others chortle at this and point to where the money lies, with the beginning of modern capitalism in the coffee houses of Amsterdam and London in the seventeenth century.

They all have a ring or two of truth to them, as do other claims about where the modern world began; however, the story of football begins in school. The tale of footeballe now enters the Age of Rules, and for most of us wild children at heart, we first encounter rules at school. For football, a wild child indeed up to this time, this was especially true.

The schools in question were the English "public schools"—a term that can be confusing to Americans and others. In this instance it means that these were schools originally founded as small religious institutions or grammar schools for a parish that had grown beyond its parochial origins. They were open to the public, as long as that public could afford the fees. Many had been founded in the sixteenth century, in Tudor times, and this reflected something of the ferment of that era. Religion had become a source of dissent, even war. The money supply, boosted by thousands of tons of silver from South America's Mt. Potosi, was growing, as was trade. "New men" were rising, and old families were falling. Printing was putting books, many different kinds of books, into people's hands. Literacy was still restricted to a tiny elite, but it was growing.

The public schools most important to our story are Rugby, Shrewsbury, Harrow, Eton, Winchester, Charterhouse, Westminster, and Merchant Taylors. The last three were London day schools, and the first five grew into boarding schools. In the eighteenth century, they expanded but also developed a reputation for various kinds of savagery, in addition to scholarship and lots of Latin and Greek. Any number of odd traditions began; some continue, and they can evoke thoughts of Harry Potter and Hogwarts, the school for wizards. Take, for example, the custom of the "Greaze" on Shrove Tuesday at Westminster School in London. This isn't a ball game, this is about a special pancake made with horsehair, as well as eggs and flour. The hair presumably holds it together during its brief ordeal. Once it's ready, the head cook ceremoniously slings this pancake over a high rail in the school hall. This rail once curtained off the Lower School in the sixteenth century. Members of the top three class years then scramble for the pancake for one minute under the watchful eyes of the dean of Westminster Abbey, the head master, and the rest of the school; he who emerges with the largest portion of the pancake is rewarded in ritual with a golden sovereign (a tiny English gold coin). The winner then hands the coin back, and it is put away for reuse the following year. The head master proceeds to "beg" the Dean to declare a "play," which is a day off school. The dean, of course, agrees.

In previous centuries—this tradition is thought to have begun in 1753—if the cook failed to sling his pancake high enough to clear the bar, there would ensue the terrible punishment of said cook being "booked," that is, having Latin primers hurled at him by the assembled students. This part of the tradition has not been enforced for many years.

Equally strange are many of the elements of the football games that developed at these schools. But before we delve into the Olde Curiosity Shoppe of Public Schools Football, let's establish a benchmark.

In 1801, Joseph Strutt, an engraver and author of the late eighteenth century, produced *The Sports and Pastimes of the People of England*. Of popular folk football he found that the game had "fallen into disrepute and is but little practised." Still, he describes the game as it was. The first requirement was a cleared field, similar to the "close" described by Francis Willughby in 1660. Then came two goals, now "made with two sticks driven into the ground about two or three feet apart." The ball, "commonly made of a blown bladder and cased with leather" was "delivered," i.e., thrown, into the middle of the ground, and each team proceeded to attempt to "drive" the ball through the opposition's goal. One goal decided the match. Strutt felt that the game could be "exceedingly violent" when the players would kick one another's shins "without the least ceremony." This appears to be much the same game described by Willughby. I suspect it was very similar to kicking-camp from the fifteenth century as well. This game, for its own practical reasons, had settled into a pattern with recognizable rules long before the concept of "rules" had really taken hold in the popular imagination.

Two teams of equal size were formed, with as many as 40 on a team, but this was probably dependent on the size of the field of play. A round ball of leather, with an inflated pig's bladder inside to give it bounce, was used. The field consisted of two goals, quite small, at either end of an area that was at least 80 to perhaps 120 yards long. Coincidentally, such smallish farm fields, often called "closes," could usually be found near villages as a result of the "enclosure movement."

This briefly saw common lands being purchased or seized by manorial lords or others and "enclosed" into fields rather than the "strips" of the manorial two- and three-field system. While enclosures were vilified in popular imagination, they were not always formed without the consent of villagers, in part because they allowed better farmers to farm even better and production to grow. It was a complex process that spanned several hundred years, with many causes. The chief complaint against enclosures came from the Midlands of England, where former plowland was turned into pasture for sheep and a considerable number of villages disappeared. The outlines of former houses can still be seen from the air, ghosts beneath the pasture.

In places without enclosures, an area would be marked off, probably with sticks thrust into the ground, although this is not mentioned in any sources. From the standpoint of simple practicality, however, I have to assume this was done, otherwise the game would have been like the old village game, with goals miles apart and so on.

The rules of the simple country game were few but instructive. The ball, when kicked out of the field, was to be returned at the point where it had gone out. It was usually kicked back in. If a player caught the ball "on the full," that is, before it bounced, he could call a "mark" and mark the spot with his heel, and then take a free kick from that spot.

Punching an opponent was generally frowned upon, especially without specific provocation. Kicking shins seems to have been allowed in some places and not others. Rough play was generally part of the game and expected. Since there were not usually referees, dastardly foul play might be punished by simple ejection from the game by everyone else.

This basic game was known and understood pretty widely throughout the English landscape. Also known were many traditional Shrove Tuesday-style games, some with bizarre traditions, as at Haxey or Hallaton.

And so when the young men of the aristocracy and the sons of wealthy farmers, merchants, doctors, and others "in trade" were sent to further their education at the public schools, they took with them their understanding of the games from their own regions.

But life in the great schools was not exactly gentle and sweet. In the school rooms, the "beaks," or masters, ruled with the birch and the cane in one hand and the Greek or Latin primer in the other. Outside of class, however, the schools were run by the older boys. Younger boys, termed "fags" (not a term with sexual meaning), were appointed servants for the older boys. As recounted by Thomas Hughes in *Tom Brown's Schooldays*, there was considerable room for cruelty in this situation.

Indeed, the young scions of the aristocracy and business world were fond of the notorious eighteenth-century vices. Drinking, cockfighting, card playing, horse racing, whoring, gambling, and even dreaded homosexuality were common and pretty much horrifying to the growing sentiments of what was soon to become Victorian England.

Physical activities, sports, and even football were seen by educators of the day as a way to channel youthful energies away from the vices and encourage manliness and "muscular Christianity."

Inevitably, perhaps, the football games at the public schools came to reflect the social order among the boys. The older boys "played up" and were the forwards, the kickers, the big men behind the ball. The youngsters, the "fags," were shoved to the rear and told to guard the goal with their lives. This set up many a moment when a top upper classman, perhaps six foot two and close to two hundred pounds, would hurtle through and crash into the line of 14 year olds trying to be brave and protect the goal. Keen eyes would pick out those youngsters who exhibited "pluck" and picked themselves up quickly after being trampled into the dust. Those with less pluck would be carried off, often with broken limbs, to be patched up and made ready for the next rough game on the close.

We'll start with Rugby School, because Rugby, quite simply, gave the world one of the modern codes of football, and from that game three others evolved, including American football.

Rugby School was founded in 1567, from the will of one Lawrence Sheriff, who had been grocer to Queen Elizabeth I. Sheriff had apprenticed to a London grocer and been elected to the Worshipful Company of Grocers, a guild in all but name. Queen Elizabeth's patronage raised him to the status of a gentleman, with a coat of arms. He bought property in both London and in Rugby, where he had grown up. He died childless and left much of his fortune to endow a free grammar school for local boys in Rugby. In time, and after epic legal battles over the endowment, the school expanded and slipped away from being purely parochial and began to cater to a wider clientele.

We don't know when football was first played at Rugby, but in the early nineteenth century the game was pretty close to the game of country football, as recorded by Strutt and Willughby. The ball was round, inflated, and mostly kicked. It could be caught and then punted as well. If caught "on the full" without a previous bounce on the ground, he who caught it could call a "mark," and everyone stood still while he took a run up and kicked the ball from that spot, either at the goal or upfield. No one was allowed to move until the ball was kicked.

Scoring goals came from either a dropkick in play or by getting the ball over the opponents' end line and touching it down. This earned a "try" at dropkicking a goal. Many games remained scoreless, sometimes for days. The game would end at dusk and continue the following day. In at least one case, possibly legendary, this went on for five days before someone scored the two goals necessary for victory.

The games were played on the "Close," which was then a set of three fields where sheep and cattle grazed. Indeed, sheep grazed these fields until the 1900s.

In 1823 came the apocryphal, transformative event, when William Webb Ellis is said to have caught the ball and run with it instead of immediately kicking it, as was customary. He was probably not the first boy to try this, but his was the legendary run that made history and began the process that changed the game. We should note that with a mob of 50 to 100 boys on the field, running with the ball would not normally last for long, and the runner would quickly end up buried under a pile of bodies. However it went, it is Webb Ellis's statue that stands outside Rugby School today and whose name decorates the Rugby World Cup. Ellis went on to become an Anglican clergyman.

Thomas Hughes, our next vital character in the saga of Rugby School football, arrived at the school in 1834. The second son of a Berkshire gentleman, he attended a preparatory school near Winchester and moved to Rugby at the age of 11. He arrived as Thomas Arnold, the headmaster, was moving the school in the direction of his ideals, which were to become the foundation for not only English schooling of the nineteenth century, but also, less probably, the Olympic movement.

Hughes is best known for his semiautobiographical novel *Tom Brown's Schooldays*, which contains a record of how football was played at Rugby School in the 1830s. At the time, School House, 65 strong, traditionally played against the rest of the school, more than 200 strong. The game was pretty close to mob football, with the ball occasionally soaring above the mass as someone got hold of it and punted it one way or the other. Players could stop the ball with their hands and put it on the ground. Some may have tried to run with it, but this would have been unusual. Nor would anyone get very far. Hughes does not mention anyone running with the ball to score a try.

The actual basis of the game was constant scrummaging—not the organized scrum seen in modern rugby football, but loose mobs of as many as 50 forwards, packed together, pushing and shoving their opponents, probably kicking them, too. Moreover, these scrums were not about heeling the ball back so the running backs could take it and run with it for the end lines and tries. Instead, the scrums were out to heave the opposition aside and take the ball, usually kicked along the ground or dribbled within the scrum to the opposition's goal line, where it could be touched down for a "try." When the ball broke out of the scrummage, it was either punted downfield or dribbled madly toward the end line. Now and then someone may have tried picking it up. Once tackled, the scrum would resume as soon as the ball was placed on the ground. Scrums would last for considerable stretches of time and might go this way and then that, much like the "hug" at Ashbourne or the "sway" at Haxey still does.

Hughes excelled at sports, particularly cricket. In later life he became an attorney and then a judge. He became involved in Christian socialism, which he joined in 1848.

In 1839, there were two interesting developments. The School House team adopted a uniform—a red velvet cap—which was then joined by white trousers and white jerseys. This is the first known uniform in football. Rugby's choice of all white is said to be origin of the England rugby team's white uniform.

Also in 1839, at Cambridge University, a Mr. Arthur Pell organized a rugby team, composed of Old Rugbeians. They challenged the Old Etonians at Cambridge to a football match. The fallout was momentous, because the Etonians were incensed at the Rugbeians' use of their hands. This led to the effort to draw up the "Cambridge Rules."

What the Etonians were objecting to, however, was not rugby played as it is today, with the ball being carried for the most part and kicked in a supplementary fashion. It was that the Rugbeians were touching the ball at all, which, in the Etonian game, was strictly forbidden.

However, during Rugby's slow drift from a barely organized kind of mob football to a game with rules, other schools were also developing their own approaches to football. In terms of their importance in a national sense, neither Rugby School nor its football were of any consequence at this time. The schools that mattered were Eton College, to the west of London near Windsor, and Westminster School, next to Westminster Abbey, a stone's throw from the Houses of Parliament and Big Ben. From these schools came the leaders of the House of Lords and the House of Commons. Eton, in fact, has produced more prime ministers than any other school, including the current premier, David Cameron (2015).

Nor was football important in these schools' sports hierarchies. Rowing was the one that counted, and then came cricket.

But, unglamorous as it was, football was being played at Eton and Westminster. At Eton, a uniquely weird game, the "wall game," had evolved, first recorded in 1766. This one is played on the "furrow," a strip of ground 15 feet wide and 330 feet long, next to a slightly curved brick wall. The action is all about a long, fierce scrum, called a "bully," moving along the wall. Hands are not allowed to touch the ball, and only the feet and hands can touch the ground. Players are also forbidden from grabbing opponents' jerseys, nor are they allowed to punch them. There are strict offside rules. A goal is rarely scored, as in about once in 10 years on average.

This game developed, it seems, because the wall, built in 1717, was there, and the boys had no other area in which to play football. Then a field was purchased, and the Eton boys developed the Field Game.

Eton College is, in many ways, a special case. Founded in 1440, by Henry VI, as a feeder school for King's College, Cambridge (which he founded the following year), the school has always exemplified the English public school. Like these schools, the primary education before the late nineteenth century was in Greek and Latin. Discipline was enforced through flogging, and at Eton there were some famous events of that nature. Dr. John Keate, headmaster beginning in 1809, took stern measures to improve discipline. On one occasion he flogged 80 boys in a single day.

The rules for Eton's Field Game were first documented in 1815, well before any other school football game. Many of the unique aspects of the Field Game are elements brought from the wall game. Thus, there is an organized scrum, called the "bully," formed by seven players. There are the three corners, two sideposts, one post, and one bup. Behind the bully is positioned the fly, who acts like a scrum-half does in rugby, except, of course, not touching the ball with his hands. With the fly wait the behinds, which consist of two shorts and one long. The long is deputed to stand back by the goal and keep the ball out of the goal, but only with his feet. The shorts' job is to kick the ball over the bully if and when it emerges.

The ball itself is round and a little smaller than a soccer ball. A size four soccer ball can be used today.

In the bully, the players shove against the opposition and seek to "furk" the ball back with their heels. The bully is sometimes able to push the opponent's bully backward, in which case the ball can be kept in the bully and dribbled downfield.

If the ball is furked back to the behinds and then kicked forward, all the players can run onto it and either take a shot at the goal—which is like a soccer goal, but smaller—or strike the ball off a defensive player so it goes behind the end line. This makes it "rougeable," and if an attacker touches it first, he scores a rouge, worth five points. A goal is worth three, and a converted rouge, done with a free shot at goal, is worth another two.

The Field Game also has a restrictive "offside" rule. The ball cannot be passed forward to a player standing ahead of the ball. Only players who are behind the ball (or in the bully) when it is kicked are onside and can legally play the ball.

The Eton game takes us a long way from the free and easy style of country footeballe. Organized scrums, players with named positions and roles, and a strict offside rule are elements way out on an evolutionary branch from the mainstream.

The two day schools in the city with the largest contribution to football history are Westminster and Charterhouse.

Westminster, already in a built up area in the eighteenth century, was better known for cricket than football in the early days. Westminster played Charterhouse, at that time another closed-in London school, in the first school cricket match in 1794.

Charterhouse, founded in 1611, developed two football games, as well. One, played outdoors, was simple mob football, called "runabout," with an emphasis on dribbling the ball. Another game, played indoors in cloisters, was more akin to the wall game. Played in a corridor with a stone-flagged floor, two teams piled up in a scrum and tried to push the opposition back and get the ball to one or other of the doors at either end of the corridor. When Charterhouse moved out of London in 1872, to larger, more spacious quarters in Godalming, Surrey, the cloister game died out.

At Westminster, where football was recorded being played on the green in 1710, a game that featured passing forward, as well as drib-

bling, came to predominate. Westminster and Charterhouse would contribute this aspect of the game in the eventual negotiations for the new
game of association football.

Another school with an important contribution to association football rules was Harrow School. Harrow also continues to play its own
unique "Harrow football." Located in northwest London, the school
was founded by a wealthy local farmer, John Lyon, with a charter from
Elizabeth I in 1572, to found a free grammar school for boys from
Harrow. The original key subjects were Latin and archery. Archery was
abandoned in 1771.

Harrow football is an "open play" game, without scrums. Teams are
11 a side, and the goals are called "bases," consisting of two poles in the
ground six yards apart, but without a crossbar. The field is rectangular
and, at Harrow, legendarily muddy. The game consists of two 40-min-
ute halves.

The oddest thing is the ball, a flattened sphere 18 inches in diameter
but only 12 inches deep. It is inflated but can become very heavy with
rainwater.

Play follows much the same pattern as country footeballe. The ball is
mostly kicked and dribbled but can be caught on the full, that is, if it
hasn't bounced. After such a catch, the player calls, "Yards!" The referee marks the spot with a yardstick, and the player with the ball can take
a run up to that spot and then launch himself forward for three long
jumps. He can then take a shot at goal from wherever he ends up. Most
bases are scored from yards.

Kickoffs after bases are scored are taken in turn, not by the team
scored against each time. Throw-ins are one-handed, and if the ball
goes over the end line after touching a defender, there is a corner
throw. This is taken halfway between the corner of the pitch and the
nearest goalpost along the end line.

Finally, and perhaps most important of all, there was Shrewsbury
School. Set way off in Shropshire, on the border with Wales, Shrewsbury was another Tudor-era foundation, this time with a Royal Charter
in 1552, from King Edward VI. It began as a Calvinist protestant school.
Shrewsbury's football culture had to survive the reign of Dr. Samuel
Butler as headmaster (1796–1836), for as he wrote in a letter, he
thought football "more fit for farm boys than young gentlemen." But

despite the disapproval of the headmaster, football flourished at Shrewsbury.

The game appears to have been pretty similar to country footeballe, but it came to be called "douling to football." The word *doul* comes from the Greek word for "slave" and was the Shrewsbury term for youngsters conscripted as servants to older boys, called "fags" in other schools.

Shrewsbury "douling" was played with a round ball of leather around a pig's bladder. It was kicked, and the object was to score goals. The ball could be caught "on the full" and played afterward with certain restrictions. There was a tight form of offside and no forward passes. Players dribbled the ball and attempted to charge through the opposition, while their teammates "followed up." If a player lost possession, teammates would attempt to regain it or kick it forward, and everyone would rush on, while the other team would seek to control it, either with their feet or by catching it on the full and calling for a free kick, or, if space and time allowed, simply punting it.

And so by the mid-nineteenth century, three groups of schools, with distinctive approaches to football, had emerged.

First was the rugby group, in which Rugby School was joined by Cheltenham and Marlborough. Second was the Eton–Harrow axis, which emphasized dribbling, but with tight offside rules that prevented forward passes. Third was the dribbling and passing group, led by Charterhouse and Westminster.

Finally, in passing, we should note the outlier, Winchester College, another ancient school with a game more similar to *episkyros* than country footeballe. Although Winchester old boys would be involved in the negotiations that would eventually give birth to association football, their own game would contribute very little because it was so different from the rest.

Moving on from school to university, which for public-school boys almost universally meant going to one of the many colleges at Oxford or Cambridge, many students only remained for a year or so, sometimes even less, but the experience was regarded as an essential element in the education of young gentlemen of the time. Taking a degree was less important.

However, everyone arrived with a different style of football in their head, and no common game existed. The demand was there, so supply would inevitably eventually provide the rules.

7

THE AGE OF RULES
Part II

While the young men of the upper classes were slowly sorting out rules to make their games of football easier to organize, play, and enjoy, the traditional games, from "mob ball" games in towns to "footeballe" in the fields, were coming under increasing pressure from the "authorities." As noted in prior chapters, those good people had generally seen football as a nuisance, even a danger, since 1300 or even earlier. What had been lacking, from their point of view, was some way to enforce the bans and laws directed against mob games of ball, whether played in the streets or on the commons.

The small states of medieval Europe simply had no effective police forces. There were sheriffs, and manorial lords, whether barons or bishops, had a few armed men to enforce their will. The king's writ could sometimes be followed up by visits from sheriffs or even special parties of knights dispatched to find, and perhaps slay, evildoers, but the expense and risks of law enforcement were significant. On the whole, the authorities could no more stop football than they could stop theft, adultery, or crimes far worse.

However, something began to happen in the eighteenth century that would eventually change all that. This was the time of the Industrial Revolution, which for many reasons, all of which have been challenged and argued over, began in Britain. Was this a coincidence? Was it due to the relative success there of the Agricultural Revolution, which partly preceded and accompanied it? Or was it, challenging thought, part of an agency by which during a period of hundreds of years of a Darwinian process had transformed society because the upper classes outbred the lower?

In societies caught in the "Malthusian trap"—where improvements in living standards simply led to more people, negating the improvements—the steady downward movement of upper-class children infused education and upper-class values into the population at large. This argument, framed by Dr. Gregory Clark in his groundbreaking book *A Farewell to Alms*, has certainly set the opinion mills briskly whirling among economic historians. In a nutshell, Clark posits that with a few setbacks here and there, literacy and the ability to postpone gratification and save, accompanied by the acceptance of hard work, with self-control, had slowly ousted earlier cultural values, which had featured impulsivity, carelessness with money, and violence.

Why did this happen first in Europe, not China, India, or Japan? Clark suggests that Europe was simply harsher, Darwinian to the extreme. Thus, the difference in birth rates between the social classes in China was never as great as it became in England, for instance.

Clark points to the history of humankind prior to the Industrial Revolution as being largely the same, in as much as its effect on the living standards of the vast majority of people. From the Stone Age through early farming to the times of pyramids and empires, Rome and Han China, and until the end of the seventeenth century, most people, that is everyone who was neither an aristocrat nor a wealthy merchant, lived at pretty much the same level. Hence, good times coincided with good harvests; hard times came with a poor season in the fields. In Clark's view, the increase in agricultural productivity simply brought about an increase in population, to return the situation to the previous stasis. Clark also notes that the Black Death, by killing off a third of the population, brought about a period of increased prosperity for most people in the succeeding two hundred years. It seems perverse at first to read that plague and pestilence produced improved living standards, while good farming and good harvests lowered them. Much of the opposition to these views may simply be rebellion at the thought of such pure, Darwinian measurements being drawn on human populations.

However it may be, by the early nineteenth century, something was changing in the more civilized parts of Great Britain. The Industrial

Revolution had produced a sudden explosion in consumer goods. The industrial working classes now spent long hours bent over machinery, earning cash wages. The countryside had lost population to the towns. Life was still hard, but few mill hands would have preferred to move back to the villages and farm labor.

And the new middles classes—the management, shopkeepers, craftsmen, and traders—were demanding a share in the government. Until this time, Parliament had been completely dominated by the upper classes and aristocracy. Members of the House of Commons represented "boroughs," and the number of voters in these boroughs varied from as few as 12 to 12,000. Powerful members of the nobility controlled the House of Commons. The Duke of Norfolk, of the long-lasting Howard family, controlled 11 boroughs. The franchise qualifications varied from borough to borough, as well, from property ownership in varying degrees to simply having a hearth capable of boiling a pot of water.

Reform came after a long period of pressure, resisted to the end by the aristocracy. The Great Reform Act of 1832 began a process by which the franchise steadily spread to more and more members of the population. For all the fervor on both sides, the 1832 act only increased it marginally, from less than half a million to about 813,00, or one in five adult British men.

This was but one of many reforms and new laws that set out to change and improve social conditions in the country. For the story of football, the Highways Act of 1835 would have a serious and lasting impact. Following a pattern, British society was slowly losing its taste for horrible public spectacle. Signposts on the road to the new tone might include in 1789, the end of the practice of burning at the stake, wives convicted of murdering their husbands; and, in 1832, the custom of "gibbeting" the bodies of executed criminals, in particular highwaymen, whose remains, slowly decaying in iron cages hung from poles, had enlivened the roadside on the King's Highways. In 1835, bear baiting, cock fighting, and bull baiting were banned as well. Of course, these activities had been banned before but were now being addressed with a greater degree of enforcement. Bear baiting disappeared; bull baiting became secretive; and cock fighting took place at night, in someone's barn, out of view of the local constable.

The rise of the middle classes meant more and better clothing shops and more shops in general—butchers, grocers, and fruit and vegetable shops, as well as stores for clothing, shoes, general goods, and tools. That meant streets full of shoppers, with money changing hands, which, in turn, meant prosperity in town centers, with new classes of workers, both in the mills that made the goods and the towns that sold them.

The middle classes also needed servants, which pulled another segment of the working classes out of complete poverty and pressed them into a disciplined regime of service, with regular hours and duties.

A change in the general mindset of the population was taking place, just as in the great public schools, where the wild ways of the eighteenth century were slowly being eliminated with Latin, Greek, and the cane.

Against this backdrop we can see that the persistence of the great mob ball games on Shrove Tuesday was now running against the cultural tide.

Another facet of this should be considered, however. Football games had, for some time, been used as a way of inciting a politically pointed demonstration, even a riot. Enclosures, particularly in the East Midlands, were the targets of some of these events. Others were spurred by attempts to go against custom and traditional rights in other ways. In the eighteenth century, what mattered most was food—grain, or "corn" in British terminology. In the nineteenth century the emphasis shifted to wages, and in this alone we can see the transformation wrought by the Industrial Revolution. But in earlier times, efforts by landowners to break convention and overturn long-settled customs were seen as a direct threat by the peasantry.

In the eighteenth century, where wheat gradually became the standard cereal of the overwhelming majority of the country, half of a laborer's weekly income might be spent on bread. That meant the price of wheat was the most vital statistic in the land.

English historian E. P. Thompson wrote about the "moral economy" of the rural working class in the eighteenth century. Widespread food riots were a feature of the time, either to prevent wheat ("corn") from being moved out of a region or the country, or to keep wealthy farmers from selling the goods at prices deemed higher than what was seen as the traditional "fair price" in the market. These riots, often instigated by women, were quite disciplined, usually with a fixed objective, for instance, wrecking a baker's shop or destroying a mill that cheated small customers by perhaps mixing lower-grade grain with the farmer's, or simply by shorting his take.

Football provided a useful cover for riotous events of this nature. In 1638, during the era when the marshlands, known as the fens, of the east coast, above East Anglia, were being drained, a football match had been organized to bring in a big enough crowd to then tear down the levees being built for a local drainage project. The customary economy of the fens was a pastoral one, with some arable farming, allied with fishing, harvesting wild fowl, and cutting reeds for thatch. Drainage yielded rich soil but destroyed the pastoral livelihoods of many. Developers and landlords, sometimes called "projectors," were the bad guys in this scenario, which might strip a village of wetlands that for centuries had contributed protein and thatch to the common people.

Mills were another target, of course. As mentioned, with the price of grain so significant, millers and mill owners were the object of constant scrutiny and suspicion. In *Popular Recreations in English Society, 1700–1850*, Robert W. Malcolmson states that in 1740, an informant in Northamptonshire reported to the secretary of state that, "A match of futtball was cried at Kettering of 500 men of a side, but the design was to Pull Down Lady Betey Jesmaine's Mill."

In 1768, three "political" football games were organized in one month to protest an enclosure at Holland Fen in Lincolnshire. This was the end piece of a long battle begun in 1720, by Earl Fitzwilliam, to drain fens and create prime agricultural land. The Haute Huntre of Holland Fen was drained and enclosed in 1767. On July 1, 1768, about two hundred men "threw up a football" and played for about two hours, until a troop of cavalry ("dragoons") arrived with constables and some gentlemen from the nearby town of Boston. (This part of England, from the fens to Essex, was heavily represented among the Puritan emigrants to New England in the previous century.) Five rioters were arrested and taken to the jail in Spalding. Three women among them were given their liberty, and the men made bail. Two weeks later, another ball was thrown up, and hundreds of men played football. This time the dragoons did not show up. At the end of the month, on the 29th, yet another football game was held, again without opposition. The football players do not seem to have tried to break the drainage system or do any other damage, but their appearance had to have been seen as a threat.

Of course, the fens continued to be drained. Today as much as half of England's best agricultural land lies in the region of the former fens. With the demand for grain increasing, the urge to drain what were described by some authors as "sterile swamps" to produce wheat fields was irresistible. The customs of the local people were overridden by laws written in Parliament, for example, the Enclosure Act for Holland Fen, passed in 1767.

"Improvement" was the concept that covered much of the movement to suppress custom and institute laws in its stead. Lands were "improved" by their owners, especially if the customary uses by the peasantry had been severed. But in the towns, popular customs were also being drastically purged or changed. By the nineteenth century, a great many old customs were being curtailed or abolished. Gathering wood in the forest was now forbidden, because the forest was no longer "common" land. Gleaning in the fields was forbidden, too. Even Maypole dancing was being suppressed, as it was associated with unlicensed sexual activity, as well as a certain degree of drunkenness.

Consider Christmas Day. The day of the birth of Jesus had been placed on December 25 by the fourth-century AD Roman Catholic Church, despite evidence that his birth actually took place in the spring; however, it took over such pre-Christian wintertide festivals as Yule, falling near the winter solstice. In the Middle Ages, Christ's Mass day was often a drunken carnival, when people took to the taverns and streets. Some folk football games, like the one in Kirkwall, in the Orkney Islands, were played on Christmas Day, as was the game we discussed earlier at Llanwenog, in far western Wales.

During the nineteenth century, Christmas was stripped of the drunken revelry and converted into a family event, with Christmas trees and gifts, Christmas cards and carols, holly and mistletoe, and a big dinner in the evening.

Just as Christmas was changed, so the customary Shrovetide football games were due to be changed and, if they resisted, stamped out.

In the eighteenth century, the greatest, maddest, most dangerous town ball game was that played in Derby. It was so famous that it leant its name to any fierce game played between local rivals in football. Today, when Liverpool plays Everton or Manchester United plays Manchester City, the games are called "derbies." (Note: This does not apply to horse races; the Epsom Derby takes its name from the 12th Lord Derby and was first run in 1780.)

The small city of Derby lies 13 miles to the east of Ashbourne, and the Derby Game was similar to that of the Ashbourne contest, but on a considerably larger scale. The town of Derby was founded by the Danes in 873 AD. The "-by" suffix is a clear sign of Danish provenance. Before that, the Romans had a fort there, called Derventio, on the east bank of the River Derwent.

Derby was a town of 2,000 by the time of the *Domesday Book* (1086), which at that time indicated a solid middle England town, with a market and craftsmen, coopers, blacksmiths, carpenters, and so forth. The town gained a charter in the twelfth century and became a center for woolens production in the later Middle Ages. In Tudor times it became a brewing center as well, and in the seventeenth century it became known for clock making. Silk manufacture began in 1717, and porcelain was later produced there. Municipal improvements came too, with street lamps, fueled by oil, being installed beginning in 1735. Beginning in 1768, a municipal force for street maintenance and lighting existed. In 1821, the oil lamps were replaced by gas lamps. In 1839, the railway arrived.

But set against this gathering modernity was the annual madness of Shrove Tuesday and Ash Wednesday. By noon on Shrove Tuesday, large crowds gathered in the heart of the town. Large quantities of ale flowed down thirsty throats. The following song was sung, over and over, each time the city's many church bells sounded out:

> Pancakes and fritters
> Say All Saints and St. Peters
> When will the ball come?
> Say the bells of St. Alkmund's
> At two they will throw
> Says St. Werbaro
> Oh! Very well
> Says little St. Michael.

The game was nominally between the young men of the parishes of All Saints and St. Peters. In fact, every man capable of getting out of a chair was expected to turn out. It was a fierce game, with the honor of the parish resting on the outcome, in much the same way that the Blaenus and Paddy Brothers battled for their honor every Christmas

Day in Llanwenog. But it also pulled in hundreds of men from the surrounding area. All Saints, in the northern end of the town, is a cathedral, the seat of the bishop. St. Peters is an old church, initiated in about 1100 AD, perhaps earlier, and lies on the southern edge of the center of the old town. This really became a battle between north and south, with adherents from throughout the region. There might have been as many as several thousand people in the streets on a fine, sunny Shrove Tuesday, waiting for the game. The goals were Nuns Mill for All Saints and the Gallows Balk, on the Normanton Road, for St. Peters.

The ball, stuffed with cork shavings, was thrown up outside the Guildhall in central Derby, and then all hell broke loose. Glover's *History of Derbyshire* from 1829 records it pretty well:

> None of the other parishes in the borough take any direct part in the contest, but the inhabitants of all join in the sport, together with persons from all parts of the adjacent country. The players are young men from 18 to 30 or upwards, married, as well as single, and many veterans who retain a relish for the sport are occasionally seen in the very heat of the conflict.
>
> The game commences in the market-place, where the partisans of each parish are drawn up on each side; and, about noon, a large ball is tossed up in the midst of them. This is seized upon by some of the strongest and most active men of each party. The rest of the players immediately close in upon them, and a solid mass is formed. It then becomes the object of each party to impel the course of the crowd towards their particular goal.
>
> The struggle to obtain the ball, which is carried in the arms of those who have possessed themselves of it, is then violent, and the motion of this human tide heaving to and fro, without the least regard to consequences, is tremendous. Broken shins, broken heads, torn coats, and lost hats are among the minor accidents of this fearful contest, and it frequently happens that persons fall in consequence of the intensity of the pressure, fainting and bleeding beneath the feet of the surrounding mob.
>
> But it would be difficult to give an adequate idea of this ruthless sport: A Frenchman passing through Derby remarked that if Englishmen called this playing, it would be impossible to say what they would call fighting. Still the crowd is encouraged by respectable persons attached to each party, and who take a surprising interest in the

result of the day's sport, urging on the players with shouts, and even handing to those who are exhausted, oranges and other refreshment.

In fact, much of the game took place in the Markeaton Brook or the River Derwent. All in all, it was an exhausting, muddy monster of a game and quite terrifying to behold if you were a property-owning householder of good Victorian rectitude.

We should note the detail about the crowd being "encouraged by respectable persons attached to each party." This is yet another point about the movement from custom to laws in the eighteenth and nine-teenth centuries. Some members of the upper classes, hewing to tradi-tion and possibly disliking the increase in manufactures and growing organization of daily life, encouraged the old game and its wildness. They joined the masses in throwing down the gauntlet to the town authorities, the mayor, the mill owners, and the new middle class. Those parties would soon take it up. Indeed, as early as 1731, the mayor tried to stop the game. A legend has it that the mayor bought in some paid toughs to cordon off the area in front of the Guild Hall and stop the game being played, but an old lady concealed the ball under her skirts and smuggled it past them, and it was thrown up again and the game resumed. Another legend has it that the ball was broken into pieces on one occasion and smuggled in a lady's skirts all the way to the goal, where it was quickly put back together and used to score the winning goal.

In 1796, a man was killed during the game. According to the inquisi-tion and postmortem of John Snape at Derby Town Hall, the game was promptly condemned as "disgraceful to humanity and civilization, sub-versive of good order and Government and destructive of the Morals, Properties, and very lives of our inhabitants."

More unsuccessful attempts were made in the early nineteenth cen-tury to stop the great games, which were held both on Shrove Tuesday and Ash Wednesday, two whole days of terror for the middle class and the shopkeepers on Iron Gate and Sadler's Gate. The melee caused a loss of trade and an increase in thefts and assaults, not to mention damage to property, including shattered windows and broken gates. And with all this, the reputation of the town was forged, as one stuck in the older world, where law could not be maintained and brutes from the lower orders ran untamed along the public thoroughfares.

In 1845, the town fathers tried another tack: holding a sports day on the Holmes, a park by the river, with sack races and jumping competitions. On Ash Wednesday a greasy pole competition to fetch down a prime joint of beef was added, and for the less athletic, an eating match featuring plum pudding was incorporated. In addition, a football competition was added, with a prize of £10 to the winning team, no small sum in 1845. Finally, anyone found being abusive or drunk, or just spoiling the fun, was tossed in a blanket.

But the townsfolk ignored all this, perhaps because the town fathers banned beer and liquor from their event. Instead, the usual drunken hordes gathered by the Guildhall, where they were met by a new force, the borough police, allied with some cavalry troopers. It was still not enough. But the town passed a law specifically forbidding the old game, and in 1847, dragoons—heavy cavalry armed with sabers—were brought in to clear the streets and stop the game.

There were subsequent attempts to revive the great old melee, but they failed. The local law still stands, and it is, technically speaking, illegal to play football in Derby on Shrove Tuesday or Ash Wednesday.

So ended the most famous of the old town ball games, although other games persisted and indeed still continue. Still, the tenor of the Victorian Age was such that this kind of customary, uncontrollable public violence was to be brought to an end wherever possible.

And while customary town ball was being stamped out, the old boys of the public schools were now working on coming up with rules to make their games of football comprehensible to anyone and playable anywhere a suitable field could be found. This was a profound development, a sure indication of the gathering pace of this civilizing intent spreading throughout the nation. Now boys at the great schools were less keen on cockfighting, horse racing, and possibly even whoring, and more interested in sports that stressed athletic prowess.

Rugby football's first set of rules was written between August 25 and August 28, 1845. Three schoolboys at Rugby did the job: William Arnold, 17-year-old son of the great headmaster Thomas Arnold; Frederick Hutchins; and 16-year-old W. W. Shirley. They came up with 37 rules, which were passed by the Sixth Levee (equivalent to the modern 6th Form, or in United States, the senior high school class), and a Rule Book was printed. The rules were regularly updated throughout the next decade.

The first rule? I—FAIR CATCH: A fair catch is a catch direct from the foot.

Second? II—OFFSIDE: A player is off his side if the ball has touched one of his own players behind him, until the other side touches it.

So here the old rule from country footeballe persists in the fair-catch routine. No "mark" is mentioned, but the concept remains that a fair catch stopped all play until he who'd caught the ball had taken a kick.

And the offside rule here was tight; to be onside meant staying behind the ball. By the way, "offsides" comes from a British military term. When a soldier was absent for one reason or another from his unit, he was labeled "off the side," usually for reasons to do with pay.

Some other rules that are still relevant or interesting to consider are as follows:

IX—CHARGING: Charging is fair, in case of a placekick, as soon as the ball has touched the ground, or, in case of a kick from a catch, as soon as the player's foot has left the ground, and not before.

XVIII—A player having touched the ball straight for a tree, and having touched the tree with it, may drop from either side if he can, but the opposite side may oblige him to go to his own side of the tree.

XIX—A player touching the ball off his side must throw it straight out.

XX—All matches are drawn after five days, but after three if no goal has been kicked.

These first rules were very much Rugby School-specific rules, down to concerns about particular trees growing in the field of play. Several were about making sure that everyone required to play showed up. No excuses, not even for fagging, were allowed. Football was serious business now.

Rugby began to be played in venues other than Rugby School's "close." It grew in popularity among the old boys of the public schools, mostly residing in and around London, who became the test bed for the new sports that were evolving around the theme of "football."

Thus, the rules as of 1862 were more comprehensive, much less concerned with trees and so on, and quite portable to other fields of play, anywhere in the world. This time the idea was to come up with a code, more than just rules.

The ball? A gradual shift had taken place at Rugby. A pig's bladder is naturally oval; making it into a sphere requires skill and patience to carefully heat it over a flame and stretch it out in the necessary direction. This was the breakthrough achieved by an unknown Greek sometime in the seventh or eighth century BC. At Rugby the ball had been round, but by Tom Brown's schooldays, sometime in the 1830s, the ball was capable of "pointing": "The new ball you may see lie there, quite by itself, in the middle, pointing towards the school goal." Still, the ball was closer to round than the oval of the modern rugby ball. In 1851, a rugby-type football was exhibited at the first World's Fair, the Great Exhibition in the Crystal Palace, set up in Hyde Park, London (later moved to South London). It was no longer spherical but had not moved very far in the direction of the oval ball that was to become standard.

In 1862 came the next revolution, affecting all forms of modern-day football, when Richard Lindon introduced the first balls encasing a rubber bladder. This led to standardized sizes and shapes for the various balls used in the modern-day codes.

Next came an example of the way things were organized in England in that time. A letter was published in December 1870, in the *London Times*, from Edwin Ash, secretary of the Richmond Football Club, suggesting that a code be established for "those who play the rugby-type game," because "various clubs play to rules which differ from others, which makes the game difficult to play." Indeed, too much time was being spent "jaw-jawing" and not enough time playing rugger!

A month or so later, on January 26, 1871, representatives of 21 clubs and schools from London and surrounding counties met to hammer out a common code of rugby rules and, in so doing, formed the Rugby Union. It still exists, and Rugby Union is now the second most widely played code of football in the world.

Meanwhile, on the other side of the great divide between those who allowed handling the ball and those who did not, there had also been movement toward codification.

As mentioned, the 1839 Cambridge Rules are an important milestone. Key points established by these rules included that there was to be no running while holding the ball; when the ball was kicked out of play at the end line by an attacking player, it would be kicked back into play by a "goal kick"; if the ball was kicked out of play on the sidelines, it would be thrown back in by the opposing team; and forward passes were allowed.

So, in 1846, again at Cambridge, J. C. Thring and H. De Winton, Old Salopians (Shrewsbury School), gathered some Old Etonians to form the Cambridge University Foot Ball Club. In 1848, they came up with a set of rules; alas, no copy of these exists. How far they propagated is not well understood, either. But the need for common rules was a growing problem for the old boys of the great schools who wanted to continue playing football in their 20s and 30s.

A set of old rules, dated to 1856, was discovered in the school library at Shrewsbury. These rules are thought to be closely modeled on the Cambridge Rules. In these guidelines, the offside rule states that if the ball has passed a player and has come from the direction of his own goal, he may not touch it until the other side has kicked it, unless there are more than three players from the other team in front of him. No player is allowed to wait between the ball and the adversaries' goal.

The following are the rules discovered at Shrewsbury, called the "Laws of the University Foot Ball Club":

I. This club shall be called the University Foot Ball Club.

II. At the commencement of the play, the ball shall be kicked off from the middle of the ground: After every goal there shall be a kick-off in the same way.

III. After a goal, the losing side shall kick off; the sides changing goals, unless a previous arrangement be made to the contrary.

IV. The ball is out when it has passed the line of the flag-posts on either side of the ground, in which case it shall be thrown in straight.

V. The ball is behind when it has passed the goal on either side of it.

VI. When the ball is behind it shall be brought forward at the place where it left the ground, not more than 10 paces, and kicked off.

VII. Goal is when the ball is kicked through the flag-posts and under the string.

VIII. When a player catches the ball directly from the foot, he may kick it as he can without running with it. In no other case may the ball be touched with the hands, except to stop it.

IX. If the ball has passed a player, and has come from the direction of his own goal, he may not touch it till the other side has kicked it, unless there are more than three of the other side before him. No player is allowed to loiter between the ball and the adversaries' goal.

X. In no case is holding a player, pushing with the hands, or tripping up allowed. Any player may prevent another from getting to the ball by any means consistent with the above rules.

XI. Every match shall be decided by a majority of goals.

These rules retain the fair catch but do not include the "mark." They also allow the ball to be "stopped" with the hands.

The offside rule, IX, is looser than the offside rule in the Etonian Field Game, but it still requires three defenders to be ahead of an attacker in the event that the ball comes to him from one of his teammates.

In 1862, J. C. Thring, one of those involved in the early effort at Cambridge to come up with common rules, published his rules of the "Simplest Game." By then, Thring was assistant master at Uppingham School, a minor public school in Rutland, about eight miles from Hallaton, of the bottle kicking, as it happens.

There were just 10 rules.

1. A goal is scored whenever the ball is forced through the goal and under the bar, except that it be thrown by hand.
2. Hands may be used only to stop the ball and place it on the ground before the feet.
3. Kicks must be aimed only at the ball.
4. A player may not kick the ball whilst in the air.
5. No tripping up or heel kicking allowed.
6. Whenever a ball is kicked beyond the side flags, it must be returned by the player who kicked it, from the spot where it passed the flag, in a straight line towards the middle of the ground.
7. When a ball is kicked behind the line of goal, it shall be kicked off from that line by one of the side whose goal it is.
8. No player may stand within six paces of the kicker when he is kicking off.
9. A player is "out of play" immediately when he is in front of the ball and must return behind the ball as soon as possible. If the ball is kicked by his own side past a player, he may not touch or kick it, or advance, until one of the other side has first kicked it, or one of

his own side has been able to kick it on a level with or in front of him.

10. No charging allowed when a player is out of play; that is, immediately the ball is behind him.

The rules of the Simplest Game and the Cambridge game are an intriguing halfway house between the long-established country footeballe and the new game, still in gestation in the minds of a few hundred young men who liked to play football on the weekends in and around London and a few other cities in England. This game had a tight offside rule, with no forward passing, and the ball could not be "volleyed," or even kicked, while it was off the ground. The intent was to make a game for dribbling, one player at a time, rushing forward, attempting to dribble or force his way through the opposition. Behind him, alongside him, were his teammates, ready to intervene should he lose possession and the ball come to them off the feet of an opponent. Then, whoever received the ball would resume dribbling and rushing toward the opposition goal or, if close enough, take a shot at goal.

The Simplest Game dropped the concept of a catch and a "mark," with a free kick thereafter. The ball could only be handled to stop its progress and lay it on the ground for dribbling to resume. The throw-in was clearly in an early stage of development, but it was an advance on the old kicking in of the ball. Finally, it is important to note that there was some progress in the ban on kicking other players and tripping and heel kicking.

In 1857, Sheffield Football Club was founded and, in 1858, codified a set of rules, the "Sheffield Rules." The club grew out of pickup games that had begun some years before among members of a local cricket club. Nathaniel Creswick and William Prest were the drivers of the foundation of the football club. Neither were public school old boys, but both were keen cricketers and sportsmen in general. Creswick's family was in the silver plate business; Prest's family became wine merchants.

Football in Sheffield had existed for some time but in the unorganized, mob format. The earliest known game was in 1794, between Sheffield players and those of the village of Norton. This game is said to have lasted three days before someone scored a goal. No one, however, was killed.

From Sheffield Football Club's 1858 meeting, the Sheffield Rules are an interesting contrast with those of Thring's Simplest Game and the supposed Cambridge Rules found at Shrewsbury:

I. The kick off from the middle must be a place kick.

II. Kick out must not be more than 25 yards [23 meters] out of goal.

III. A fair catch is a catch from any player provided the ball has not touched the ground or has not been thrown from touch and is entitled to a free-kick.

IV. Charging is fair in case of a place kick (with the exception of a kick off as soon as a player offers to kick), but he may always draw back unless he has actually touched the ball with his foot.

V. Pushing with the hands is allowed, but no hacking or tripping up is fair under any circumstances whatever.

VI. No player may be held or pulled over.

VII. It is not lawful to take the ball off the ground (except in touch) for any purpose whatever.

VIII. The ball may be pushed or hit with the hand, but holding the ball except in the case of a free kick is altogether disallowed.

IX. A goal must be kicked but not from touch nor by a free kick from a catch.

X. A ball in touch is dead; consequently the side that touches it down must bring it to the edge of the touch and throw it straight out from touch.

XI. Each player must provide himself with a red and dark blue flannel cap, one color to be worn by each side.

Some of these rules are a step back toward country footeballe. The fair catch is allowed, but goals cannot be scored from the resulting free kick. The ball may be minimally handled, but not carried, and hacking the oppositions' shins is out, as is tripping, holding, and pulling over opponents.

And a degree of uniformity is now required, as colored caps are to be worn, with a single color for each team. What's missing is a rule regarding offside. The Sheffield Rules originally had no guidelines on this. Thus, players called "kick-throughs" were stationed by the opposition's goal, awaiting an opportunity to strike. Sheffield later dropped the kick-throughs by first making it offside, unless there was at least one defender between a forward player and the goal when he touched a ball kicked by a member of his own team. Sheffield then switched to the "three defenders" standard adopted by the Football Association (FA).

Sheffield Football Club, by the way, currently plays in the Northern Premier League, Division One South. They have always remained an amateur football club; the team won the FA Amateur Cup in 1904 and were runners-up in the FA Vase in 1977. The Northern Premier League Division One South is on the eighth tier of English football, with the Barclays Premier League at the top, where such giants as Chelsea and Manchester United play. There are 11 tiers altogether.

In October 1863, the Cambridge Rules were updated by the Cambridge University Football Club Rules Committee. They make for interesting reading:

1. The length of the ground shall not be more than 150 yds. and the breadth not more than 100 yds. The ground shall be marked out by posts, and two posts shall be placed on each side-line at distances of 25 yds. from each goal line.
2. The GOALS shall consist of two upright poles at a distance of 15 ft. from each other.
3. The choice of goals and kick-off shall be determined by tossing, and the ball shall be kicked off from the middle of the ground.
4. In a match when half the time agreed upon has elapsed, the side shall change goals when the ball is next out of play. After such change or a goal obtained, the kick off shall be from the middle of the ground in the same direction as before. The time during which the game shall last and the numbers in each side are to be settled by the heads of the sides.
5. When a player has kicked the ball any one of the same side who is nearer to the opponent's goal line is OUT OF PLAY and may not touch the ball himself nor in any way whatsoever prevent any other player from doing so.
6. When the ball goes out of the ground by crossing the side-lines, it is out of play and shall be kicked straight into the ground again from the point where it first stopped.
7. When a player has kicked the ball beyond the opponents' goal line, whoever first touches the ball when it is on the ground with his hand may have a FREE kick, bringing the ball straight out from the goal line.

8. No player may touch the ball behind his opponents' goal line who is behind it when the ball is kicked there.

9. If the ball is touched down behind the goal line and beyond the line of the side-posts, the FREE kick shall be from the 25 yds. post.

10. When a player has a free-kick, no-one of his own side may be between him and his opponents' goal line, and no one of the opposing side may stand within 10 yds. of him.

11. A free kick may be taken in any manner the player may choose.

12. A goal is obtained when the ball goes out of the ground by passing between the poles or in such a manner that it would have passed between them had they been of sufficient height.

13. The ball, when in play, may be stopped by any part of the body, but it may NOT be held or hit by the hands, arms, or shoulders.

14. ALL charging is fair; but holding, pushing with the hands, tripping up, and shinning are forbidden.

Rules 5 and 7 have much of the Eton Field Game about them, and indeed, two members of the committee that drew up the rules were Old Etonians. But there were old Rugbeians and Harrovians, and the chairman had been to Shrewsbury. It is also worth mentioning that the dimensions of the field of play and the goals are now being specified. Moreover, the dimensions are roughly those of the modern association game and have decisively moved away from country footeballe.

And so we come to October 26, 1863, and a meeting of 13 London football clubs at the Freemason's Tavern on Long Acre, in Covent Garden. The tavern, by the way, is still there and packed with football memorabilia.

The impetus for the meeting came from Ebeneezer Cobb Morley, founder and captain of the Barnes Football Club. His letter was published in *Bell's Life* newspaper and sparked interest from clubs as diverse as the Blackheath Football Club, Kensington School, the War Office, Forest (later "Wanderers"), Crystal Palace, and the No Names of Kilburn. Charterhouse School sent an observer to the meeting.

The meetings were long and acrimonious. There were many different rules and interpretations of the rules. Two rules in particular sharply divided the group:

1. IX. A player shall be entitled to run with the ball towards his adversaries' goal if he makes a fair catch, or catches the ball on the first bound; but in case of a fair catch, if he makes his mark (to take a free kick) he shall not run.
2. X. If any player shall run with the ball towards his adversaries' goal, any player on the opposite side shall be at liberty to charge, hold, trip, or hack him, or to wrest the ball from him, but no player shall be held and hacked at the same time.

We clearly have gone back to the good old country footeballe with these two. Running with the ball from a fair catch, but with no "mark" called, is allowed, and if one dared do this, then tackling, kicking, hacking, and just about anything would be legal to stop an opponent. Oliver Cromwell probably would have approved; however, note the concern about holding and hacking the same person at the same time. It was one or the other, because if you're being held and someone also kicks you hard in the shins, you're likely to end up with a broken leg. We may take this as evidence of social progress from the eighteenth to nineteenth centuries.

Hacking was particularly important to the Blackheath representative, F. W. Campbell, who regarded this to be a vital part of "masculine toughness." When the group voted 13–4 to ban hacking, he resigned from the infant FA. A few years later, he helped form the Rugby Football Union.

On December 8, 1863, the FA published its first attempt at "laws":

1. The maximum length of the ground shall be 200 yards, the maximum breadth shall be 100 yards, the length and breadth shall be marked off with flags, and the goal shall be defined by two upright posts, eight yards apart, without any tape or bar across them.
2. A toss for goals shall take place, and the game shall be commenced by a place kick from the centre of the ground by the side losing the toss for goals; the other side shall not approach within 10 yards of the ball until it is kicked off.
3. After a goal is won, the losing side shall be entitled to kick off, and the two sides shall change goals after each goal is won.

4. A goal shall be won when the ball passes between the goal-posts or over the space between the goal-posts (at whatever height), not being thrown, knocked on, or carried.

5. When the ball is in touch, the first player who touches it shall throw it from the point on the boundary line where it left the ground in a direction at right angles with the boundary line, and the ball shall not be in play until it has touched the ground.

6. When a player has kicked the ball, any one of the same side who is nearer to the opponent's goal line is out of play, and may not touch the ball himself, nor in any way whatever prevent any other player from doing so, until he is in play; but no player is out of play when the ball is kicked off from behind the goal line.

7. In case the ball goes behind the goal line, if a player on the side to whom the goal belongs first touches the ball, one of his side shall be entitled to a free kick from the goal line at the point opposite the place where the ball shall be touched. If a player of the opposite side first touches the ball, one of his side shall be entitled to a free kick at the goal only from a point 15 yards outside the goal line, opposite the place where the ball is touched, the opposing side standing within their goal line until he has had his kick.

8. If a player makes a fair catch, he shall be entitled to a free kick, providing he claims it by making a mark with his heel at once; and in order to take such kick he may go back as far as he pleases, and no player on the opposite side shall advance beyond his mark until he has kicked.

9. No player shall run with the ball.

10. Neither tripping nor hacking shall be allowed, and no player shall use his hands to hold or push his adversary.

11. A player shall not be allowed to throw the ball or pass it to another with his hands.

12. No player shall be allowed to take the ball from the ground with his hands under any pretense whatever while it is in play.

13. No player shall be allowed to wear projecting nails, iron plates, or gutta-percha on the soles or heels of his boots.

You can see that we're a long way from the rules of association football as we, and FIFA, understand them today. There are rules with a distinct hint of one public school game in particular, for example, rule 4, which hints at Harrow football's "bases," with their lack of a crossbar. Rule 13, banning nails, iron plates, and gutta percha (then used to case golf balls) poses the question, Did players really have projecting nails and other bits of metal sticking out of their shoes? Rules 5 and 7 seem strange to modern eyes but contain elements of the Eton Field Game, for instance, the "rouge," as well perhaps as an incentive to get players to pursue any ball that went out of play and thus quickly return it to play. Rule 6 is a tight offside rule, with a strong echo of Eton about it.

The age-old concept of the fair catch and calling a mark to earn a free kick remains, but Webb Ellis–like players need not apply—there will be no running with the ball in one's hands. Pushing, holding, tripping, and hacking are all out—although referees, of course, routinely hand out free kicks and yellow, and even red, cards for the same offense every match day on every continent on Earth.

Another point should be made: These rules weren't terribly good. The game they provided was unsatisfactory for several reasons. The tight offside rule (6) denied forward passing, so the game was still one of dribbling and trying to push through the opposition or kick the ball downfield and have everyone run after it to try and prevent the opposition from kicking it back. In practice, it appears to have often descended into "bee ball"—a circle of players kicking away at the ball, which was trapped and could not be extricated. In fact, it's claimed that these rules were hardly ever precisely followed and that arguments about how to play the game continued unabated on the fields and heaths around London. In other words, most clubs continued to play by their own rules, and only occasional games were played by the association rules.

But having an association and a set of rules to work from was still a vital step. Improvements continued. Pressure from old boys from Westminster and Charterhouse in favor of loosening the offside rule and allowing forward passing finally earned its reward in 1867, when the FA chose to allow both. In 1871, after much argument, the fair-catch use of the hands was ended. At about the same time, a Scottish innovation, the header, was becoming widely used. Indeed, the Scots, particularly those of Queen's Park Football Club, which formed in 1867, had a tremendous effect on the early development of the game. These Scots were not public-school boys and had no preconceptions or loyalties to the peculiar games of their schools. The Queen's Park players passed the ball; in fact, they passed it a lot. They called it "combination play"—dribbling, passing, dribbling, passing. It was still difficult to pass forward, because the offside rule was still very strict, but passing had arrived. And with it came an important tactical shift, because now the entire field was just one pass away from being in the center of play, whereas before the ball and most players had been jammed together in one place or another.

This caused consternation among the old boys from Eton and Harrow. Passing was just not done. It was even considered "unmanly."

Instead of dribbling directly at the defenders and trying to go through them, knocking them aside if necessary, the Scots passed the ball to one another, found the player with no opposition in front of him, and "followed up" alongside. The advent of passing and heading produced the next tactical revolution. Up to this point, most of the clubs, which were mostly in Southern England and filled with old boys, had played with seven or eight forwards, a goalkeeper, and two "backs." This didn't work against a team that moved the ball around the field. Players had to be pulled back into a "midfield" defensive system, and teams had to spread out and cover the entire field.

Formations slowly evolved from a goalkeeper, one full-back, one half-back, and eight forwards to a goalie, two backs, two midfielders, and six forwards, although there were those who tried to play with just two in midfield, who were told to dribble at "their discretion." Otherwise it was still a game of kicking the ball downfield and hurtling after it in a pack, trying to knock it free and keep it moving, either with dribbling or long kicks. The idea of a modern-day team setup, like the 4–4–2 or the more sophisticated 3–2–3–2, would have horrified the Old Etonians and their ilk, if for nothing else, because of the emphasis on defense.

Queen's Park didn't lose a single game in their first nine years as a club or give up a goal for eight years. The Scots proved again and again that they were too good for the English. England and Scotland played the first-ever international match in 1872, which ended in a thrilling 0–0 draw; however, during the next 15 internationals with England, the Scots won nine, drew four, and lost just twice.

Despite this progress, however, the association code was clearly losing out to rugby football in terms of popularity at this point. The fact that no two sets of rugby rules were exactly the same made no difference. Rugby was preferred by the press, and on any given game day in the 1860s, four times as many fellows were playing rugby or rugby-like games on fields and parks around London as were playing the dribbling association game.

It may seem improbable to us now, with rugby and soccer so well differentiated and with rugby clearly the more physical game, but at this juncture, the association game still carried the freight of criticism for "brutality." There were those drawn to it for the pleasure of kicking other players, or worse. In 1862, the Blackheath Club included a rule that said, "Though it is lawful to hold a player in a scrummage, this does not include attempts to throttle or strangle, which are totally opposed to the spirit of the game."

But with the arrival of the 1871–1872 season, a transformative competition was to begin that would bring many changes in its wake and ultimately lead to the association game achieving an astonishing worldwide popularity.

Before we tackle that tale, we must catch up on the progress of football in the rest of the world.

8

THROUGHOUT THE WORLD

Moving on from the muddy fields around London and the English public schools where rugby and association football were taking shape, the rest of the world had undergone some amazing changes between 1700 and 1900. New nations had arisen, new empires now spanned the globe, and older domains had gone into decline. France, which had dominated Europe until the final defeat of Napoleon at Waterloo in 1815, now found herself confronted by the might of united Germany, under the Prussian Kaisers. Italy, which had also been fragmented, was now united, too. The Netherlands, which had fought for freedom from Spain in the seventeenth century, briefly soared to the top as a global trading nation, before being trimmed back by another new power. England, now Great Britain, following Cromwell's conquest of Ireland and the union with Scotland in 1707, had become a global player through the power of the Royal Navy, which, in 1800, was the largest single industrial organization in the world.

Across the Atlantic, the early English colonies had grown into small states with higher levels of prosperity than the home country. Once Britain had finally defeated the French, in what was really the first global war (known in Europe as the Seven Years War [1756–1763] and America as the French and Indian War), the need for British protection from the French had been lifted. The American colonies soon began to feel overtaxed and underrepresented in the government in London. British arrogance led to war, and British incompetence left the Americans on the battlefield long enough to let the French revive and enter the fray on their side. A French fleet finally blocked relief for Cornwallis's army at Yorktown and forced his surrender, ending British rule in the former colonies, although Britain held on to Canada.

In China, the Ming dynasty had suffered through a long twilight as the Manchus unified the northern tribal forces once more, and the Ming fell into the dark in 1644, with the sack of Beijing by rebel forces. The last Ming emperor committed suicide, and soon afterward the Manchu Qing emperor seized Beijing. The southern Ming were not crushed until 1662, but the Manchu Qing had already become the next major dynasty to rule China.

During the next century, the Qing rose to their peak, extending their rule over Tibet and Mongolia, as well as the traditional Chinese heartland and their original center, Manchuria. By 1900, however, Qing China faced humiliation at the hands of the European powers, which had begun the process of carving provinces out of China.

India had witnessed the decline of the Mughal Empire; while the Hindu religion had successfully resisted the tide of Islam, the younger religion would remain an important minority faith in the northwest and northeast, but the competing powers, from the Marathas to the Afghans, were to find themselves increasingly matched against an outside power with a rapidly improving technological edge—the Europeans, especially the British. In a series of short wars, the British took over Bengal and defeated the other central Indian powers. In time, the entire subcontinent—today's Pakistan, India, Bangladesh, Burma, and Malaysia—came under Imperial British Rule.

South and Central America remained locked in the unprogressive Spanish colonial empire until it began to come apart in the early nineteenth century. Africa, source of slaves, ivory, gold, and romantic mystery, remained largely unexplored and unknown deep into the nineteenth century, although the Europeans had dotted the coastline with forts and small colonies. The effect of the slave trade on West Africa had been extensive, leading to the rise of such powers as the Ashanti and the demise of many smaller ones.

The British had gained control of the Atlantic slave trade in West Africa following the Treaty of Utrecht in 1713, which ended Louis XIV's imperial ambitions toward Europe. Early British manufactures were of little interest to Qing China or Mughal India but could be exchanged for slaves in West Africa. The slaves produced sugar in Brazil and the Caribbean, which was a hot commodity in both Europe and North America, where it fueled the distilling of rum. The massive increase in sugar production went hand in hand with the rise of tea and coffee drinking in Europe. The brutality of the slave labor model at the base of this took place far from where tea was sweetened and sipped, morning, noon, and night. The use of caffeinated beverages was a stimulating change from earlier times and quickly became universally popular. After 1670, the slave economic model was imported into the Carolinas from the sugar islands and, in America, transformed into a cotton production model that built the southern states and led to the agonies of the American Civil War in the 1860s.

Through the latter part of the eighteenth century, the Industrial Revolution gathered speed in Britain, adding further weight to British influence throughout the world and influencing the longtime struggle in Britain between custom, tradition, and the new rule of law. Beginning in about 1800, the revolution finally began to lift British incomes, which took a rising trajectory, a beacon of the great uplift that industrialization was to bring to Europe and North America.

But while great kings and emperors came and went, and steam engines led to locomotives and inexpensive cottons, in the wilder parts of Northern France, *les souliers* continued to gather for their ancient, traditional games. In the eighteenth and early nineteenth centuries, *la soule* was reported as being played in Normandy, as well as Brittany, the heartland of the tradition. Another game, called *choule*, was also reported as being contested in Normandy and seems to have been more of a hockey variant. Games of both were reported to last for considerable periods of time. But it was in Brittany, especially Morbihan in southern Brittany, where *la soule* was most often seen and recorded.

We have accounts from two British writers. The first is from the older brother of famous Victorian era novelist Antony Trollope. T. A. Trollope wrote in *A Summer in Brittany* in 1840, that the Morbihannais were well known for their adherence to elements of ancient Celtic, perhaps druidic worship. They were also known for the fierce games of *la soule*, which, due to illegality, were played less frequently and in secrecy.

In 1877, another travel writer, Katharine Sara Macquoid, added intriguing detail to the tale in her *Through Brittany*. She writes,

Vannes, which is entirely Celtic in its features, represents Morbihan. The Vannetais were the fighting men of Brittany. Caesar said, when he tried to conquer them, that they had bodies of iron and hearts of steel.

The Vannetais played the fearful game of Soule long after it had been given up by the other provinces.

The Vannetais are, of course, the descendants of the shipbuilding Veneti, who once controlled the trade in tin with Cornwall.

Brittany remains distinct—the Wales and Cornwall of France—where the Celtic past and independent ways are never far from the surface. The game of *la soule*, like *cnapan* and Cornish hurling, is an echo of that past.

However, French education, while the equal of what was available in England, did not see local grammar schools of medieval foundation grow into schools for the wealthy in the way that Eton, Winchester, Harrow, and Westminster had. Until the French Revolution in 1789, schools and colleges were largely Catholic Church enterprises. They were then nationalized and the priests dismissed. Both the Republic and Napoleon set up schools and lycées, and spread liberal arts education more widely. Education remained a political battleground through the nineteenth century. While sports activity must have been part of the lives of young people, especially boys, it does not seem to have involved games of football until later in the nineteenth century, when the French took up rugby, followed by the association game, both imports from across the English Channel.

Across the Atlantic, however, other games were stirring that would eventually influence football in a powerful way.

The rough "mob football" tradition had inevitably crossed the ocean with some of the emigrants from England. There are tales of early settlers at Jamestown kicking a football around. This might not have been so obvious among the Puritans who went to Massachusetts or even the later Cavaliers who went to Virginia, but the third great wave of emigrants, the "Borderlanders," often called the "Scotch Irish," most certainly took the concept with them. In the nineteenth century, many upper-class American boys were sent to England to be schooled at Eton, Harrow, and the other large public schools. There they encountered the burgeoning culture of football games in their different forms.

When the games arrived in the New World, they percolated upward, remaining below the cultural radar until the early decades of the nineteenth century. As had been the case in England, "mob football," in its many variations, and the football concept in general arose at the elite American universities.

The early American colleges tended to be founded by religious groups with a strong sense of moral purpose, and they had an atmosphere reminiscent of sixteenth-century Eton. When young men were not studying, they were meant to be praying or asleep on their hard beds in freezing dormitories. Conditions were, at best, uncomfortable, and the food was ghastly. At Harvard, the earliest and best known American college, it was referred to as the "commons" and was the cause of riots leading to its abolition in 1849.

The faculty at most of these colleges also acted as provosts or sheriffs, determined to keep order and prevent any of the "vicious" immorality that so beset the English public schools in the late eighteenth century. Duels, drinking, cock fighting, gambling, and sexuality of all varieties were evils to be kept at bay. This drawing of lines naturally pitted faculty against students in endless warfare, and throughout the nineteenth century, tales of riots and rebellion emerged from American colleges. At colleges in the more recently settled states to the west, professors were sometimes shot or stabbed to death. Duels were fought on campus and unpopular students put to the sword. In light of this kind of cultural feistiness, even football could be seen as preferable.

At Harvard, beginning in 1827, there was a wild mob game known as "Bloody Monday," pitting incoming freshmen against sophomores, watched over by the senior class. A similar battle took place in early autumn at Dartmouth College in New Hampshire, where it was called the "Usual Game of Football." These games were a pretext for the older boys to hammer into the younger ones some respect and understanding of their position in the hierarchy. They were violent, without rules, and frightening to behold; however, a form of loosely organized football, somewhat similar to what would later be soccer, was common at Dartmouth and other New England colleges.

At Dartmouth, rules eventually evolved for something they called "Old Division" football, which pitted students from even-numbered class years against those of odd-numbered years. In the issue nine of the

October 1871 installment of the college newspaper, *The Dartmouth* 5, a set of rules was published by the students.

I. Five umpires, one from each class in the Academical, and one from the Scientific Department, shall be elected annually by the college. The senior umpire present shall settle all disputes which arise concerning the game.

II. The ball shall be warned from the second base of the college grounds and towards the buildings. No warn shall be valid until both parties are ready.

III. Until the ball is kicked the warning party shall stand behind the ball and their opponents in front; the latter at a distance of at least two rods (a rod is 5.5 yards). These positions, and the warn as well, shall be changed each game.

IV. No player shall kick, trip, strike, or hold another for any cause during the game. It shall be considered foul when the ball is caught on the bound, or fly, or picked from the ground; when it passes the fence at the north or south end of the common, or at either corner, or when knocked past the east or west fence.

V. In case of a foul the ball shall be tossed up by the umpire at the place where the foul occurs, unless it be within two rods of either fence, in which case the ball shall be brought directly in a distance of two rods before umpiring.

VI. The game shall be won when the ball is kicked past the east or west fence.

At Yale, a similar mob game took place often enough to raise angry complaints from the surrounding town of New Haven. The town refused to allow Yale students to hold the annual "rough house" game on the village green in 1858. In 1860, Yale bowed to the pressure and banned football of all varieties. Harvard followed suit the next year. And at Harvard, a mock funeral was held for dear old "Football Fightum," who was laid to rest in a ceremony around a mock grave. The following verse has survived from this moment:

> Beneath this sod we lay you down,
> This sign of glorious fight;
> With dismal groans and yells we'll drown
> Your mournful burial rite!

In miniature, and within just a few decades, the elite students of the East Coast colleges had repeated the history of mob football in England, establishing a wild, violent game and settling it into "tradition," followed by having it banned by the authorities.

At about the same time, on Boston Common, just a mile or so from the hallowed precincts of Harvard, a group of young men was setting about playing their own style of football, which became known as the "Boston Game." They were students from elite Boston schools, including Dixwell's Latin School, Boston Latin, and English High School. Boston Latin and English High School were "public schools" in the American mode, not private "fee paying" schools like Eton, Harrow, and Rugby in England. They were schools for the sons of the elite in New England.

The Boston Game lay somewhere on the spectrum between the ball-carrying rugby style and the old country footeballe tradition. The game was the special province of the Oneida Football Club, founded by Gerrit Smith "Gat" Miller of Dixwell Latin School. Tiring of the rather chaotic cast of the games then played between the Boston schools, Miller pulled together a select team, and they produced some rules. They played the Boston Game on Boston Common. The rules were few. Harking back to *episkyros*, a point was scored for kicking the ball over the opponent's end line. A point could also be scored for carrying the ball over that line. Thus, ancient met modern, with an element of the rugby carrying game amid a game that had a lot of kicking, like something from a field in Sparta in approximately 400 BC. The rules were not recorded, but it was agreed that the ball could be kicked, thrown, or handed to teammates rugby style. There was an offside component, but it doesn't appear to have been written down, or to have survived. The teams were 12 a side.

Miller went on to Harvard after 1865, and the Oneida Club folded, retaining an unbeaten record; indeed, the proud boast was that no one had even managed to score against them. Gat was also instrumental in beginning the Holstein dairy cow herd in the United States, importing four cows from Schleswig-Holstein, part of Prussia by that point, to upstate New York.

The Boston Game's importance in our story lies in the way it predisposed Harvard to prefer the ball-carrying mode of football. In effect, the Boston Game became the football that Harvard men played in the 1860s and early 1870s.

This was a momentous time for the United States of America, which fought the bloodiest war in its history between 1861 and 1865, as the issue of slavery and fear of its suppression drove southern states, dominated by planter aristocracies, into rebellion and secession. From Bull Run to Chickamauga, Shiloh to Antietam to Gettysburg, the war transformed the young nation and put 750,000 men into early graves.

Football might have seemed beside the point next to the casualty lists coming back from the Wilderness or Spotsylvania. But even during the awful war years football of a sort continued to be played, and afterward the passion for a vigorous contact sport increased. Among the most literate, well-off classes—those who sent their sons to the eastern colleges and had sent them to England as well—the doings of the football playing old boys in and around London were definitely known, if perhaps not entirely understood. The concept of agreed upon rules for a rough game involving a large ball was infectious among young men.

In 1866, Beadle & Co., in New York, publishers of popular dime novels, published the rules of both association and rugby football. Within a year, New Jersey College at Princeton had adopted the association rules. Fellows up and down the turnpike were playing one kind or another of the new thing; football had arrived.

This inevitably brought about a challenge between two colleges. In 1869, William Leggett of Rutgers College sent a message to his counterpart at New Jersey College (Princeton), William Gummere. A three-game series was proposed, with the first game to be played at Rutgers on College Field, which today is underneath the college gym and parking lot in New Brunswick, New Jersey. This is seen as the first "college football" game.

The rules were idiosyncratic, with elements from country footeballe and the Eton Field Game, mixed with the London Football Association rules of 1866. The game was broken into 10 separate "games" on the basis of the old country football rule that a single goal decided the game. The ball could be kicked, dribbled, or, apparently, headed and punched. There were 25 players a side, which crowded the pitch considerably, and there was no offside rule. That meant that two players from each team took up the role of Sheffield-style "kick throughs," lurking by the opposition's goal. Each team had 11 "fielders" who played defense and 12 who played in attack and were called "bulldogs" for some unknown reason. According to an account of the game, Rutgers played in the manner of the Eton Field Game, not with an organized bully or scrum, but by forming a mass of players, with the ball brought along close behind, but not kicked over, until there was an opportunity to shoot at goal. The New Jersey Tigers were said to have a distinct size and weight advantage, but that did not count for enough in the end, and Rutgers ran out victors with a score of six "games" to four.

The following year, Columbia joined the two New Jersey colleges. The rules were still a curious mix of old and new, with elements from various sources. Rutgers beat Columbia but lost at Princeton.

In 1872, no games were played; perhaps it just too difficult to schedule that time around. But the next year saw Yale enter the lists, along with Stevens Technical College. In 1873, a team of Eton old boys joined in, although they were beaten by Yale. The game was still being played by a set of rules floating somewhere between the London Football Association rules, the Sheffield Rules, and old country footeballe traditions.

However, the still-tiny world of football enthusiasts, a few thousand strong in Britain, the United States, and faraway Australia, had been lifted by the news from England. For those leaning toward rugby, there was the January 1871 meeting that produced the Rugby Union and a code of rules for rugby football. For those attuned to the association game, there first came the initiation of the Football Association Challenge Cup in 1871–1872, leading to the first cup final, watched by 2,000 spectators, in which Wanderers won the cup. Later that same year, the first "international" football match, pitting England against Scotland, was fought to a scoreless draw on a misty day. In addition there was the Scottish revelation of "combination play," which featured passing the ball and using the entire field. These events fueled the fire in the hearts of the band of young men who were passionate about football of some sort and determined to bring it to the United States.

In 1873, at a meeting between representatives from Columbia, Yale, Rutgers, and Princeton at the Fifth Avenue Hotel in New York, new rules were worked out. Teams were to be 20 strong, although Yale argued for 11 and was overruled.

The 1873 American Rules, from the Report of the Intercollegiate Football Rules Committee, were as follows:

1. The ground shall be 400 feet long and 250 feet broad.
2. The distance between the posts of each goal shall be 25 feet.
3. The number for match games shall be 20 to a side.
4. To win a game six goals are necessary, but that side shall be considered victorious which, when the game is called, shall have scored the greater number of goals, provided that number be two or more. To secure a goal, the ball must pass between the posts.
5. No player shall throw or carry the ball. Any violation of this regulation shall constitute a foul, and the player so offending shall throw the ball perpendicularly into the air to a height of at least 12 feet, and the ball shall not be in play until it has touched the ground.
6. When the ball passes out of bounds it is a foul, and the player causing it shall advance at right angles to the boundary line, 15 paces from the point where the ball went and shall proceed as in rule 5.
7. No tripping shall be allowed, nor shall any player use his hands to hold or push an adversary.
8. The winner of the toss shall have the choice of the first goal, and the sides shall change goals after every successive inning. In starting the ball it shall be fairly kicked, not "babied," from a point 150 feet in front of the starter's goal.
9. Until the ball is kicked no player on either side shall be in advance of a line parallel to the line of his goal and distant from it 150 feet.
10. There shall be two judges, one from each of the contesting colleges, and one referee; all to be chosen by the captains.
11. No player shall wear spikes or iron plates upon his shoes.
12. In all matches a number six ball shall be used, furnished by the challenging side and to become the property of the victor.

The number six ball was made of heavy duty canvas impregnated with rubber and was the chosen ball of the London Football Association.

No offside rule is included, and rule 5 strikes the modern eye as both bizarre and unworkable. In the end, however, none of this mattered. The assembled colleges only played by these rules for a season or so, and that was because Harvard had taken another path.

But first, the Harvard men expressed their dislike for the new game being organized by the other colleges. Harvard had refused to send anyone to the New York meeting. Mark Bernstein's *Football: The Ivy*

League Origins of an American Obsession gives the explanation provided by Harry Grant, Harvard's captain of football:

> Harvard stands entirely distinctly by herself in the game of football.
> You perhaps wonder on your side at our rules; but I assure you that
> we consider the game here to admit of much more science, accord-
> ing to our rules.
>   We cannot but recognize in your game much but brute force,
> weight, and especially "shin" element. Our game depends upon run-
> ning, dodging, and position playing,—i.e. kicking across field into
> another's hands. We are perfectly aware of our position in regard to
> other colleges. I assure you we gave the matter a fair discussion last
> spring. We even went so far as to practice and try the Yale game. We
> gave it up at once as hopeless.
>   I would send you a copy of our rules, but we do not have a spare
> copy.

Arrogant and stuck-up perhaps, but Harvard's loyalty to their old
Boston game and refusal to play by the modified association rules
agreed to by the others would swing the entire North American continent away from making them part of the soccer-playing world and in
another direction, as yet uncharted in 1873, with unpredictable but
enormous consequences for global sport.

Despite the refusal to attend the meeting, Harvard did play a couple
of games in 1874, losing once and winning once. Something like a
critical mass was starting to emerge.

Tufts College and New York University joined in, while the Eton old
boys disappeared. Still, eight teams competed, although teams played
wildly varied seasons, with Columbia playing six games and losing five,
and Yale playing and winning three.

We should note that by this point, balls made with rubber lining
were becoming common. This had two important effects. First, it was
now possible to simply buy a football at a department store in New
York, London, Boston, and other large cities. Obtaining a football had
previously required knowing someone who could make one. This skill
might have been common in a Welsh village, where a *crydd* made
everyone's shoes and everyone knew someone who would soon be
slaughtering a pig, but it was much less available to upper-class youths
in the 1870s. The second effect was that the balls were now regular,

perfectly round or in whatever shape was desired, and this affected how one might play. The dribbling game, with passing, heading, and control being carried out with entire the body, other than the hands and arms, took on a more consistent nature. The regular ball could be trusted to do what players wanted it to do as they moved it around with their feet.

At this juncture in the narrative of football in the United States, it would have seemed likely that the Americans would join the British nations and play both the association game and rugby. If that had been the story, then truly, the history of the world would have been somewhat different, because, quite simply, a powerful aspect of American "exceptionalism" and difference with the rest of the world would not have arisen. It's also likely that the United States would have become a dominant power in association football; "soccer" and the American football league(s) would have quickly rivaled those of England and Europe. There might have been a real "World Series" or Club Cup fought between English, Scottish, and American champions, and later with the various European champions as they arose. Rugby's development would have taken a different course as well, if Australia, New Zealand, and South Africa had been joined by an American team in challenging the nations of the original rugby heartland. And with intense American competition, the English rugby authorities would have been forced out of the amateur mold long before they actually were. English rugby would have been forced to either give up competing with the Americans or accept that real competition, a real league, and professionalism were essential if English rugby was to hold its own in the world. This might have fostered the spread of rugby beyond its strongholds in England and the English upper-middle class, also giving soccer a run for its money.

That these things did not happen are the result of some specific small-scale twists in the history of football. Crucial to it all was the peculiar stature of Harvard College among American universities. Harvard, founded in 1636, is the oldest and most special. In the 1870s, it was *the* elite school, with particularly close links to the Boston and New England ruling classes.

Another point should be made here. In 1869, Charles William Eliot became president of Harvard. He would hold the position for the next 40 years and oversee the college's transition from the nineteenth century to the modern world. In his inaugural address, he spoke of an

American "aristocracy, which excels in manly sports, carries off the honors and prizes in the learned professions, and bears itself with distinction in all fields of intellectual labor and combat." Eliot set a tone for Harvard that demanded "manliness" from the students. This was the era of "muscular Christianity" in the Anglo-Saxon world. Elites were concerned that the rising tide of prosperity and luxury would make their young men effete, flaccid, decadent. To combat this it was seen as necessary to school elite youth in "scholarly manliness," and by that measure it was required that they play "manly sports."

Said Eliot, "[E]ffeminacy and luxury are worse evils than brutality."

So, at this critical point in the history of America's own football game, a certain tone, ringing from the battlefields of the Civil War, demanding sacrifice and pain in the pursuit of higher callings, was coming from the very top of Harvard's hierarchy.

The infant "game" in the United States was now to be impacted by a challenge from the north. Canada had seen a bit of the new kinds of football, beginning with a game in 1861, recorded at the University of Toronto. The rules they employed are unknown.

Trinity College, of the University of Toronto, was playing with the rugby rules, presumably those of 1862, in 1864; however, the first-known game of real "rugby" played in Canada was in Montreal in 1865, contested between British army officers and a locally formed team. This game set off rugby fever in a certain social milieu in Montreal.

The Montreal Football Club was founded in 1868, the first known from Canada.

Rugby football was being played at McGill University in Montreal from some point in the mid-1860s. In 1874, McGill was playing by the rugby union code, and hearing that Harvard played the Boston game, which was said to be similar—although, of course, it wasn't—the McGill senior boys challenged Harvard to a game.

The Harvard men were apparently not allowed the time away from school to travel to Montreal, so McGill came to Boston. Harvard easily won the game on Boston rules and managed to eke out a draw (tie) on the second game, played by rugby rules. The second surprise was that the Harvard men were deeply impressed by the rugby rules. That game was more complex, rougher, and just more fun than the game they'd been playing.

Also watching were young men from Tufts College, from the nearby suburbs of Boston. They, too, were so impressed they immediately adopted the rugby union game. They then beat Harvard in the spring of 1875.

Harvard and Yale played that fall in New Haven, Connecticut, using rules that blended elements of the two codes, and something like 2,000 people paid 50¢ each to watch the Harvard men in crimson defeat Yale in blue.

Harvard announced that they would no longer play the variant association game that had been played by the colleges for the past few years. To play with distinguished Harvard, it was rugby or nothing.

Princeton and Columbia switched games. Then, during Thanksgiving break in 1876, representatives from Harvard, Yale, and Columbia met with those from Princeton in Springfield, Massachusetts, to set up a college football association. While they agreed in principle on the rules of the 1871 Rugby Union of England, they immediately began to argue about some of them. Yale, in particular, wanted to reduce the size of teams from 15 to 11. The round ball was out, and the new oval ball, with a rubber bladder and leather casing, was in. Long arguments persisted about the relative weight of "tries" or "touchdowns" versus field goals. In the end, four touchdowns were ruled equal to one field goal, which could come from a dropkick in free play or a set piece kick from a placement. The field size was set at 140 yards long by 70 yards wide.

For a few years, the American colleges played by the rugby rules of the time. The season for college football ran from mid-October to Thanksgiving in late November. In 1878, 12 colleges participated. In 1879, this number decreased to only seven, but in Chicago, the University of Michigan Wolverines defeated Racine College in the first game played in the Midwest. The U.S. Navy had also developed a team. By 1882, there were 13 teams.

Changes were coming, however, primarily from the mind of Walter Camp, a perfectionist Yale student who had played as a freshman in the 1876 game against Harvard.

Camp campaigned for a reduction in the number of players from 15 to 11. The idea was rejected, but Camp's biggest objection to the rugby rules was the scrum. The scrum, which lives on in rugby union, locks eight players per side together in a great heaving beast, into the center of which, on the line between the two sides interlocked, the scrum half of the team with possession carefully tosses the ball. Supported on either side by the biggest men on the team, the two prop-forwards, is the hooker, whose job it is to get his heel to the incoming ball and knock it back through the scrum, through the legs of the other scrum members. If the hooker accomplishes this and retains possession, the scrum-half darts around to the rear of the scrum, waits for the ball to emerge from the heaving mass, picks it up, and either runs with it or immediately passes it, angled just a little backward, behind a line running through his position, to the first of the running backs. They run at their opposite numbers and drop the ball off or pass it back along the line of the other running backs, who are racing toward the opposition's end line. Along the way they may be tackled, the ball may be lost, a penalty may occur, and another scrum may be called for. Indeed, in many situations in the flow of a rugby game, a player will punt the ball forward, seeking a major gain in ground position and accepting that the other side may win possession. Thus, there are only two ways to gain ground in rugby, running the ball forward or kicking it forward.

Camp simply found the scrum too chaotic and laborious. A scrum will collapse. Sometimes one set of scrum forwards is too strong for the other, pushing them over, while at other times, the pressure in the center is so strong that a scrum disintegrates, the players in the center going down to their knees.

The free-flowing nature of rugby, with the chance of possession being lost at any moment and the possibility of losing possession in a scrum at any time, also didn't sit well with Camp. He felt that a higher level of organization was possible, with more intricately worked "plays" and tactics.

Instead of the scrum, Camp proposed that restarts from open play should come from a "scrimmage" line, on which the ball carrier last tackled to the ground would stand, put the ball on the ground, and heel it back to a "quarter-back"—a back closer than a half-back and much closer than a full-back. The quarter back would then take over the duties of the former scrum-half.

Camp won over the other colleges, and they not only chose to accept this change, they also reduced the size of teams to 11, the long-standing Yale demand. They also reduced the size of the field of play by 53 yards, to 110. (Note: This form of restart lives on in the rugby league variety of rugby, a game of constant running and tackling.)

Alas, the change produced the unexpected. Teams soon learned that they could hold the ball forever, denying their opponents any possession. In an 1881 game against Princeton, in which Camp played, Princeton held the ball the entire first half, never scoring a single point. Yale did the same for the entire second half.

This set Camp to work on the system of "downs," by which the team with possession had just three attempts to move the ball five yards forward or be required to give it up to the other team. This produced the "grid iron" stripes on football fields, set at five-yard intervals. The five yards on three downs rule would last 24 years, until 1906, when it was doubled to 10 yards.

Camp also set in motion changes in scoring methods. In 1884, the colleges settled on five points for a field goal, scored with a dropkick from open play. A touchdown was worth four points, and if converted with a goal kicked afterward, six. A safety was worth two points.

Camp coached Yale football for a decade, unpaid, just for the love of the game. He went on to a long career with the New Haven Clock Company. He died in 1925, and attended every football rules convention to that point.

Nonetheless, the American game was about to become extremely brutal, although this was not entirely the fault of Walter Camp.

Since the game was now all about running with the ball, teams began to try and protect the ball carrier, running "interference" against tacklers. At Princeton, they had used a system with two men flanking the ball carrier, blocking tacklers. Now there developed the "v-trick" and the "flying wedge."

The ball would be tossed into play from the line of scrimmage, caught, and passed to the designated carrier, and teammates would form up in front of him as they charged downfield. The flying wedge was particularly terrifying, because it began well back from the line, and the players accelerated to full speed in time to pick up the ball carrier and then hammer into the defenders. Needless to say, there were many injuries from this kind of mass play, and in 1894, these tactics were prohibited by a special rule.

By this time, the United States was well and truly on her own, playing a kind of football that was born from rugby but changed into a game with different patterns. In addition, the new game had become popular not only with the upper crust, who sent their sons to the top colleges, but also with a more general audience, who showed up as paying customers to watch the biggest games.

The United States and Canada were not the only British colonies to develop distinctive football cultures. Far away, on the other side of the world, lay Australia and New Zealand. Along with South Africa, both were to become important parts of the world of rugby union, and also of rugby league, of which more will be learned in the next chapter.

But first, to Australia, which developed its own variant of football.

Australia had been rumored to exist for centuries, millennia before it was located and mapped by Europeans. Aristotle had theorized that a southern continent, a "Terra Australis," must exist. It is believed that Chinese and Indian traders had visited the shores of the mysterious land in the southern ocean. Controversial modern theories propose that Ming admiral Zheng He visited Australia, as well as North America, although the evidence for this is slim.

However it went, it was primarily Dutch sailors who recorded visits in an accurate way, beginning with Willem Janszoon in 1606. Through the seventeenth century, a number of Dutch vessels visited and explored the western and southern coasts of the unexplored continent. Abel Tasman discovered Tasmania in 1642, sailing west to east across the great southern ocean.

The Dutch were not to turn these visits into anything more concrete. For them, the great prize was the "Spice Islands" of Indonesia and cargoes of pepper and cloves, and later coffee and tea, which brought a fortune to the wharves of Amsterdam.

It was left to the British, following Captain Cook's visit in 1770, with naturalist Joseph Banks aboard, to come up with a colonizing plan.

In 1788, the "First Fleet" arrived, carrying 751 convicts, sentenced to "transportation." More than 162,000 British and Irish convicts would be transported to Australia during the next 70-odd years. Transportation was as awful in its way as the slave trade, and many convicts perished aboard the ships, long before they reached the distant new colony of New South Wales. Once there they were essentially worked as slave labor.

Convicts formed the majority of the population of the colony for the first few decades, but throughout time they also gained their freedom; some opted to return to England, but others, either because they were forbidden from doing so or had adapted to the new surroundings, stayed.

By the 1820s, there was a growing population of freed convicts who could own land and win appointments in governing the colony. The population was also spilling out of the original colony area in New South Wales, where the city of Sydney now sits, and into the Murray River basin and southward into the lands that would eventually become the state of Victoria. In 1835, the city of Melbourne was founded on the southern coast.

That same year, Thomas Wentworth Wills was born, the grandson of one Edward Spencer Wills, who had been transported to Australia for life on conviction of highway robbery in 1799, accompanied by his wife and eldest child. If American football can trace its origins to Walter Camp, Australian football looks back to Tom Wills as its founding light.

Tom Wills grew up in what would become the state of Victoria and, from an early age, befriended the Aborigines who lived around the properties his father had obtained. He learned many aspects of their unique culture before, at the age of 14, being plucked from this idyll and sent to England to be educated at Rugby School. A natural athlete, Wills became captain of Rugby's cricket team, and he played Rugby football by the rules of the 1850s. He was seen as one of the best young cricketers in England at the time and played for the prestigious Marylebone Cricket Club. Returning to Australia in 1856, he immediately became a star on the Australian cricket scene. In 1858, Wills brought up the idea of starting a "foot-ball club" as a way for cricket players to keep fit during the winter months. He and two other members came up with the first set of rules for Australian football. The rules from May 1859, which are held by the Melbourne Cricket Club, were as follows:

I. The distance between the goals and the goal posts shall be decided upon by the captains of the sides playing.

II. The captains on each side shall toss for choice of goal; the side losing the toss has the kick off from the centre point between the goals.

III. A goal must be kicked fairly between the posts, without touching either of them, or a portion of the person of any player on either side.

IV. The game shall be played within a space of not more than 200 yards wide, the same to be measured equally on each side of a line drawn through the centres of the two goals; and two posts to be called the "kick off posts" shall be erected at a distance of 20 yards on each side of the goal posts at both ends, and in a straight line with them.

V. In case the ball is kicked "behind" goal, any one of the side behind whose goal it is kicked may bring it 20 yards in front of any portion of the space between the "kick off" posts, and shall kick it as nearly as possible in line with the opposite goal.

VI. Any player catching the ball "directly" from the foot may call "mark." He then has a free kick; no player from the opposite side being allowed to come "inside" the spot marked.

VII. Tripping and pushing are both allowed (but no hacking) when any player is in rapid motion or in possession of the ball, except in the case provided for in Rule VI.

VIII. The ball may be taken in hand "only" when caught from the foot, or on the hop. In "no case" shall it be "lifted" from the ground.

IX. When a ball goes out of bounds (the same being indicated by a row of posts) it shall be brought back to the point where it crossed the boundary line and thrown in at right angles with that line.

X. The ball, while in play, may under no circumstances be thrown.

These rules are a long way from Rugby football, starting with the size of the field of play, which derives from playing the game on cricket grounds. Cricket is played on a large oval field; the dimensions vary, but the fields are usually about 450 to 500 feet in width. What strikes the eye about these rules is the way they hark back to country footeballe. There was the calling of a "mark" if a catch was made directly from a kick. The ball could be carried, it seems, and handled, but only on the bounce, and it could not be picked up if it was rolling on the ground. The ball was mostly to be kicked. There's also the first rule, setting up the goals, the distance of which could be anything the two captains agreed on. This was a break from the old country game, where the goals were just small gates at either end of a "close"—an enclosed field—but this left a lot of latitude to the captains. In time, Australian football would refine its rules and define its goals but retain many of these elements, for example, the large field of play and the calling of a "mark." One change that soon appeared was the rule requiring players to bounce the ball every few steps while in possession.

In summary, the period beginning in the 1840s had seen a steady movement toward creating rules and organized varieties of football. While the threatening, even terrifying, mob ball games of the cities in England were being suppressed, the young men of the upper classes were creating something new. There was divergence—the rugby game and its descendant, the new American one, were on one side of the divide. The association game, after a fruitless period where the rules hardly made the game playable, was beginning to find its feet and was now set on a path to a game that did not allow any handling of the ball except by a goalkeeper. And far away in the antipodes, Australians were creating their own game, with roots in the old country football of England, but with new ideas, too.

9

THE FOOTBALL ASSOCIATION AND FOOTBALL LEAGUE

The year 1872 was a fateful one for association football. It was the rugby style of football, now organized by the Rugby Union and being played with one set of rules, and with a standardized oval ball with a rubber bladder encased in leather, that was easily the most popular game on the fields around London. That said, there were football clubs forming throughout the country, with hot spots like Glasgow in Scotland, Manchester, and Newcastle, as well as Shropshire and North West Wales. For any group of young men keen to play a rough but skilled game on the weekends, the first thing to hammer out was what to play—rugby or association. And in the decade or so since the rules had begun to be written, the two tribes had moved ever farther apart. The idea that the two codes might somehow be reconciled to bring everything back into one game called "football" was dead and buried.

The association men were still absorbing the lessons taught by the Scots, particularly those of the groundbreaking Queen's Park club of Glasgow. The original game, as codified in 1863, had been closer to the Eton Field Game and the Harrow Game, with one player after another dribbling the ball at the defenders or kicking it over their heads and sending everyone charging after it. As the Harvard men in the United States were to so eloquently complain, there was a considerable degree of "shin element" in all this.

At this time there were many critics of football, in particular the association game, who claimed that it was brutal and somewhat dangerous. In fact, they were behind the times—the truly brutal era has passed, although legs were still being broken now and then and young men were being carried off the field with bruises and bloody noses. Set against this was the fun several hundred others were up for on the weekends, pursuing a bouncing round ball.

In the early stages of the 1871–1872 season, at a meeting of the Football Association, the Wanderers club, with support from the Harrow Chequers, called for a knockout competition to be played along the same sort of lines as the "cock house" games at Harrow School.

At this point, we must introduce Charles W. Alcock, who was to be as influential in the development of the association game as Walter Camp of the American game and Tom Wills of the Australian one. Alcock was the moving spirit within the Wanderers club.

Alcock had grown up in Chingford, Essex, just north of East London. He attended Harrow School and was a keen player of Harrow football. After school he and his older brother, John, were key in the formation of the Forest football club in 1859, which played its games at Snaresbrook, near Epping Forest. In these early days, when the rules varied from club to club, teams played in long trousers and shirts, and usually fielded 15 men a side. Charles was known as a center forward with a good shot and a high work rate.

Forest was among the clubs that gathered in 1863 for the first go-round of rules and the formation of the Football Association. After that meeting, Forest evolved into their famous successor club, Wanderers FC, in 1864. Early on, Wanderers were largely made up of Harrow old boys. The concept of Wanderers was that they had no home ground, unlike Forest. They would play other clubs on their grounds. This would save the costs of owning a field to play on; however, there were others on the Forest club who clung to both the name and their home ground until after the 1865 season, when the Forest name disappeared from records. Wanderers struggled for a while, sometimes not even having 11 players show up for a game. They resorted to the use of Battersea Park as a "home" ground and, in 1869, began playing at Kennington Oval, where they recorded 151 games. The Oval, a cricket ground during the summer, was to become the home for association football's most important games for many years to come. It remains a premier cricket ground and is also used for outdoor concerts.

A year or so later, the Wanderers began to rise again. In the 1870–1871 season, they played 37 games, losing five.

C. W. Alcock has another claim to fame, in the "official" big match between a London team and a team from Sheffield, on March 31, 1866: He was the first player ruled offside and thus became the first "officially" offside center forward in association football history.

In 1870, Alcock, then 28, became the first secretary of the Football Association. He organized the first "international" game on November 19, at Kennington Oval, where England beat a team of Scots, or "London Scots." Historical curiosity note: The Scots fielded W. H. Gladstone, the son of Prime Minister W. E. Gladstone. The football playing Gladstone remains the only sitting member of Parliament to have played in an international football match.

So Alcock and the Old Harrovians, who were prominent in London football circles, next campaigned to have a knockout competition for a challenge trophy. At this time there were about 50 football clubs in the association. Twelve were persuaded to add the Football Association Challenge Cup fixtures to their schedules. A cup was purchased for £20, at a time when the average working man received less than £50 a year and working women rarely made even £20. This cup, called the "little tin idol," was made by the firm Martin, Hall & Co. and used until it was stolen in 1895, from a shoe shop window in Birmingham. Aston Villa was the holder of the trophy, and it was being displayed to the public in the shop window. Villa had to pay £25 for the replacement. Almost 60 years later, the man who stole the first cup admitted that it had been melted down to make counterfeit coins.

A glance at the list of the original 12 clubs gives the flavor of the game at this point: Hampstead Heathens, Harrow Chequers, Harrow School, Civil Service, Royal Engineers, Wanderers, Lausanne, Windsor Home Park, Crystal Palace, Clapham Rovers, Upton Park, and Barnes. All are London clubs; there's a strong presence of Old Harrovians and Old Etonians, as well as old boys from other famous schools.

Three entrants withdrew, for various reasons, before the competition even began, leaving just nine clubs. Six other clubs agreed to enter, including the Scottish club Queen's Park. (Note: This was not Queen's Park Rangers FC, founded 1884, in West London.) The Crystal Palace club of this time is not related to the current Crystal Palace FC, which played in the Premier League in 2014.

While most of these early clubs have long since disappeared, a few still exist and compete. Queen's Park plays in Scottish Division Two and is the only amateur club in the Scottish League. Maidenhead and Marlow, two of the six later entrants, are still alive and playing amateur football. So is the Civil Service club, and Hitchin, another late arrival, still plays as Hitchin Town.

And so on park fields and borrowed facilities around London, the first cup competition was played during the winter of 1871–1872. In the great scheme of things, this hardly featured as important news. It was merely seeding the ground for what was to come.

Across the Channel, in the other half of the cradle region, where *les souliers* still played their ancient, wild game, it had been a terrible year. The Franco–Prussian War, which had begun in late 1870, had demonstrated all too clearly that a united Germany, under the leadership of a Prussian dynasty, was far more powerful on the battlefield than France. The days of Napoleonic glory were truly over. Indeed, Napoleon III, the autocrat of the Second Empire and nephew of the first Napoleon Bonaparte, had gone into exile in London after the crushing defeat at Sedan, which led to his capture. Meanwhile, Count Otto von Bismarck had seen his life's work completed with the crowning of Wilhelm I of Prussia as emperor of Germany in the halls of Versailles, the very temple to French imperial dreams built by Louis XIV. The siege of Paris had ended in January, an armistice was signed in February, and the people of Paris had risen to establish the Paris Commune in March. For two months, an avowedly revolutionary socialist government held sway in the capital, until it was suppressed in bloody fighting by the regular French army on May 28. The events in Paris were to produce echoes that would linger long into the twentieth century. Another exile in London, Karl Marx, wrote about the civil war he saw between the communards and the French bourgeoisie, and the realization that the revolution would be accompanied by violence. Marx and the First Socialist International, based in London, came under heavy attack from rightwing London newspapers through 1872.

In terms of Europe's concerns, it should be noted that in North America, the United States had reached its final dimensions with the purchase of Alaska from Russia in 1867. British Canada became a self-governing dominion that same year. In South America, the War of the Triple Alliance had ended with the utter defeat of Paraguay by Brazil,

Argentina, and Uruguay, and the loss of two-thirds of its population. Mexico was recovering from the French-supported Habsburg Imperial Adventure of 1864–1867, while the wound inflicted by the defeat by the United States in 1848–1849 and the loss of Texas, New Mexico, Arizona, and California remained raw.

In the United States, while industrial sectors were growing and railroads stretching throughout the continent, in the South the white population had regained the whip hand over the freed black slaves. African Americans were no longer slaves, but they were now placed under a new tyranny designed to keep them subordinate to white supremacy.

In far off China, the Qing dynasty was fast decaying from within, ravaged by such events as the Taiping Rebellion. India was now entirely held by the British Empire in one way or another. Japan, however, had been shaken out of the isolation and torpor of the later shogunate period, and the Meiji Restoration of 1868 put the Imperial family back in control. The former Tokugawa shogun forces were defeated in the Boshin War in early 1868. The young emperor put Japan on the path to rapid modernization, seeing that the world, following the Industrial Revolution, had utterly changed. Qing China failed to follow Japan's lead.

It is perhaps important to mention that at this time, in about 1870, London was the world's largest city, with a population of 3.8 million. Paris was second, at 1.8 million, and New York was coming up fast at 1.4 million. Older cultures that had normally held this particular title had been left behind because of the singularity of the industrial/scientific/agricultural revolution in the West. For now, the Royal Navy enforced a Pax Britannica in the world's oceans, and Queen Victoria reigned over an empire that stretched throughout the world as no previous empire had ever done. The changes in British and European culture described by Gregory Clark in *A Farewell to Alms* had set Britain, France, and Germany on a fateful trajectory. The United States was already catching up and would eventually surpass them all.

Elsewhere in Europe the new pattern of civilization was taking hold: Railways, industry, highly efficient agriculture, trade, the rule of law, efficient banking, and stock markets and commodities trading, with secular education exploding throughout the middle classes and science, always science, holding up a light to guide the world forward. To what, one might ask? The first underground railway in London in 1862 and antiseptic surgery, also in London, from Joseph Lister, would seem marvels enough, as would the Suez Canal and the transcontinental Pacific Railroad spanning the United States. Thomas Edison's electric light, the Eiffel Tower, and the Benz Motorwagon of 1888 all pointed upward, but Sir Hiram Maxim's machine gun and the Krupp 15-centimeter field howitzer pointed to another trajectory with potentially fatal implications.

An important sociopolitical movement was also gathering strength—that of women's suffrage, the right of women to vote. Indeed, the rights of women in general, from owning property and receiving inheritance to the ability vote and protections from violence within marriage, were both gaining increasing acceptance and facing mounting resistance from conservative men. Throughout this period, as Impressionism shook up the world of art and literature, music, mathematics, and science underwent revolutions in everything from popular taste to fundamental concepts, the struggle for women's rights remained a constant talking point.

This fast-moving, quickly changing world of the late nineteenth century was the background to the progress of the various codes of football now being played throughout the Anglo-Saxon nations.

The Football Association Cup culminated in the final, played on March 16, 1872. Royal Engineers, who had adopted the combination game pioneered by Queen's Park, and before them, by the old boys of Charterhouse and Westminster schools, faced the Wanderers, lead by C. W. Alcock. The Wanderers remained wedded to the dribbling game, with limited passing. The combination game saw forwards pair up and pass the ball back and forth as they moved downfield, sometimes trying a longer pass across the field. The Wanderers played in the traditional 1–1–8 formation, with eight forwards. A man in possession of the ball would seek to dribble through the opposition, while teammates "followed up" around him. Should he lose possession they would seek to win it back or kick it clear and downfield for everyone to run after. The combination teams usually played with just six forwards, two midfielders, and two backs.

Wanderer's path to the final involved two other sides withdrawing. In the first round, the Harrow Chequers withdrew, unable to find 11 members prepared to make the trip across London to the Kennington Oval. Engineers also had a walkover when Reigate Priory, their opponents, withdrew for similar reasons. Wanderers then beat Clapham Rovers, 3–1, while the Engineers crushed Hitchin, 5–0. In the quarter-final round, Wanderers drew 0–0 with Crystal Palace, and both teams were allowed to go through to the semifinal round. Crystal Palace lost to the Engineers, 3–0, in a replay, after a 0–0 draw the first time out. Wanderers drew 0–0 with Queen's Park from Glasgow, but the Scots could not afford the expense of traveling south for a second match in London and withdrew.

The final was played at Kennington Oval, on a pitch with little in the way of lines. There were no halfway lines, no center circle, no penalty area or six-yard box, and the goals lacked both nets and crossbars. A crowd of about 2,000 came to watch.

Alcock, captain of Wanderers, won the toss and chose the southern goal, leaving the Engineers playing into the sun and wind. The Engineers played with seven forwards, the Wanderers in the classic eight-forward formation. Early on, Edmund Cresswell of the Engineers suffered a broken collarbone. He refused to leave the game but could contribute little thereafter and moved out to the wing. The Wanderers played the classic dribbling game, while the Engineers played the combination game with passing.

After 15 minutes, a long dribble by a Wanderer led to a shot from an acute angle by Morton Betts that went in. Betts played under the pseudonym A. H. Chequer. With that the teams changed ends; however, the Engineers could not capitalize. Five minutes later, Alcock put the ball through the posts, but it was disallowed due to another player handling the ball before the shot.

The Engineers pressed for the equalizer and had a late rally, but the Wanderers held on to keep the victory. According to the game report in the *Field* newspaper, the Wanderers displayed some of the best play that had ever been seen in association football.

In April, Wanderers received the trophy at the annual dinner of the Association held at the Pall Mall restaurant in Central London. (The Pall Mall restaurant was also the site where the Rugby Union had been formed.)

We should perhaps note that the Wanderers included several Old Harrovians, and the Engineers included two men with the rank of captain and nine lieutenants.

The FA Cup was a new thing under the sun, or in England's case, under the gentle rain. At this time the only sporting occasions that drew large crowds were the major horse races, like the Epsom Derby. Cricket attracted crowds for certain matches, and boat races, in particular the Oxford versus Cambridge race on the Thames, drew thousands to line the riverbanks. Boxing was still absorbing the Marquess of Queensberry rules, published in 1867, and had yet to become a large-scale spectacle. One problem for cricket attendance was the leisurely nature of the game in an era when few working people had the time for it. In this era, working men and women had little time off; many worked six days a week. The cup offered something quite different in an exciting, rough game, with relatively simple rules, played with a large ball, and games lasted just an hour and a half. Still, it would be a few years before the crowds grew much beyond two or three thousand for the biggest games. Football remained an exotic pursuit, with many critics thundering in newspaper letters and columns about the beastly brutality of young men charging about in parks and fields on weekend afternoons.

The other code organization, the Rugby Union, never followed the lead of the association clubs in setting up a national knockout competition. Rugby instead followed the model of cricket in England, with county championships and county-wide cups.

While football of both varieties spread throughout the land, with hotspots like North Wales becoming obsessed with association football, while South Wales turned into rugby country, the association game got a powerful boost from having the great industrial city of Glasgow go nuts over the game. Glasgow would spawn giant clubs of Scottish football, Rangers and Celtic, plus a number of lesser lights, from Clydebank to Partick Thistle. The Glasgow football players were generally not public school old boys, but were drawn from all walks of life.

The Queen's Park club, in south Glasgow, organized the next important rallying point for association football—the November 30, 1872, international match between Scotland and England. Four thousand spectators came out and paid a shilling to watch an absorbing 0–0 draw. *Bell's Life in London, and Sporting Chronicle*, the leading chronicler of the English sporting scene at the time, described the game as "one of the jolliest, one of the most spirited and most pleasant matches that have ever been played according to association rules."

In 1873, the Scottish Football Association was formed, with eight clubs. That year also saw the rule overturned that had allowed Wanderers to get a bye right to the final the year before by virtue of being cup holders from that first year. From now on, everyone, cup holders included, would have to enter the preliminary rounds.

With generally agreed upon rules in place, the association game began to spread. Soon there were hundreds of clubs forming almost everywhere in England, Wales, and the central parts of Scotland. County organizations arose to start up local competitions. It had taken a decade or so, but the working class had at last discovered the association game. Throughout Lancashire and the Midlands, young men were playing football at every opportunity.

At this point, clubs arranged fixtures with other clubs on an informal basis, unless they entered either a county cup or the FA Cup, in which case they were duty bound to show up and play. Not that they always did, of course, and walkovers were common in the early years of the FA Cup; however, there was a degree of discontent with this lack of accountability among players and people who might show up to watch a game. There was a growing sense that some kind of order ought to be imposed, especially for the clubs that were getting a significant spectator response.

The FA Cup grew year by year, although crowds remained small at first. Many players, former public-school boys, found having strangers turn up to watch the games quite unsettling. The concept was another new thing under the sun and one that many of the early football players never adjusted to. Indeed, quite a few of the early clubs did their best to discourage casual onlookers.

At the same time, the clubs were moving to renting or buying their own places to play. For years they had used public parks, which brought some complications. Youths out for a lark could interfere or even run off with the ball. Other members of the public might casually stroll onto the pitch, not comprehending that where they were walking was temporarily out of use and then strenuously objecting when a band of players came thundering down on them. The first move was to private fields, sometimes set up specifically for football games by their owners and rented to the clubs. The second was to get one's own field.

There was an added factor to this process. As had been shown in the FA Cup, you could charge a shilling or sixpence a head, and thousands would willingly pay up. A few games with that kind of crowd and the rent was paid.

Not that paying spectators got comfortable seats or even cover from the rain. Far from it. Some clubs might put down duck boards to spare people from standing in mud, while others set up wooden rail sleepers for people to stand on, providing the first "constructed" stands, but other than that, amenities lay in the future.

Oxford University defeated the Royal Engineers for the cup in 1874, and the following year the Engineers defeated Old Etonians in two games, with a 1–1 draw first time around and a 2–0 win in front of 3,000 at the Oval. C. W. Alcock was the referee for both games.

Seeds of the near future were also being sown in Lancashire and other industrial areas. Old boys from Harrow School founded Darwen FC, an early Lancashire club. But the first Lancashire club, and an incubator for the game there, was Turton FC, founded in 1871, with two Old Harrovians prominent from the beginning. Now it wasn't just public-school boys who were playing the game. Grammar school boys were starting the same process of founding clubs that would soon become prominent and, in some cases, still are.

In 1878–1879, 43 clubs entered the fray. Among the quaint-sounding names like the Pilgrims or the 105th Regiment were two that would stand the test of time: Notts County and Nottingham Forest. County was one of the earliest clubs to form, in 1862, and today they play in the Football League One, the third tier of English football. Nottingham Forest, founded in 1865, currently plays in the Championship, the second tier. Forest enjoyed a period under the management of Brian Clough where they soared to the zenith of European football, winning not only the English League title, but also back-to-back European Cups, before slipping out of the Premier League in the late 1990s, yet to return to top flight.

In 1879, Forest made it to the semifinals, where they lost to Old Etonians, who went on to win the final, 1–0, at the Oval.

The following year, more familiar names appeared: Blackburn Rovers and Sheffield Wednesday. Still, these northern clubs had yet to break the grip on the cup held by the public school old boys. That year, Old Carthusians (Charterhouse) defeated Old Etonians, 3–0, at the Oval. In 1882, Old Etonians beat Blackburn Rovers, 1–0, in the final.

This would be the last time that a team devoted to the old "dribbling" style and playing in a 2–1–7 formation would win the cup or even reach the final. The future lay with the passing game, which was growing more sophisticated with long passes woven in among the short combinations. Moreover, the 2–3–5 formation was becoming the standard.

In the 1880s, the FA Cup began to produce the golden eggs. The number of clubs participating started to climb dramatically, from 73 in 1881–1882, to 100 in 1883–1884, to 130 in 1885–1886. Crowds began to grow, too; the final in 1884, in which Blackburn Rovers beat Queen's Park, 2–1, was watched by 12,000 people.

Another turning point had also been reached—the age of professionalism had arrived. The 1881 final between Old Carthusians and Old Etonians was the last played between two amateur southern sides. The teams from the north, like Blackburn Rovers, were not public-school boys; they were often factory hands, and they trained hard and practiced in every spare moment. Those that were special began to receive a bit of money to make sure they stayed with one club and didn't shift to another.

At a meeting of the FA in the summer of 1884, the representative from Blackburn Rovers said that players had to be compensated for lost wages or it would doom football for the working men of Lancashire. This proposal exposed a canyon between the gentlemen players of the old boys' southern clubs and the working men of the north. The southern clubs voted against any payments to players. Professionalism was illegal, and players could not be compensated for any more than out-of-pocket expenses, for instance, a railroad ticket. But under the table, professionalism was commonplace in the north.

The FA believed the core of the problem was the player brought in from another town. They set up a ban on clubs offering inducements to players from towns more than 12 miles distant from their own. Clubs were to list any players from outside their immediate town or district, giving the names, residence, occupations, and incomes. The Lancashire clubs fiercely resisted, and when the FA forbade clubs who failed to comply from participating in the FA Cup, the northern clubs formed the British National Football Association (BNFA) and gave outward signs of rebellion. Anxiety arose on both sides, for while the FA didn't want to see a split in the organization of the sport, the BNFA needed the FA even more. In particular, they wanted the chance to win the FA

Cup; however, their ploy worked, as the issue came to a grand meeting of 221 clubs in January 1885.

C. W. Alcock announced that professionalism needed to be controlled under the most "stringent of conditions." Proposed rules would allow a certain amount of professionalism, with an eye to keeping it visible and monitored. Objections followed the line that professionals would ruin the sport. The representative from Sheffield FC said the association had been formed without clubs from Lancashire, and if they didn't want to conform to the rules they were free to leave. The representative from Preston North End, where professionalism was already in the door, admitted that paying the players was already common practice in Lancashire, but when you drew big "gates," i.e., crowds, there would be money, and when there was money at stake there was bound to be professionalism. Scottish and Welsh representatives abhorred professionalism, and many amendments were offered to the rules that might allow it.

A two-thirds majority was needed to pass these rule changes, and it could not be found at this meeting, nor at the next, in March of that same year. Alcock didn't give up, fearing that hidden professional practices would proliferate unless a degree of professionalism was allowed. A summer meeting in July drew fewer clubs, partly because so many winter football men played cricket in the summer. Alcock finally got his way, and the door was opened. It is also likely that the opponents of professionalism had realized it was inevitable. The momentum had moved to the north and the Midlands, and the clubs there were growing, both in terms of the quality of the teams they fielded and the crowds they attracted. The horse, in other words, was out of the barn.

The Scottish and the Welsh associations voiced their displeasure, knowing full well that the first, immediate impact would be for the best players from Wales and Scotland to be drawn to Lancashire and Birmingham by the inducement of good cash money.

Another aspect of the shift to allow a degree of professionalism also became quickly apparent. Pulling in a good crowd was now essential, as clubs needed a lot more money. This put selection pressure on fixtures, and clubs only sought to play other clubs that could draw a crowd. Less attractive or lesser- known clubs were ignored.

Within a couple of years the Lancashire clubs had become the dominant voices within the FA, eclipsing the old boys of the south. The days of Old Etonians and Old Carthusians reaching the Cup Final were over. From that point onward it would be the northern clubs who would fill the latter fixtures of the cup competition.

In 1885–1886, a replay between Blackburn Rovers and West Bromwich Albion after a 0–0 draw was held in Derby, the first time the final had been played outside London. This was also about 40 years after the terrible old Derby Game of Shrovetide mob ball had been suppressed. It already seemed to belong to another age. Rovers won, 2–0. In 1886–1887, West Brom was back, and again they lost, this time to Aston Villa in an all-Midlands final. West Brom finally got their name on the trophy the next year, beating Preston North End, 2–1, at the Oval. This game was a sellout, forcing the gates to be shut, with 17,000 spectators on hand.

Preston had arrived at that final after 434 consecutive wins, including a 26–0 hammering of Hyde FC, which is still a record in English football. They brought with them an air of invincibility, but West Brom had been to the final two years in a row, only to lose, and they were not to be denied the third time.

Preston, and Burnley, had begun life as rugby football clubs during the rugby boom of the 1870s but had switched to the association game and were now pulling in audiences of 10,000 or more for their games.

However, this 26–0 result caused the FA to restructure the competition, introducing the qualifying rounds and then the competition proper. This continues today, so that only the strongest of the small, nonleague clubs make it into the competition with the more established clubs and then the giants, who enter in the later rounds.

But by this point, something else new had appeared: the Football League, to which our attention must now turn.

The problem of fixture cancellation due to poor weather, problems with transportation, or injuries to key players required some form of discipline, something to ensure that the big clubs would show up for their games. The answer came from William McGregor, a Scot from Perthshire who had a shop in Birmingham, near the Aston Villa ground. McGregor joined Aston Villa, not as a player, but in a management role. In the winter of 1887–1888, he wrote to the leading clubs from Lancashire or the Midlands, including Villa, of course, suggesting home and away fixtures between them the following season. In March and April of that year, meetings bore fruit. Twelve clubs, six from Lancashire and six from the Midlands, were invited to form the Football League. No southern clubs were invited, because none south of Birmingham were yet professional.

McGregor was voted the first president of the league. With kickoffs on September 8, 1888, it began.

It became the season of seasons for Preston North End. They were the first team, it appears, to see the importance of having the half-backs step up and support the forwards. The standings for that first season are fascinating for various reasons. Preston played 22 games, won 18, drew 4, and lost 0. Goals for were 74, against 14, points 40.

Preston also returned to the FA Cup Final that season, and this time they made sure of things, beating Wolverhampton Wanderers, 3–0, before 23,000 spectators, a new record for attendance.

Thus, by the end of the 1880s, the football association game was well and truly launched.

The term *soccer* had also been coined. It arose from college slang, via the way football games were reported in the daily papers of the time. By the mid-1880s, there were dozens, even hundreds, of matches being played and the results printed. Newspapers in London divided their reports into football—rug. and football—assoc. Oxford college men are said to have come up with the slang terms *rugger* and *soccer*.

The game was also being exported. When British engineers and military men embarked on foreign travel, they took cricket, rugby, and association football with them. These three sports were launched throughout the world during this period. Tennis and golf followed shortly thereafter.

It is time to turn our attention back to the rugby game, which had also passed through the period of crisis concerning professionalism, but with a different result.

10

RUGBY UNION, RUGBY LEAGUE, AND GAELIC FOOTBALL

The 1873 *Football Annual* (edited by C. W. Alcock, of course) claims that there were 230 football clubs in England. Of these, 132 were rugby clubs, and 91 played association football. Twenty-two association football clubs were still playing the Sheffield variant of the rules ("kick throughs"), leaving only 69 as pure "association" rules clubs. The annual adds that there were now 16,313 registered players, of which 7,638 were rugby and 6,767 association; however, as reported by Kenneth Sheard and Eric Dunning in *Barbarians, Gentlemen, and Players*, 28 of the rugby clubs were school clubs, and they contributed 3,836 players to the rugby total.

This finding would seem to show that rugby's earlier dominance on the playing fields of England had vanished. The association game was simpler to play, and after the 1863 rules meeting and formation of the association, the game had grown less brutal.

A major part of the brutality factor came down to "hacking," which was kicking your opponent in the shins. In rugby, there was also the practice of "hacking over," where you came in and booted the ball out of a ruck on the ground and out of anyone's hands who might be holding onto it. A great many injuries occurred as a result. This began to change with the January meeting at the Pall Mall restaurant, at No. 1 Cockspur Street, near Trafalgar Square.

Twenty-one rugby clubs from in and around London attended. They included the exotic—the Mohicans, the Wimbledon Hornets, and the

Flamingoes—as well as clubs that still exist today—Blackheath, Civil Service, and such college and school teams as St. Paul's School and King's College.

Missing were representatives from major clubs outside London, for instance, Bath. Also missing were Wasps, the famous London club, whose representative it is thought went to the wrong place, got drunk, and never made it to the meeting.

Cockspur Street in and of itself serves as an interesting marker of historical change. Today it sits on the western edge of Trafalgar Square. Before the square was cleared and built in the early nineteenth century, that area was the "Great Mews," a stables area for the Palace of White-hall. In 1748, a female dwarf, described as the "Corsican Fairy," was exhibited in a "show" on the street for half a crown a head—that is, two shillings and sixpence—which would be around $30 in 2010 American terms. The fairy was a rousing success, apparently drawing crowds of the wealthy.

There was a long tradition of such spectacles. In their book from 1872, *Old and New London*, George Walter Thornbury and Edward Valford mention that during the reign of Queen Anne, some 50 years before the debut of the Corsican Fairy, there was a "collection" shown near Charing Cross, by royal permission, of "strange and wonderful creatures from most parts of the world, all alive." This included

> a black man, a dwarf, a pony only two feet odd inches high, several panthers, leopards, and jackalls, and a strange monstrous creature brought from the coast of Brazil, having a head like a child, legs and arms very wonderful, and a long tail like a serpent, wherewith he feeds himself as an elephant does with his trunk.

This last item was probably a spider monkey. Of course, one's heart goes out to that poor black man, who may have been a captive or slave bought in some foreign market and brought to be exhibited to the London nobs in 1700.

The name of the street most likely stems from a connection with the cock-pit in Whitehall, which, of course, was a venue for cock fighting, a popular entertainment in earlier times but one that was illegal by this time.

During the meeting at the Pall Mall, attendees agreed on a set of rules and cut a few of the most violent aspects of the Rugby School game, including hacking, hacking over, and tripping. It also led to the formation of the first Rugby Union. Of course, these were just the first steps on the road to a uniform code of rules obeyed by everyone and the end of hacking over. Fifty-nine rules were laid down for rugby, a far more complicated set than for any other code up to this time. Many clubs continued to play by the older rules, and it would take time for hacking over to disappear.

At this point there were still 20 players on a team, and with the abolition of hacking over, the ball tended to end up stuck in scrums, or scrummages. These were not like the full, organized scrum, but heads-up-in-the-air knots of men struggling to push things one way or the other, a bit like miniature "hugs" from of the Ashbourne Game. This also put a premium on brute strength, and bigger players tended to gravitate to the rugby game. When games of rugger descended into endless scrummage, with the ball invisible within the battling mass of players, the spectacle value declined. And indeed, the association game, which had begun to sort out its own problems of congestion and chaos in the rules, began to look more attractive.

In March, some English players organized the first international game of rugby, against Scotland, and it was held in Edinburgh. The English players paid for their own rail tickets and traveled third class on bare boards to make the game. Part of the impetus for this match lay in the scornful reaction of the rugby men to C. W. Alcock's "international" game the previous year, of English association players against a Scotland team largely composed of Scots living in England, some of whom had never been to Scotland. It is also of great import to mention that of the England Rugby XX, 10 were Old Rugbeians. (Note: English football teams are traditionally described as First XIs and in rugby as First XVs.)

The "international" rugby game went Scotland's way by a single try, which was not converted.

And now rugby began to spread throughout the world. We've seen that it was being played in Montreal beginning in the mid-1860s and that the Rugby Union rules had been adopted there by 1874. Early rugby games in Australia, perhaps as early as 1840, had led to the Sydney University Football Club being founded in 1864. Five years later, Newington College and the University of Sydney recorded the first "official" rugby match. Of course, farther south, in Melbourne and

Victoria, Australians were playing their own kind of football, then called Victoria rules.

But rugby had also reached Ireland, where Wanderers Ireland was formed in 1870. That same year, the first-known game was played in New Zealand, between the Nelson Football Club and Nelson College. Other clubs were soon to follow. The game had come to New Zealand courtesy of Charles J. Monro, who, although born in New Zealand, had been sent off to school at Christ's College in Finchley, London, where they played rugby.

In Wales, the first Welsh Club, Neath, was formed, inspired by Scottish doctor T. P. Whittington. Rugby had been growing steadily in Wales since 1850, when the Reverend Professor Rowland Williams came to St. David's College in Lampeter. Williams had learned the game at Cambridge and was a keen proponent. Lampeter, you may recall, lies in the heart of the wild football country of West Wales, and it was in the Lampeter Workhouse that Charlotte Sophia Burne had recorded the tale of the *bwl troed* game of Llanwenog from an elderly man who remembered it. The industrial towns of South Wales would soon become one of rugby's heartlands.

In 1872, British residents of Le Havre, in France, formed a club, Le Havre Athletique, which played a combination game but allowed some handling of the ball. French interest in rugby began to grow. In Wales, the Swansea and Llanelli clubs were formed the same year as Lansdown in Ireland.

In 1873, the Scottish Rugby Football Union was formed in the aftermath of a 0–0 match against an England XX.

In Ireland, in a sign of the political divisions that remain to this day, two rugby unions formed. The Irish Football Union controlled clubs in the south, in Munster, Leinster, and Connaught, while the Northern Football Union of Ireland controlled the game in protestant-leaning Ulster; however, they agreed to each select players for Ireland's international team. The Irish Rugby Football Union would eventually unite Ireland's rugby players under one organization with four provincial bodies, a rare element of unity on the fractured isle.

In 1874 came the aforementioned matches between McGill and Harvard, games that would send Harvard into the rugby channel and eventually give rise to the singular game of American football.

This year also saw the first rugby played in South Africa and the formation in Australia of the South Rugby Football Union in New South Wales.

In 1878, the first genuinely French rugby club, the Paris Football Club, was formed. In 1882, Racing Club de France was established, followed by Stade Francais a year later.

In 1875, a team selected from the clubs in Auckland went on a two-week tour of South Island, New Zealand, and played against clubs in Dunedin, Wellington, Christchurch, Nelson, and Taranaki. New Zealand was well and truly set on the path to becoming a rugby nation.

From 1875 onward, many clubs cut the number of players to 15 a side, opening the game up and reducing the amount of pure scrummage. International matches between England and Ireland and England and Scotland were being played fairly regularly.

The next technical shift in the game would come from Cardiff, in Wales. After retrieving the ball from a scrum, the scrum-half would fire a short pass to a half-back, already in motion. That player became known as the fly-half.

In 1878, a white ball was used in a county match, Surrey versus Middlesex. The match was also illuminated by four lamps.

In 1879, a floodlit game was played in Scotland, at Hawick, in their local derby with Melrose. In 1880, the Canadian Rugby Football Union was founded.

Meanwhile, the same seeds of discontent and division that had begun to sprout in the ranks of association football clubs were growing in the rugby world. Starting with Bradford in 1863, rugby football clubs had sprung up throughout the north, in the same way that association clubs had done. By the end of the 1870s, Huddersfield (1864), Hull Football Club (1865), St. Helens (1874), Widnes (1873), Wakefield Trinity (1873), Wigan (1879), and many others were playing rugby football. There were more rugby clubs in the northern towns, where working men made up the teams, than in the south, where young gentlemen—old boys from schools that played rugby football—and college men were the primary groups that came out to play on the weekends.

Again the issue of "broken time"—the loss of earnings players suffered when they missed work to travel and play for their club—arose. Some form of compensation was sought for this, but as in the world of association football, there existed a profound divide between the gentlemen and the players. This division had overtones of not only social class, but also regional antagonism, south versus north.

Nevertheless, the committee that drew up the rules regarding amateurism in 1886 had a majority of men from Lancashire and Yorkshire on it. Moreover, many northern clubs were begun by industrialists seeking a way to put their towns on the map with a successful football team. Players were sometimes given leave from work to play without losing any pay. This, combined with the rapid growth in crowds paying to watch local games, led to charges of "veiled professionalism." The opposition to full-on professionalism came from several points of view. First, was the gentlemanly disdain for the working man, expressed in the idea that if you couldn't afford to give up a day's work to play then you shouldn't play at all. Then came the concern of the lesser northern club chairmen, seeing bigger clubs with bigger industrial backing as a threat. And finally came the concern that financial inducements would lure the best players from one club to another, forcing everyone to pay more to keep the best team on the field. Meanwhile, the top clubs in the north were forming small leagues, playing more games, and training their players with professional trainers.

In the early 1890s, there were many reports of players in the north receiving payments for playing. And in the eyes of the southern gentlemen, a new evil had begun, for southern clubs, concerned about the quality of their own sides, were starting to approach northern star players and offer them money to move south.

Another different problem was posed for the working men who played rugby. If injured they had only themselves to fall back on. If they were too badly hurt to work, they faced poverty. Clubs wanted their men to give their all but could offer no assistance if that led to serious injury.

The situation began to move toward a crisis point when the Cumberland County Union complained that a big club had lured a player away with offers of money. Cumberland is a rural county, to the north of Lancashire. The Rugby Football Union (RFU) set up a committee of inquiry to gather evidence. Then came warnings that if there was punishment for the club involved, the big clubs of Yorkshire and Lancashire would leave the union. We should recall that the association game had already cracked opened the door to professionalism in 1885, and the professional Association Football League had formed in 1888, to become a considerable success.

According to RugbyFootballHistory.com, at a meeting at the Westminster Palace Hotel on September 20, 1893, two Yorkshire men proposed that "players be allowed compensation for bona fide loss of time." The amount involved was hardly generous, a mere six shillings, about £30 or $50 in today's money.

A counteramendment was proposed, stating that, "[T]his meeting, believing that the above principle is contrary to the true interest of the game and its spirit, declines to sanction the same." It passed by 282 to 146 votes.

The bylaws were changed: "[O]nly clubs comprised entirely of amateurs shall be eligible for membership." An all-out war was on within the union, because, of course, there was a healthy measure of hypocrisy at work. The southern clubs of gentlemen asked for large financial guarantees for away games, published no accounting of their finances, and were known to pay expenses to their players far in excess of the small amounts that would go to working men in compensation for broken time.

The southern domination of the game simultaneously came under criticism. Although there were far more northern clubs, the RFU committee was stuffed with southerners. Indeed, RFU meetings were always held in London.

Efforts to broker a peace went nowhere. It is possible that the lack of a dominating figure like association's C. W. Alcock was crucial here, because without someone to hammer things back together, the split inevitably widened.

By the end of July 1895, 12 Yorkshire clubs, including Bradford, Leeds, Halifax, and Hull, had resigned from the Yorkshire Union. A month later, at a meeting in Manchester, nine of the leading Lancashire clubs declared support for the Yorkshiremen. And just two days later, at the George Hotel in Huddersfield, 22 clubs met to form the Northern Rugby Football Union, which came to be known as the Northern Union (NU). Twenty clubs resigned from the RFU.

The RFU reacted badly to this challenge and sanctioned players and officials, even amateurs, who played against NU clubs. This deepened the divide and drove more northern clubs to the NU. In less than a decade, the NU had more clubs than the RFU.

At first, the league clubs stayed with the established rules of the Rugby Union, but bit by bit, the game began to change. The flankers, who join the scrum on either side, were done away with, reducing teams to 13 a side. Line-outs were dropped. Instead of a ruck after a tackle, the game would stop momentarily until the tackled player, who had possession of the ball, could stand and heel the ball back to someone on his own side. This sped things up, ended messy rucks, and cut out a lot of the scrummages that so dominated rugby union play. The league game became more and more open, running, tackling and then running again. The Yorkshire and Lancashire leagues introduced cup competitions, and a nationwide Challenge Cup began. A playoff system was created for interleague competition to establish a national champion. By 1900, top rugby league fixtures were drawing in excess of 30,000 spectators.

Along the way, the league style of rugby was passed on to New Zealand and Australia. The key to this was a tour by a team from New Zealand and Australia called the All-Golds, who went to Britain in 1907–1908. They had never even seen a rugby league match and had to learn the new style in a matter of days, with intensive coaching. After a few games against league teams they played a "rubber" of three games against a Great Britain side and won twice.

Back home in New Zealand and Australia, similar battle lines had been drawn along the class divide. In New Zealand, the "veiled professionalism" kept rugby union on top. In Australia, a New South Wales Rugby Football League came to life in August 1907, sparking the same angry response from the union side, with lifetime expulsions from union rugby in Australia.

Rugby league, however, caught on with the spectators in and around Sydney, the heartland of rugby in Australia. The league game then spread north to Queensland. Within a few years, rugby league had forged ahead of the union game in terms of gate and receipts.

Meanwhile, rugby union, the game with 15 players to a side and the big scrum, was also spreading far and wide. At the 1900 Olympics, France, England, and Germany entered teams. France won the gold medal.

In South Africa, the rugby game had found a new group of enthusiasts, the Boers, primarily farmers of Dutch descent who had lived uneasily with the British Imperialists. Between 1835 and 1845, 15,000 of them quit the British-ruled Cape Colony and moved north and east into the interior of South Africa. They created two new states, the Orange Free State and the Transvaal. After the discovery of diamonds at the juncture of the Orange and Vaal rivers in 1867, the British determined to annex the two states and push the Boers, Zulus, and other native groups together into a dominion similar to that of Canada. Tensions eventually lead to the First Boer War in 1880–1881. The British military had become accustomed to fighting colonial wars against ill-armed and unsophisticated native forces. They found the Boers, who were used to rifles, shooting, horses, and living rough in the countryside, difficult opponents. The war went badly for Britain, and the Boers regained some elements of independence.

The discovery of gold in the Transvaal in 1886 led to the second, longer war, when France and Germany were scrambling to seize as much of the African continent as possible. The gold was too tempting. The Second Boer War broke out in October 1899, and after initial Boer successes, the British pushed into the Boer republics and took control. The period of formal battles ended in August 1890, but guerrilla war continued. The British borrowed from the Spanish in Cuba and the Americans in the Philippines and set up "concentration camps," where they herded the population to deny the guerrillas food and shelter. The guerrilla war slowly fizzled out during the next two years, and in the aftermath, a South African Union was created. Bitterness on the part of the Afrikaners (the Boers' name for themselves) would lead to anti-British sentiment and even the creation of the apartheid state after World War II.

Despite the war and legacy hatreds, rugby football became an emblematic sport for the Afrikaners beginning in 1883, with the formation of the Stellensbosch club. From that beginning, the game spread along the east coast, through Natal and into the Western Cape in the other direction. The Transvaal formed a rugby union in 1889, and that same year the South African Rugby Board was set up. The first national tournament was held, with Western Provinces rising to the top. War put a temporary stop to all this for a few years, but in time, rugby resumed, and South African rugby, in the guise of the national team, the Springboks, became a singular force in the game.

Across the South Atlantic, in Argentina, both rugby and association football had arrived with British businessmen, farmers, and engineers in the latter decades of the nineteenth century. Argentina was being developed, chiefly with British capital, and while never becoming a formal colony, it was largely absorbed into the British global economic system. Rugby was now another component in the British variant on European civilization being exported throughout the world. Organized team sports weren't as important as drains, railways, ports, schools, or even the most modern accountancy methods, but they were much more fun.

The British initially restricted membership in their football, rugby, and cricket clubs to themselves, a pattern seen worldwide; however, the Argentinians soon picked up the games and began to play them among themselves. The first recorded game in Argentina was not quite rugby union and not quite association football, played in 1873, at the Buenos Aires Cricket Club. By 1899, the River Plate Rugby Union had formed, with four member clubs, three in Buenos Aires. In 1904, a club with non-British members, primarily engineering students, was playing in Buenos Aires, signaling the movement of the game out of the realm of English public-school boys and into that of Argentina proper.

By 1914 and the cataclysm of World War I, rugby union had spread to the countries that today are top-tier lands for the sport, from New Zealand to South Africa, to Ireland, Scotland, France, Wales, and, of course, England. The game of Tom Brown's school days had become an international giant.

Along the way, as we've seen, social class and regional divisions in England had spawned a second kind of rugby, the league variant, which was to have an eventful history in the twentieth century, becoming Australia's biggest sport on television in modern times. Moreover, the amateur versus professional issue would not go away, although rugby remained wedded to amateurism until 1995.

Association football, as we will see in the next chapter, was on its way to becoming the world's most popular sport, but while these developments from the old country game of "footeballe" were taking place, another game had formed in rebellious Ireland. This was Gaelic football, an exciting variation on the basic plan of football, with interesting peculiarities of its own.

A short distance to the west, across a narrow sea, lay Ireland, long since conquered by the English crown. In 1801, the two kingdoms of Ireland and Great Britain were merged to form the United Kingdom of

Great Britain and Ireland. This never sat well with a large section of the Irish people.

Ireland has a long and disagreeable history with England. Ireland, being smaller, less populous, and remaining true to Catholicism in the sixteenth century, was always vulnerable to English depredations, colonization, and religious bigotries. England's lack of concern during the great famine of 1847, which depopulated parts of Ireland, confirmed the deep veins of bitterness in many Irish hearts. That famine came from a potato blight that virtually annihilated the potato crop, on which millions of Irish were utterly dependent. This situation had grown from their loss of lands to both English and wealthy Irish protestant owners. The productivity of the potato had allowed a large population to grow, even though most people were driven to the margins of the arable lands. But everything depended on the potato, and when the blight destroyed the harvest in the late 1840s, starvation or emigration were the only choices. The response of the Westminster Parliament can only be described as callous and indifferent.

From the 1870s to the 1920s, the Irish question was a constant issue in British politics. One response, from the liberals led by W. E Gladstone, was home rule, devolving powers from Westminster to Dublin, yet keeping Ireland within the realm. Home rule was anathema to the conservative side, which would brook no threat to protestant ascendancy or English landowners, and Gladstone's efforts to bring this reform to fruition were thwarted.

As a result, the movement for Irish independence gathered strength in the latter decades of the nineteenth century. While a certain amount of terrorism occurred, including assassinations, another aspect of the agitation for independence involved the nurturing of Irish national character. Thus, the Gaelic language became a powerful symbol. Seeing the need for Irish sports, the Gaelic Athletic Association (GAA) was founded in 1884. The GAA sought to promote sports that were not English, the central point to many. The association codified Gaelic football in 1887.

For centuries there had been a tradition of country footeballe in parts of Ireland; however, the true Irish traditional field sports were hockey games, that is, shinty in the winter and hurling in the summer. Although there is a reference to a man being charged for accidentally stabbing a player in a football game at New Castle of the Lyons from

1308, there are no "fossil games" in Ireland. This author suspects that the football games, collectively known as *caid*, were imports from the other side of the Irish Sea. The word *caid* referred to the ball, which, according to the earliest accounts, appears to have been a leather case surrounding a pig's bladder. The Irish are known for keeping pigs, and it is certainly possible that the bouncing, inflatable ball was separately invented in Ireland, or even, although less credibly, invented in Ireland, spreading east to England. But the lack of fossil games and tradition prior to that reference in 1308 is discouraging to this line of thought.

Furthermore, the accounts increase from the seventeenth century, and by this time the games had a resemblance not only to country footeballe in England, but also to the way that gentlemen were organizing games of Cornish hurling to Goles. Gentlemen "got up" teams of 20 men and wagered on their prowess in matches conforming to the game described by Francis Willughby and later Joseph Strutt. This puts the Irish *caid* in perspective. It was most likely imported from England. The earliest recorded game was in County Meath beginning in 1670, and this game was clearly country footeballe, with the ball primarily being driven by kicking but also being caught. Meath lies just north and inland of the Dublin area.

Gaelic football is played by teams of 15, on a field larger than a rugby or soccer pitch, as many as 140 yards long and 90 yards wide. The goals are like those of rugby, the "H" form, but the bottom half is netted like a soccer goal. The ball can be kicked; carried in the hands for four paces at a time but then bounced once; or dropped to the foot and kicked back up to the hands many times, called "soloing." It can also be "hand passed"—"punched" to other players or even over the crossbar to score.

Kicking the ball into goal scores three points. Kicking or hand-passing the ball over the crossbar scores one point. Players are not allowed to move the ball from left to right hand or vice versa.

The game has no offside rule; instead, to prevent "kick throughs" accumulating by the goal, there is the "square ball" rule. If a teammate is in the small rectangle close to the goal and the ball enters that rectangle, play stops and a free "out" is awarded.

The game is similar enough to Australian rules football that, since 1998, the two codes have compromised a bit to produce international rules and allow test matches.

Gaelic football has been a big success, drawing the largest crowds of any sporting event in Ireland; however, the sport is strictly amateur, and its popularity is lamented by Ireland's soccer and rugby communities, who see it as funneling away talent from those sports, which have stronger international competitions.

When it comes to international appeal, the most popular of the games that descended from country footeballe would be the association game, which, as we will see in chapter 11, spread to every continent and almost every country in the world.

11

SOCCER GOES GLOBAL

The crucial era for the spread of association football was the 30 years before World War I. This period saw European empires spread throughout the world, as well as extraordinary migrations of peoples. About 40 million Europeans emigrated to the United States, South America, Australia, Canada, New Zealand, North Africa, and South Africa. Millions of Bengalis and Chinese also migrated as laborers to the Caribbean, Africa, Australia, and even California, where the Chinese worked on the railways that were stitching together the continental United States. The Japanese migrated to Hawaii and California. Hawaii, formerly an independent kingdom, had been taken over by white American settlers by this time.

The movement of black Africans via the slave trade to the Americas and the Muslim lands of the Ottoman Turkish Empire ironically ceased in the 1880s. The British, who had formerly controlled the trade and profited from it, had turned decisively against it in the Victorian Era. The Atlantic slave trade had been banned by Parliament in 1807, and between 1808 and 1860, the Royal Navy seized at least 1,600 ships and freed 150,000 captives. Slavers were now seen as pirates and could be hanged. After David Livingston's adventures in Central Africa in the 1860s had caught the public imagination, the Royal Navy moved against the east coast slave trade, ultimately exchanging the island of Heligoland off the coast of Germany for Zanzibar, which the Germans had taken possession of. Zanzibar had been a center for the eastern trade, and the British were now moving to shut it down. African rulers inland who refused to accept the new rules were also punished and even deposed. Treaties banning slavery were signed with more than 50 African rulers.

At the same time, the world was seeing an acceleration in the development of new technologies. The telephone, the automobile, electric lighting, disinfectants, anesthetics, and the airplane were the classic hallmarks of the new age. And with them came football, which brought with it an echo of earlier, more violent times but packaged in a way that was both exciting and still safe enough for most to play.

To start this quick tour of global developments, we should check in how things went in Britain, which was between 10 and 20 years ahead of the rest of the world.

In 1890, the Scots formed the Scottish Football League, and there were now two professional leagues playing association rules football in Britain. The crowds were also growing steadily. In the English league's first season, 600,000 spectators watched the games. By 1905–1906, that number had swelled to 5 million. What had begun as a weekend pursuit for public school old boys on the heaths and parks throughout London 30 or so years prior was turning into something that was already achieving an element of social importance.

The English league would grow steadily throughout the 1890s, from the original 12 clubs to 16 in the first division and 12 in the second, and then 18 in the first and 18 in the second. The league would sprout a third division in 1920, then double that third to a third north and third south in 1921, and eventually, in 1950, to a full four divisions, involving 88 clubs.

A key element to the league, and every soccer league outside the United States, was promotion and relegation. The top two clubs in the lower division would be promoted, and the bottom two in the upper division would go down. This continues in the modern era of the Premier League, with its highly lucrative television contracts and largely sold out stadia, which makes the drop into the "Championship," as the second division is now named, particularly brutal. The fear of relegation and struggle to "avoid the drop" provided excitement and tension for clubs at the bottom of every division, and the battle for promotion added considerable zest to the competition in the upper reaches of the lower divisions.

While the league was growing, other aspects of the game were changing. First, the pitch got some extra lines. In 1892, double semicircles six yards deep appeared in front of the goals. There was also a 12-yard line, inside which penalty kicks could be awarded for certain infractions. The center circle was another innovation at this time, forcing opponents to keep 10 yards clear of the player kicking off. In 1902, the 12-yard line gave way to the 18-yard penalty area.

The size of the field of play was shrinking, too. The older field, which measured 200 yards by 100 yards, had been reduced to 130 yards maximum, with many being trimmed to 110 yards in length and between 50 and 75 yards in width.

In addition, the referee took over running the game from the pair of umpires (one from each team) that had previously done so. The ref moved from the sidelines, where he had adjudicated when umpires disagreed, to the interior of the field. He was also given a whistle, replacing the flags that had previously been waved to mark infractions. The umpires were replaced by linesmen, who were to police the crucial offside rule, as well as judge who had last touched the ball before it went out of play and award, via the referee, throw-ins and either goal kicks or corner kicks.

Penalty kicks, basically free shots at goal from wherever the infraction took place, were now awarded for handling the ball, deliberate tripping, kicking, pushing with the hands, charging from behind, holding onto an opponent, and jumping onto an opponent. If inside the 12-yard area, this meant a free shot at goal with no opponents standing in between.

Moreover, the actual goals had evolved. First a tape had been put across the top at a height of eight feet. In 1882, the fixed crossbar had arrived. That year also saw the halfway line added to the layout.

Players were now being fitted with uniforms. Things had come a long way from the early days, when players wore long, white cricket trousers and shirts, and were only distinguishable by the different colored caps they wore. Everyone now wore shorts, and shirts were generally a single color—usually red, blue, or white—or broad stripes of red and white, black and white, blue and white. Less common were green, black, and yellow.

It was still permissible to barge into the goalkeeper—"grassing" the keeper was, in fact, a bit of an art practiced by the less scrupulous forwards. The idea was to arrive at the same moment your teammate was taking a shot and knock the keeper off his feet, clearing the goal mouth. On corner kicks, goalkeepers were regularly hammered to the turf by leaping forwards.

The offside rule remained that you needed to have three opposing players between yourself and the goal at the moment a teammate struck a pass for you to run onto and play.

In summary, the game had left behind the rather violent dribbling style characterized by a herd of players surrounding the ball and little passing. Instead, teams used the wings, where quick players with dribbling skills would receive a pass and move downfield and send in a cross from close to the byline. Forwards would seek to either head the crossed ball toward the goal or gain control close to goal for a shot. Everything had become faster, and play had begun to resemble what we see today, albeit at nothing like the modern pace, nor with the sophistication of modern systems of attack and defense.

A look at the league table of 1901–1902 shows a first division full of clubs that still play in the Premier League and the Championship today. Sunderland was at the top; Everton, Newcastle, Aston Villa, Liverpool, and Manchester City were also there. It isn't until fourth place in the second division that we meet a southern club, Woolwich Arsenal, which had first joined the league in 1893–1894. Of course, they would eventually move across London to Highbury and simply become Arsenal.

Another signpost to the future from 1901 was the FA Cup Final, played between Tottenham Hotspur, then a nonleague team, and Sheffield United, which drew a crowd of 110,820 to the Crystal Palace. That game ended in a 2–2 draw but demonstrated the drawing power of a successful London club with a popular story behind them. The replay was held in Bolton and drew 20,470, even though the clubs involved were not from Lancashire. Tottenham won, by the way.

Spurs were the last nonleague club to win the cup. Of course today, the competition remains open to nonleague teams, but the likelihood of one surviving to reach a Wembley final against a giant like Manchester United or Chelsea is remote, and to carry off the cup against one of today's top sides, with several hundred million pounds worth of star players on the field, is unimaginable. Still, at the beginning of each season the qualifying rounds for the FA Cup are chock full of hopeful nonleague amateur teams. And indeed, every so often, one of them, by dint of hard work and some luck, will make it to a great day when they play against an elite club from the Championship or even the Premier League.

While association football was becoming big business and highly popular in England and Scotland's great cities, it was also starting to embed itself in the countries of Europe, indeed the world, with some interesting and notable exceptions. The game was first spread by the English upper classes, in a process similar to that by which Old Harrovians kicked off clubs in the North of England. A few English chaps, dedicated to cricket in the summer and either association or rugby football in the winter (plus tennis, golf, squash, polo, and badminton), would form a club, and this could be almost anywhere, Buenos Aires, Milan, Calcutta, or Philadelphia; the British upper classes were everywhere, it seems, either planting flags for the empire, constructing railways, or setting up trade associations and founding schools for the local upper classes, where the English language and ways could be taught, along with classical Greek and Latin.

Now that is a broad statement, and the details were slightly different based on locale, but in this era, roughly from 1880 to World War I, the people of Great Britain, rather improbably considering the size of the place and its location, were leading the world on the march into modernity. London, at 6,226,000 inhabitants, was by far the largest city in the world, sitting at the center of webs of trade and finance that ran from the docks of Shanghai to those of Sydney, and to Cape Town and just about anywhere you could name. This moment would not last; World War I would shatter this world of global trade and free markets led by the British, and indeed, the Americans and Germans had already caught up and surpassed the British in terms of industrial output. But no other country or culture had quite so much to offer the world in terms of sports and outdoor activities as the upper-class British culture of this time.

Other European powers contributed their own elements to the growing global culture: German classical music and motor cars; French painting and bicycle racing; German and Czech lager beer; and French, Spanish, and Italian wine and cuisine. And in time, other cultures would add their own components, especially in terms of popular restaurant food.

As previously mentioned, this was also the era of emigrations and migrations that helped shape the modern world today. Italians, especially from the south, moved to the United States and Argentina. In the United States, they learned English, in Argentina, Spanish. In the United States, they played baseball, in Argentina, soccer.

The British, now that the trade in African slaves was dead and buried, began to move large numbers of indentured workers from India and even China throughout the world to satisfy labor demand from large plantation companies, creating new ethnic mixtures in the Caribbean, South Africa, and even Uganda.

And we should always remember that this empire, like all those before it, was based on violence. The British approached foreign lands with ships of war and guns in their hands. Like the French, Germans, Dutch, Belgians, and Italians, their imperial history was one long saga of small wars and atrocities, whether in the conquest of India or putting down rebellions in Africa and Jamaica. The United States took the same path, with war in the Philippines, war against Mexico, and war for Cuba. And let's not forget the Russians, who pursued their imperial dreams throughout Central Asia with musket and cannon.

The British Empire was simply the largest and most varied of these harsh, capitalist combinations, involving military conquest, exploitation of resources and native labor, and frequent savage bouts of repression, complete with massacres.

Naturally enough, the history textbooks of the former imperial powers skirt around this difficult knot in the topic, but the peoples on the receiving end remember these things all too well.

Many of the foot soldiers of the empire, especially in this phase, were Irish and Scots, Celtic peoples who were often forced off their own lands by either Scottish lairds or Irish lords and given little choice other than to take the king's shilling and sign up for a regiment. Beyond those who joined the army, the Irish continued to migrate to the United States and Australia in considerable numbers, while Canada took on a Scottish hue. The Scots became a prominent part of the British Empire, serving as soldiers, administrators, and merchants.

And wherever the British congregated in sufficient numbers for a club to be formed, then it soon was, and on weekends some patch of green sprouted chaps chasing a ball or clad in white and playing cricket. Given time, there'd be tennis courts and even a golf course to go with a club house, with a bar and piano. In the evenings, there were amateur theatricals and sing-alongs of show tunes from London and New York. Ladies took tea time in the lounge, and gents flocked to the "water hole" after a game of footer, or golf during the season. These clubs were everywhere during this period.

The spread of football, both association and the two rugby forms, followed interesting pathways. The South American countries associated with the game today, Brazil, Argentina, Colombia, and Chile, were never part of the British Empire. Even Argentina, which for a while was tightly connected to Britain by trade and finance, always remained an independent political entity; however, there were extensive commercial links to the British world, and while coffee and beef flowed one way, British manufactures and such cultural creations as association football flowed the other.

In the "white" dominions, Australia, Canada, and New Zealand, it was rugby and cricket that became the most popular imports, while first Australia and eventually Canada added their own varieties of football. Cricket never became as important in Canada as it did elsewhere, and Canadians play baseball and softball for a bat-and-ball summer sport. An interesting element of cultural resistance to the association game was common to all three of these colonies. While soccer would be played in all of them, it would never become the national obsession that it became in Britain or elsewhere.

In South Africa, a racial divide was to grow when it came to football. Rugby was the preferred game for whites, especially the Afrikaners of Dutch descent, while soccer became popular in the black townships around the growing cities of Johannesburg and Cape Town. It would not be until the end of the apartheid era that South African rugby would begin to seriously bring in black players.

Two major exceptions to the spread of football must be declared. Neither India nor China were to take up these games in a dedicated manner, although India has become a world center for cricket. For soccer, the sport that professes to be the world's most popular, the absence at the top level of the two largest population blocs is notable.

Football, both in the soccer and rugby forms, is certainly widely played in India but has never stirred the urban masses in the way it has in Brazil or Mexico, for example. And China, despite having its own tradition of football for more than two thousand years, has yet to really get serious about soccer, while Chinese rugby remains purely amateur. Having said that, soccer is the country's most popular spectator sport and is widely played, with a professional league and teams in every region. Indeed, the game was even encouraged under the early communist regime, with the Chinese Football Association being founded in 1949. China reached the World Cup Finals in 2002 (in part because Japan and South Korea were already qualified as joint hosts) but failed to win a game in the group stage. Still, both the men's and women's game is encouraged and supported by the state. The women's team has established a reputation as one of the best in the world, challenging the United States and Germany for the top titles.

The problem for the Chinese men's national team and the professional leagues that provide the players for it has been systemic corruption. At times this has even involved fixed matches and paid-off referees. Gambling has been cited, gangster influence on clubs mentioned, and a society that has not quite come to grips with the thought of youngsters pursuing careers as professional athletes discussed.

It remains to be seen if this is the only problem and, if corrected, whether there would be some large-scale change. It does not appear to be a general problem in the region. The association game has been successful in both Korea and Japan, and Japan has also taken up rugby to a high standard. North Korea, South Korea, and Japan have been to the soccer World Cup Finals, and South Korea and Japan jointly hosted the event in 2002. To the south, soccer is widely popular, from Thailand to Singapore, although none of these countries has made it to the finals of the World Cup. In the summer of 2014, a 5–1 defeat of the Chinese men's team by a Thailand under-23 side led to widespread criticism on the Internet. China's problem with football remains unclear. In 2014, Xi Jinping, general secretary of the Chinese Communist Party and president of the People's Republic of China, who happens to be a keen football player and fan, decreed that all Chinese school children will learn the game and play it henceforth. It is certainly possible that the current situation is only temporary and that the next generation will bring a different approach. Should this happen and Chinese clubs begin to rise in world rankings with all the usual passion and money, the world of soccer will do more than just grow.

In the nineteenth century, the spread of the association game to Europe began with Scandinavia. The first fully European club, that is, a club not founded by English men, was Kjøbenhavns Boldklub, established in 1876, just outside Copenhagen. Kjøbenhavns Boldklub was a "sports club" that featured handball, cricket, and tennis, as well as association football, which began there in 1878. The Danes also founded the first European football association in 1889. They were leaders in European football for some time and even won silver medals in the sport at the 1908 and 1912 Olympics. England won the golds. Not too far behind the Danes came the Dutch and Swedes.

In fact, the "take up" of association football varied from country to country throughout Europe. But the years between 1895 and 1905 saw an avalanche of club founding. The association game had matured into a successful, exciting sport that was also interesting to watch. In a relatively short span of years, clubs sprang up from Lisbon to Munich and beyond, in South America and Africa, too.

In Bilbao, Spain, British engineers and mineworkers were involved in various projects during the last two decades of the nineteenth century. They brought football with them, the association style, and the locals gradually took up the game. The Bilbao story actually contains both of the routes that football traveled on its way to new lands.

The iron mines of Bilbao drew migrant workers, including miners from England's North East (Newcastle, etc.), as well as shipyard workers from Sunderland and Southampton. They played football in their spare time.

In addition, young men from Bilbao, the capital of the Basque people in Spain, had been going to English schools and colleges. There they learned to play the game and brought it back with them.

Beginning in 1898, a group of students founded the Athletic Club, which, through meetings during the next few years, became Athletic Bilbao Football Club. They defeated FC Barcelona in the first Copa del Rey final.

Meanwhile, in Madrid, more Basque students formed the Athletic Club Madrid, which had become Atletico Madrid by 1901.

At the same time, academics, including graduates from Oxford and Cambridge at the Institucion libre de ensenanza of Madrid, had started up Football Club Sky in 1897. It broke in two three years later, and one half was now called the Madrid Football Club. In 1902, this was formally founded as the Madrid Football Club, and the group adopted the white shirt and white shorts home kit, which has remained ever since.

In 1920, the club became Real Madrid when King Alfonso XIII granted use of the royal title.

To mention Real Madrid means we have to consider FC Barcelona, the other giant of Iberian football. The Catalan club was founded in 1899, by a group of Swiss, English, and Spanish men led by Joan Gamper. It remained an amateur club for 10 years and slowly but steadily became a focal point for the Catalan national consciousness. This increased considerably after 1925, when Spain became an autocracy. Later still, after dictator Francisco Franco banned the Catalan language, the stadium of FC Barcelona became one of the few places where that language could be freely used and heard.

Other famous European football clubs were being founded in this same period.

Juventus of Turin, Italy's most successful club, was founded in 1897. In 1899, the Milan Cricket and Football Club was started by a couple of Englishmen. The official colors were red and black. This club eventually became the famous AC Milan. In 1905, Juventus changed their uniform to broad black and white stripes, inspired by the shirts worn by Notts County.

In Munich in 1900, some young men left the Münchner Turnverein, a gymnastics club that frowned on football. They started Bayern Munich. In 1906, they merged with Münchner Sports Club and stopped wearing black and started wearing the red shirts they still wear today.

The German case is interesting in many ways. Football, or fußball, did not really take off there until the 1930s, although there were at least two hundred clubs founded in the period around 1900. In the nineteenth century, Germans were caught up in a wave of enthusiasm for gymnastics, and they were slow to switch to the games invented by the English. German rugby clubs had started up in the 1870s, but Germany has never really taken to rugby in a major way; however, once they caught the bug for soccer they took to it with characteristic discipline and flair, and have become Europe's leading national team at World Cup tournaments, while Bayern Munich is one of the top-10 clubs in the world.

In South America, the association game spread rapidly, too, but before the locals picked it up it was played by British workers and expatriates.

It is also important to touch on the proselytizing work of Corinthians FC, of London. An amateur club, it was founded in 1882, with the express mission of building a team that could challenge the Scots and mighty Queen's Park. Corinthians players soon became a dominant flavor in England sides, and the club began to take tours to European nations, South Africa, the United States, Canada, and South America.

By that point, the game had been played in some parts of South America for decades. The first game played under association rules, in Buenos Aires, was between two teams of British workers in 1867. A quarter-century later, the Argentine Association Football League was formed, with primarily British players.

For an interesting comparison, consider three clubs named "River Plate." That's the English name for the grand Rio del Plata, which flows through Buenos Aires in Argentina and through a wide estuary, past Uruguay's capital, Montevideo.

First was River Plate FC of Montevideo. Founded in 1897, this was a club of British players and one of the giants of the early years of Uruguayan football, along with Montevideo Wanderers. In time these clubs gave way to another generation of Uruguayan football and clubs. River Plate FC dissolved in 1929, by which time the British influence in that region had dwindled drastically following World War I.

In 1932, River Plate de Montevideo was formed from a merger of two other clubs. This club still plays in Uruguay's Primera Division. It was composed of Spanish-speaking players, all Uruguayan.

Meanwhile, Club Atletico River Plate, a multisport club up the river a bit, in Buenos Aires, was going strong. This club, known widely as simply "River" or the "Millionairos," was founded in 1901, and although its founders were Spanish-speaking Argentines, they still took the English name for the Rio del Plata and kept it. Today River is one of the top two clubs in Argentina, and its battles with Boca Juniors are the "super-classicos" of that league.

Farther north, in Brazil, the early clubs were usually rowing clubs, and the full names of the great clubs of Rio de Janeiro, for instance, are usually Clube de Regatas do . . . Flamengo or Vasco da Gama, and so on. Flamengo began this way in 1895, and officially took up football in 1912. Vasco da Gama, their great rival, was founded in 1898, as a club for the Portuguese immigrant population in the city, and took up football in 1915.

The same held true in Sao Paulo, where Corinthians began as a multisport club with an emphasis on rowing, still visible in the club's badge, with crossed oars and an anchor in red behind the black and white emblem of the football club. The club is officially Sport Club Corinthians Paulista. And yes, the five railway workers who founded the club in 1910 borrowed the name from the touring Corinthians FC of London, who had played a number of games in Brazil that year.

The multisport aspect of many great soccer clubs should not be forgotten. Barcelona is a strong force in European basketball, as are Real Madrid and Greek soccer giants Panathinaikos and Olympiacos, and in South America, the clubs still race in sculls and participate in several other sports.

In South America, once the game made the transition from an amateur activity among British workers to the surrounding population, it began to take off, to become the leading sport in most countries on the continent. Only in the far north, where American baseball influenced Venezuela and cricket was popular in Guyana, was there any real competition for soccer.

Across the Atlantic, to the east, the vast continent of Africa took to the game as well. As in South America, the first clubs were founded by and for Europeans. In this case, however, they were French, and the first club was Club Athletique Liberte d'Oran, in Algeria, in 1897. The first Muslim club was begun the following year in the city of Constantine, formerly Cirta, and was renamed in honor of Roman emperor Constantine the Great. The club CS Constantinois began as Ikbal Emancipation, and thereby hangs a tale of colonialism and politics. The club existed under that name until 1909, when it was shut down by the French rulers of Algeria. Seven years later it started up again as Etoile Club Musulman Constantinois and survived for two years before the French closed it down again. It reopened a third time in 1926, as Club Sportif Constantinois, and this time, because it had Europeans as members and players, it was allowed to stay open. The club continues today in Algeria's top division.

Other top teams were founded during this same period, on either side of 1900. In Egypt, El Ahly Sporting Club of Cairo was founded in 1907. El Ahly has been the leading club in Egypt for decades, and the team nickname is the Red Devils. This author has not been able to determine if El Ahly or Manchester United were the first to use that name.

In Ghana, then the Gold Coast colony, thousands of miles south and west of Egypt, Hearts of Oak Football Club formed in Accra in 1911, and in 1922, Sir Gordon Guggisberg, governor of the colony, started the Accra Football League. Football spread quickly through West Africa, which, in modern times, has been a source of many star players for the European leagues.

With football clubs springing up throughout Europe, South America, parts of Africa, and beyond, it was inevitable that someone would think of creating an organization to oversee the game, guard the rulebook, and uphold standards. Enter the Federation Internationale de Football Association (FIFA), which was founded in Paris in 1904. The first members were France, Belgium, Spain, the Netherlands, Denmark, Sweden, and Switzerland.

England had been invited, and the secretary of the Netherlands Football Association had reached out to F. J. Wall, secretary of the English Football Association. Wall thought the proposal was worth following up on, but the English ran into a problem—the associations of Scotland, Wales, and Ireland needed to be involved, and action was also required from the Executive Committee of the Football Association. This could not be achieved in time for the Paris meeting. It seems flimsy today and was probably just an excuse. The English, with 40 years of history in the game, the primary professional league in the world, and the biggest cup competition by far, were slow to accept that an organization founded in France could be of any importance.

However, the next year, in 1905, England joined FIFA, the beginning of an often stormy relationship. England left again in 1918, after demanding that Germany, Austria, and Hungary be thrown out as part of the general punishment for having started and lost World War I. This didn't fly with the rest of the members, so England, Scotland, Wales, and Ireland left instead. They would rejoin in 1924, and leave once more in 1928, in a fuss over "broken time" payments to working-class players. The Football Association in London was led by men who had been great amateur players, Kinnaird, Clegg, and their ilk. They were never comfortable with the football league because of its professional nature and viewed the spread of professional football elsewhere with unease. But in 1945, England joined FIFA for the third time, this time to stay. By this point the professionalism issue was truly dead and buried.

Also, by this point, the game was well and truly established throughout the world. FIFA's brainchild, the World Cup, was beginning to assume some of the importance that would later turn it into the gargantuan sporting spectacle and television event that it is today.

12

THE UNITED STATES
The Exception and the Rule

As we've seen, both the association game and the two kinds of rugby spread throughout the world, riding the wave of Britain's imperialism and also the following waves from France. These sports had faced the challenge of professionalism and reacted in different ways, with the association game seeing the establishment of professional leagues, while rugby union decisively turned its back on professional play, leading to the creation of rugby league and a decisive move into professionalism. Meanwhile, the Australians and the Irish (not yet independent) had developed successful football variants of their own.

In all this, we've left out the United States, and it's time to catch up on progress there, because not only had there been progress of a sort, but the American game was also fast approaching a great existential crisis.

The association game, "soccer," had once again reached America's shores but was now being carried by the tribes of new immigrants from Europe. Rejected by the elite colleges of the East Coast in the 1870s in favor of rugby, the association game continued to be spurned by the colleges in the decades thereafter. Their focus had moved to the evolving sport of American football, called the "gridiron" by some due to the pattern of lines laid on the field. That game spread west through the college system and primarily became identified with "college football" for the next 40 or so years.

An important aspect of the continuing American rejection of soccer lay in the rise of a strong cultural nativism and resistance to things European at the end of the nineteenth century. This is a complex issue worked over by many cultural historians. At a time of mass immigration, with a flood of foreign languages, accents, and cultural mores appearing in the great cities of the Eastern Seaboard—in particular, New York— elite American society was concerned with establishing a clearly defined American culture, different and separate from those of Europe. Relations with Britain, always complicated, had evolved as the United States grew from a set of colonies on the Eastern Seaboard to a continental-sized power with an unlimited future and an economy larger than that of the mother country. Currents of Anglophobia swirled around, while British capital poured into U.S. markets and railways, as well as the beef industry and many other important sectors.

Soccer had been tried in the 1870s, in its primitive format, and was found wanting. The United States had adopted rugby and then moved on from that game to develop its own. That new game—call it gridiron or just football, as Americans did—was the game that counted. When European immigrants pulled out soccer balls and played that game on fields in and around the big cities, Americans sniffed in contempt and looked the other way. This was part of what has been called "American exceptionalism"—the belief that things were better in the United States because they were different.

Beneath that phrase bubbled some other currents, which focused ill will on Britain and everything English. The great migration from Ireland in the wake of the famine in the 1840s had left an American Irish population nursing bitter memories of Anglo-Saxon mistreatment throughout the centuries. In the United States, that population found power through the ballot box and organization through all manner of social groups, from the police and fire departments to Hibernian clubs and clubs that played Gaelic sports. Other immigrant groups, for example, the large German segment, were either indifferent to things British or vaguely hostile, reflecting the turn things were taking back home.

U.S. colleges continued to reject soccer, forcing it to spread via its own networks, through clubs and immigrant organizations, mostly in the big cities of the northeast, but also in other areas, for instance, St. Louis, which became strongholds for the game. Clubs proliferated, but a great many had an immigrant flavor in their very names, German

American Soccer Club, for example, or neighborhoods, like Kearny, New Jersey, which was once more like a suburb of Glasgow than New York. Kensington, Philadelphia, was another locale with strong Scottish connections, and the Kensington Blue Bells Soccer Club was one expression of their identity.

Clubs led to leagues and quite serious crowds of spectators in the 1920s, but the rejection by colleges and the elite cut the game off from the American mainstream. When the professional leagues crashed during the Depression years of the early 1930s, soccer in the United States dwindled to a few regions and was kept alive by the immigrant club teams in major cities.

While the great wave of immigration had altered the country, bringing new accents, foods, religion, and social mores, American football was also changing. After being formally banned in 1894, the "mass plays" changed, although they did not really go away. There was an evolutionary process at work, but it was slow.

In the 1890s, the game got big. Crowds came out for the big match-ups between Harvard, Yale, Princeton, and Columbia; as many as 20,000 onlookers packed into the Polo Grounds in New York for one of the season finales.

At this point the players did not wear helmets, and they were just beginning to adopt pads, but they were primitive, lacking hard surfaces and foam rubber. When they began to feature hard surfaces, the number of player injuries tended to increase. The game was still about moving the ball forward five yards in three attempts, called "downs." There was no forward pass and hardly any lateral passes. The ball was snapped back by the center, or "snapback," and the quarterback took it and handed it off, and bang, thud, crash, the two teams collided at the line of scrimmage. And while the V-wedge and other mobile scrum-style plays had been done away with, there were still highly dangerous practices, pushing and pulling the ball carrier to break the defensive line. Injuries and deaths were common, especially among younger players.

Some rules had changed, however. The score for a touchdown had risen from four points to five in 1898. In 1904, a field goal dropped from five points to four.

And now for a few signposts to the American future.

On December 29, 1890, at Wounded Knee, the last major "battle" between the United States and the Native Americans—actually more of a massacre than a battle—hundreds of Sioux men, women, and children were slaughtered. Twenty-nine U.S. soldiers also died.

In New York the following year, Carnegie Hall opened, and the first guest conductor was Pyotr Ilyich Tchaikovsky, the great composer and at that time the most popular figure in music, worldwide.

Ellis Island opened that same year, ushering millions of immigrants through its halls and into the New World.

In 1892, James Naismith published the rules of basketball, and the Wrigley company debuted its minty chewing gum.

In 1894, Thomas Edison displayed his "kinetoscope motion picture" device. The "movies" were about to be born.

But in May 1896, the U.S. Supreme Court, in the case of *Plessy v. Ferguson*, found that racial segregation under the "separate but equal" doctrine was constitutional. The old racial divide between white and black was now to be legally intensified.

In 1898, the United States annexed Hawaii and, shortly afterward, launched into a war with Spain, collapsing what remained of the Spanish Empire, seizing the Philippines and Cuba. A brutal guerrilla war soon erupted in the Philippines.

Something old, something new, something cool, and something brutal, these were the various flavors of the times in America.

In 1888, the rules of football had changed to allow tackling above the knees, instead of only above the waist. This change had made it easier to bring the ball carrier down, helping to popularize the v-wedge and other schemes to protect the ball carrier. Then came Harvard's "flying wedge," first deployed in 1892. Invented by Harvard supporter Lorin Deland, this became the standard kickoff play. In fact, the quarterback would simply nudge the ball, an "inchkick," and then pick it up and pitch it to the running back, who fell in behind the moving wedge formed by the rest of the team. It was quite exciting when performed properly but took a lot of practice. It was also the cause of many serious injuries and numerous deaths. The play was banned after two seasons; however, it was brought back in one form or another from time to time, because, well, it worked.

Mass plays were banned but continued. A near-constant style of play was to "push and pull" the ball carrier through the defensive line. The man with the ball would be propelled into the line like a human missile, either by being pushed from behind by one or more players, or pulled from in front by a teammate and slung into the opposition.

Pads were seen as "sissy stuff," not worthy of a real football player's time. Helmets were unknown, but nose guards, made of metal in some cases, were starting to become common and gave the teams of the era a strange appearance in photographs.

The game spread westward, even as horrified critics pointed to the death toll on the fields of play. Oberlin College was one of the first powers on the football field. The Oberlin Yeomen became a real force in the 1880s. Their talismanic coach in the early 1900s, John Heisman, gave his name to the trophy that is still awarded each year to the most outstanding college football player of the season. But that lay far in the future at this point. Heisman would go on to coach at half a dozen colleges, including Georgia Tech and Clemson.

At the University of Southern California, they started playing football in 1888. At that time they were called the "Methodists," in a nod to the origins of the university. The change of name to the "Trojans" came in 1912. In these early days it was hard to scrape up games, and matchups with high schools and local colleges were part of the schedule. In the Midwest, Notre Dame had started up, playing Michigan, an early adopter, in 1887, and losing, 8–0. Ohio State took to the field to play football for the first time in 1890.

In 1893, the University of Texas played four games of football, all against Texas opponents, and won them all.

Also in 1893, the Carlisle Indian Industrial School put its first football team on the field. Carlisle lies just west of Harrisburg in eastern Pennsylvania, about 30 miles due north of Gettysburg. In 1879, Richard Henry Pratt founded the school to help young "Indians" (Native Americans of many different tribal nations) assimilate into the American society that had eclipsed their traditional world and overwhelmed them. The teams from Carlisle would establish a presence in the young world of American football, playing against the big eastern colleges, as well as an assortment of others, and compiling impressive statistics. Jim Thorpe, the Native American Olympic athlete, played for Carlisle from 1907 to 1911. Perhaps their greatest feat came in his final year, when they defeated the heavily favored Harvard team, 18–15.

Almost unnoticed in all this activity, in Latrobe, Pennsylvania, the first game with professional players was recorded, with the Latrobe YMCA defeating the Jeannette Athletic Club, 12–0. Of course, during this time, "professional" meant working men getting the equivalent of "broken time" money, as their rugby and soccer counterparts in Northern England had sought. And, of course, by this time there was already a gathering scandal regarding sham amateurism in big-time college football. College teams frequently brought in mystery players, who would play a few games and then disappear after the Thanksgiving finale. They did not attend classes; indeed, some hardly appeared on campus, except to train and play football. Michigan's 1894 team had seven players who neither enrolled nor took any classes. The boosters and spectators didn't care, but the other colleges and newspapers had taken notice and didn't like what they were seeing.

Part of this was the increased danger to the actual scholar athletes, because many of the imported players were grown men, big and powerful. On occasion the presence of some giant could completely swing a crucial game, much to the rage of the other team's supporters.

There were also outbreaks of crowd violence, sometimes including the teams themselves. Some of these incidents from the 1890s were reminiscent of the worst soccer hooliganism from England in the 1970s or Argentina in the 1990s.

A late 1890s game between Vanderbilt and the University of Nashville degenerated into a riot when a player punched an opponent in full view of the crowd. More violent incidents followed. People spilled out of the crowd to fight one another on the field. The game was suspended. When it resumed, students appeared with knives and canes, and were barely restrained from killing one another. In Cleveland, the Oberlin team was attacked by a mob as they left the field; bricks and bottles rained down.

And then there were overly enthusiastic and rowdy celebrations following the big games. New York City was a frequent scene of disturbances and fighting in the streets after a Harvard–Yale encounter at the Polo Grounds. Boston and New Haven had recorded similar scenes, and drunken university men spending the night in jail after a big game became common enough to spark cartoons and vaudeville jokes.

These events continued bubbling in the press and public opinion as the nineteenth century gave way to the twentieth, but the hottest point of contention was the violence and deaths on the field. This eventually led to the great crisis of 1905–1909, in which the game came under threat of being banned altogether.

Still, football continued to progress in other ways. In 1896, the fore-runner of the Big Ten, the Western Conference, was formed, involving Michigan, Wisconsin, and the University of Chicago. In 1902, the first Rose Bowl was played. Mighty Michigan traveled to Pasadena and drubbed poor Stanford, 49–0, in a display that grew so dispiriting for Stanford that their team withdrew in the second half of the game. Michigan was crowned national champion with an 11–0 record. This game was a turnoff for the Rose Parade organizers for the next 13 years, and the Tournament of Roses had chariot and ostrich races and other novelty events instead. This continued until 1916, when Washington State University defeated Brown University in the first Rose Bowl, to use the name.

The 1905 season culminated with the Thanksgiving Day battle be-tween Yale and Harvard, this time in Boston, watched by 43,000. The national championship was once again on the line, and the leading newspapers reported on it as closely as they do the Super Bowl today. They also reported on incidents of brutality, broken noses, copious blood flows, and bad sportsmanship. Football came under intense criti-cism yet again.

After Thanksgiving, the *Chicago Tribune* reported that the season had seen 18 young men slain on the field and 159 seriously injured. Changes in the rules, for example, those made in 1898, had already been implemented to allow the officials to penalize players and teams that committed egregious fouls or attempted to hurt members of the opposition; however, the impact had been minimal. There were still mass plays, and everything came down to a battle at the line of scrim-mage.

Among the top critics of the game was the president of Harvard, Charles William Eliot, who held that office for 40 years and worked to turn the venerable institution into a modern university with concerns in research in a wide variety of fields. As one of his many contributions, Eliot oversaw the chartering of Radcliffe College as a college for wom-en in 1894.

In the 1870s, Eliot had spoken in favor of muscular Christianity and manliness, and he had seen the benefits of rigorous exercise. But since then, he had repeatedly come out against football, in particular, and team sports in general.

In November 1905, Eliot was quoted by the *New York Times* as saying that only tennis and rowing were "clean" enough. Part of his disdain came from the constant fouling and breaking of rules, unseen by officials, or at least unpunished, in the heaving rucks and masses on the football field. Eliot also spoke out against baseball, ice hockey, and basketball. But it was American football that really stoked his ire. He at one point said that "the weaker man is considered the legitimate prey of the stronger" and that "no sport is wholesome in which ungenerous or mean acts which easily escape detection contribute to victory."

Eliot was, in a sense, channeling the same line as his distant name-sake, Sir Thomas Elyot, back in the days of Queen Elizabeth I, with his declaration that football was "nothing but beastlie furie and extreme violence." And, indeed, there are many modern-day critics of all forms of football who agree with these gentlemen.

President Teddy Roosevelt, a Harvard graduate from 1880, was a serious football enthusiast who regarded the sport as a manly pursuit that would toughen up the young American elite. This reflected a concern among American opinion makers that the new patterns of wealth and prosperity would make the country soft, weakening it to the degree that the great powers of Europe would disregard U.S. interests and even seize on opportunities to reenter North America. Viewed objectively, these trepidations were far-fetched, but anxiety about national strength has never been an entirely rational matter.

To some extent these fears were a response to the quickening pace of the arms race between Germany, Britain, and France. In 1906, the British launched the HMS *Dreadnought*, the first truly modern battle-ship, a 20,000-ton steel behemoth carrying 12-inch guns and capable of 21 knots at full power. At a stroke, this ship consigned the rest of the world's naval forces to the scrapheap. In 1905, the German General Staff had come up with the Schlieffen Plan, a strategy designed to quickly break the French in the event of war and allow Germany to swiftly turn on the Russians, avoiding the dreaded "two-front war." Meanwhile, in another stark warning to the complacent, Japan had just made short work of Russia in a war that ended with a Japanese naval victory.

However, another issue presented itself along racial lines. The flood of immigrants—the great northward migration of millions of African Americans seeking respite from Jim Crow laws and white racist violence and, in the west, the presence of both Spanish speakers and Chinese laborers brought in to work on the railways—contributed to a set of concerns perhaps best summed up by Roosevelt's own comment in a letter to Walter Camp on March 11, 1895: "We are tending steadily in America, to produce in our leisure and sedentary classes a type of man not much above the Bengalee baboo." This dread of being overtaken by, contaminated by, or—horrors—interbred with racial and ethnic "inferiors" was a common terror among elites from Los Angeles to Berlin. Thus, toughening up the young men on the football field could be seen as a necessary antidote to luxury and comforts that had not existed 50 years earlier. Only it now appeared that there was an increasingly fine line between hardening the young on the anvil of football and actually killing them.

The president also had a personal interest in the matter. His oldest son, Ted, would be playing for Harvard's freshmen that year. A second son, Kermit, played for Groton school. Ted, at less than 150 pounds, was unlikely to make it onto the varsity squad, and the president admitted to relief that the boy would not be continuing to fight on the football field in subsequent seasons due to his lack of heft.

Hence, with public concern mounting and the season already marred with a riot at a game between Columbia and Wesleyan, as well as the ongoing deaths at school and college games, Roosevelt set off what turned into a four-year campaign to reform the rules.

Often described as the "crisis of 1905," it was actually more the crisis of 1905–1909. The meetings of 1905, which brought Walter Camp of Yale and his counterparts from Harvard and Princeton around the dining table in the White House with Roosevelt, eventually led to a genuine innovation—the forward pass, approved in January 1906. It was first used in September of that year, by one Bradbury Robinson of St. Louis University, who, although a halfback, threw a forward pass in a game against Carroll College played in Waukesha, Wisconsin.

But the innovation was firmly shackled to the floor: There was a penalty of 15 yards for an incomplete pass. And the ball could only be thrown forward from a point five yards to either side of the spot from where it was snapped. Few coaches were inclined to risk 15 yards experimenting with the darned thing. The game instead resumed its trench warfare at the line of scrimmage, only now everyone was at least somewhat concerned about preventing unnecessary injuries.

It was still possible to put most players in the backfield, to give them a running start for the impact with the defensive linemen in the hope of bowling them over like nine pins and sending the ball-carrying halfback or fullback downfield. And the ball had to be taken forward 10 yards in three downs, while tackling also came under stricter rules.

The 1906 and 1907 seasons were less lethal. Eleven football players were reported killed in action, and only 104 were seriously injured in 1906. And this was from all games—school, clubs, and college.

The serious critics of the game were not mollified. Attacks continued. At the end of each season the newspapers printed lists of the dead and badly injured, along with lots of commentary and letters both for and against the continuation of football.

Again a short glance at the background of the times is helpful: The pace of change was quickening. The Wright brothers had flown their airplane in 1903. Others followed. The age-old dream of human flight was becoming a reality. Albert Einstein had published the theory of special relativity in 1905, from which the fields of physics, astronomy, and even mathematics were still reeling. But other theories and discoveries were shaking these edifices too, from Planck's quantum theory to Rutherford's work on atoms. Ever-larger telescopes were beginning to shrink humanity's place in the cosmos by one order of magnitude after another. In Detroit, Henry Ford was working on his grand idea, an automobile for the common man, and his Model T would debut in 1908. In 1906, the National Collegiate Athletic Association was founded, in an effort to regulate the new world of collegiate sports, especially football.

But football was stuck in the mud. The new rules of 1905 had cut down scoring in the biggest games. The tactic of pulling and pushing the ball carrier had not been outlawed. At the big eastern colleges, coaches mostly used the forward pass as a decoy, trying to pull defensive players back from the line of scrimmage and then sending the ball carrier, with blockers, smashing into the line.

In 1909, casualties rose again, and with them came some high-profile fatalities. In October, Navy quarterback Edwin Wilson was left paralyzed by injuries in a game with Villanova. Two weeks later, in a game between Harvard and Army at West Point, Army's left tackle, Eugene Byrne, was killed. Two weeks after that, in Washington, DC, when Virginia came to play Georgetown, a freshman halfback named Archer Christian was taken off the field semiconscious. He died later that night.

In November, Georgetown abolished football indefinitely. This was just part of a campaign by the Jesuits to end football altogether (Georgetown is the oldest Catholic/Jesuit college in the United States).

The hue and the cry resumed. This time the flustered rules committee finally took action to end mass plays. Seven players had to line up on the line of scrimmage, and only four could be in the backfield. Offensive linemen were barred from using their hands, the beginning of the "holding" penalty, and kickers had to kick the ball forward at least 10 yards, ending the era of sneak kicks. The value of the field goal was cut again, too, this time to three points, a value it has held ever since. The momentum of the game also continued, and in 1912, the value of a touchdown rose to six points, which it, too, has held ever since.

Nonetheless, the maneuvers and brinksmanship concerning the forward pass are the key to the moment. The conservative faction, led by Walter Camp and Yale, did not want the forward pass, except behind the line of scrimmage. The violent old run-the-ball game was what they knew and had perfected. By contrast, Crawford Blagden of Harvard proposed rules to open up the forward pass, in effect changing the game forever. The committee blinked, voting no, although narrowly. A subcommittee was formed to come up with something. The result was widely seen as unworkable, with multiple players in motion in the backfield and the hope of multiple passes, also in the backfield. After considerable committee battling during the first four months of 1910—with Walter Camp noticeably absent—the forward pass was reinstated and mass play eliminated by requiring seven men on the line and restricting motion in the backfield to a single player.

Wedges were still formed, but they could not use a flying start. Players had to become far more skillful in their blocking, and ball carriers had to use their blockers more carefully. And then there was the forward pass, which would change the game at a fundamental level.

The conservatives made one last attempt to repeal the forward pass, winning a narrow vote on it in 1911. But the western and southern delegates threatened to quit the committee, split the sport, and come up with their own rules. That threat produced another vote, and the forward pass was back.

The violent old ground-grinding 1890s game was done.

However, the new rules produced something of a scoring drought, in part because of restrictions still in place on the forward pass, in particular that the receiver could not be more than 20 yards forward of the line of scrimmage.

Camp had become a convert. Despite his allegiance to the game he had virtually created in the 1880s, he came to recognize that change was inevitable. He recommended an end to the 20-yard limit. At the same time, the committee shortened the field of play from 120 to 100 yards to give fields "end zones," where forward passes could be caught for touchdowns. They also added the fourth down. The touchdown, as noted, was now the primary object of scoring, and the extra point became a single extra point. The shift from the rugby football point system was now complete, 30 years after the American game began to diverge from the rugby rules.

At this point the forward pass was primarily used to set up running plays or spread out the defenders in the area behind the line. The receiver usually came to a dead stop, turned, and waited for the pass.

Then came a revelation from Notre Dame, on November 1, 1913. In a game against Army, Notre Dame's quarterback, Gus Dorais, threw long passes to Knut Rockne, who caught them on the run, breaking free for long gains downfield. Notre Dame, the decided underdogs, won, 35-13, and Dorais connected on 13 of 17 passes thrown. The revolution had arrived.

While all this attention had been focused on the college game, which was still, at least superficially, amateur, openly professional football had been quietly percolating in its own cradle region. In a manner somewhat similar to the way that both the Rugby League and the Association Football League had risen up among the working class in Britain's industrial regions, so the heartland for professional American football lay in the steel-making region of the United States, from Pittsburgh to Cleveland.

Teams came from athletic clubs, and as competition grew fiercer with local rivalries, clubs sought to bring in bigger and better players. The first pro player was William "Pudge" Heffelfinger, who had been a star at Yale and was hired by the Allegheny Athletic Association in

November 1892, to play against their rivals at the Pittsburgh Athletic Club for $500.

Allegheny Athletic went on to become the first all-professional team by 1896, and professional football continued to grow in popularity in this key region, although the pro game was largely ignored by the rest of the nation.

An attempt by baseball owners to set up a national football league failed in 1902, unable to expand beyond Pennsylvania. Other attempts at leagues came and went.

In 1903, the Ohio League was formed, but this was never really a formal league with a regular structure, remaining an association of clubs primarily in Ohio. The Akron East Ends, Canton Bulldogs, Shelby Blues, Massilon Tigers, and Youngstown Patricians were typical clubs. The Canton Bulldogs became the most prominent team and eventually persuaded Jim Thorpe, the stellar Native American athlete, to play for them.

Thorpe's fame drew the crowds and helped build a market for the professional game in the industrial region of Ohio and Western Pennsylvania. A second successful center was the industrial belt of western New York, from Buffalo to Rochester and Syracuse.

This ultimately led to the formation of the American Professional Football Association (APFA) in August 1920. There were four teams to start, the Canton Bulldogs, Dayton Triangles, Cleveland Indians, and Akron Pros. Other teams soon joined; in September the league debuted with 10 teams in four states. In October, the Dayton Triangles beat Columbus, 14–0, in the first APFA game.

The APFA was the forerunner of the National Football League (NFL), the world's most profitable football league and guardian of America's most popular sport.

Of those first 10 clubs, only two have survived to play in today's NFL: the Chicago Cardinals, who are now the Arizona Cardinals, and the Decatur Staleys, who moved to Chicago in 1921 and became the Chicago Bears (Staley came from the Staley Starch Company).

The names of the early NFL clubs give the flavor of things: Columbus Panhandles, Muncie Flyers, Rochester Jeffersons, Kenosha Maroons, Cleveland Tigers, and, from 1921, Green Bay Packers, the only one of these early clubs that has not only retained its original name, but also plays in its original town. Indeed, Green Bay was a long way from most of the other clubs' towns, situated well north of Chicago on the shores of Lake Michigan. Their presence was a sign of quickening interest in pro football on the part of the American industrial working class.

The New York Football Giants (named thus to distinguish them from the baseball Giants) joined in 1925, and played at the Polo Grounds in northern Manhattan. Their first game was against All New Britain, in New Britain, Connecticut, on October 5.

Championships went to the teams with the best won–loss record, but it was a bit crazy, since some clubs played more games than others. The organization was a little ramshackle; the crowds were small compared to those for college football; and the professional game existed somewhere between the twilight zone of professional wrestling, carnival acts, and the world of serious sport. But for the players, coaches, and fans, it was a kind of golden age, a game still in innocent adolescence, adjusting and learning as it grew.

The arrival of Red Grange, college football's outstanding star of 1924, who joined the Chicago Bears in 1925, provided a huge boost in audience numbers. When the Bears came east to play New York, they drew 73,000 into the stadium. The Bears won, 19–7, and Grange noted that the competition in professional football was tougher, with better-trained teams than he had faced while in college. The money provided by that game also may have kept the Giants alive, as they had been struggling in the days leading up to it.

Part of this increased interest in football also had to do with the rise of radio broadcasting. College football became part of radio programming in the early 1920s, in New York beginning in 1922, relaying games to thousands of people who never would have made the trek to the Polo Grounds, Princeton, or Yale to see one of the big games.

Grange had soared to stardom in 1924, leading the University of Illinois to an upset victory over Michigan. He started things off by returning the kickoff 95 yards for a touchdown. The second time he received the ball he ran 56 yards for another touchdown. He ran back yet another kickoff for a score, notching five touchdowns in all, as Illinois triumphed, 39–14, over the powerhouse of the Midwest. That performance captured the imagination of the country, and when Grange switched to play for money, his presence gave the infant NFL a major boost.

To show that professional football was not immune to social pressures, the NFL banned the signing of African American players in 1927. This was the period when Jim Crow and segregation were rising to a peak. Following the nationwide success of the openly racist motion picture *The Birth of a Nation* in 1915, which glorifies the original Klan, the Ku Klux Klan (KKK) had been refounded in Georgia. The film set off a nationwide surge in Klan membership, as well as racist and nativist sentiment. The new KKK demonstrated against Roman Catholics and Jews, and promoted outright discrimination against blacks. The Klan membership was overwhelmingly drawn from the old, established white communities, Anglo-Saxon and Protestant Germans. Two-thirds of national Klan lecturers were Protestant ministers. The Klan was most prominent in the Midwest, particularly in Indiana and Michigan, and, of course, it was active throughout the South.

Along with racial discrimination came lynchings, and these increased in number and spread to a wider area during this period. U.S. involvement in World War I intensified tensions. In the South, black soldiers returning from the war were lynched while still in uniform. The Klan promoted itself as fervently patriotic, although anti-immigrant. It supported prohibition, and this was perhaps the strongest bond between Klan organizations everywhere, which harked back to a rural America now lost; yet, most Klansmen were urban middle-class whites who thought they could protect their jobs and neighborhoods from immigrants, especially "negroes" and Jews. This reborn Klan initiated the burning of crosses as a method of intimidation, something not associated with the original Klan of the 1860s.

The KKK declined during the late 1920s, but Jim Crow and open racism did not. While the immigrants from Europe could become simply "white" within a generation or two, the blacks migrating north to the cities could not. Herded into ghettoes, kept out of unions and better-paying work, African Americans were forced to live in a separate world, decidedly unequal in every way, and they were not welcome in the American sportscape. Black players could not be seen in the major baseball leagues, and few were seen anywhere else white spectators gathered. It would take 20 years and another even more cataclysmic world war for this wave of racist sentiment to begin to ebb.

The NFL, by the way, would open its doors to black players again in 1946. The last NFL club to integrate would be the Washington Redskins, in 1962, and then only under duress from John F. Kennedy's secretary of the interior, Stewart Udall. Udall threatened to boot the team from DC Stadium (later RFK Stadium), which was federal property, unless the owner, laundromat magnate George Preston Marshall, gave way.

In the world of college football, the power had shifted to the giant Midwestern institutions, Michigan, Ohio State, Notre Dame, and the University of Chicago. Newer powers were rising even farther west or south, in Oklahoma, Alabama, Nebraska, and the Carolinas. Stadiums were being built or rebuilt everywhere and were filled when completed.

Even while this growth was continuing, an old problem, and one that continues to haunt the college sports industry, even in the twenty-first century, came under scrutiny: the practice of sham amateurism, with payments and subsidies in various forms given to athletes to play football for one college or another.

This had been around since at least the late 1880s, and had been something of a scandal in the 1890s. In the 1920s, the Carnegie Foundation investigated college sports in a most thorough and professional way. Compiled from exhaustive interviews, the report came to 347 pages and was convincingly damning. College football, to a considerable degree, depended on payments of one kind or another, as well as a variety of tricks. These might have been as simple as putting a good football player, who didn't have the grades to be in college, through a year at a top prep school, where he could catch up, or as complicated as finding an alumnus who would hire a prospective college player and give him a job that he never had to show up for, along with other benefits. A few colleges were ruled "clean"; a subset, including Harvard and Yale, were found to refrain from paying the majority of their players, but they were seen paying one or two outstanding stars. Another band of colleges were seen assisting many members of their football squads, and then there were the numerous colleges that were quite open about it and freely provided athletic scholarships and allowed alumni to top things up as needed. Many of these were in the south, including Alabama, Florida, Texas, Virginia, and many more.

The Carnegie Report came out just as the stock market imploded in October 1929, and ultimately had little effect on the practices it described. Yet, it had made it all too clear that college football had grown too big to be controlled by the academy. In many states, "coach" was the most important man on campus, not the president of the college.

By the time World War II erupted, the landscape of American sports had been established. Most of the patterns that we see today had been laid down. In time, and with television boosting it, the professional game, marshaled by the NFL, would become the most popular form of sports entertainment. Other sports would rise and fall; boxing would decline from a peak of interest in the decades after World War II to near insignificance by 2000. Basketball would take its place, filling sport space on television with its long winter season. Ice hockey would grow, and baseball, still popular, would slowly lose ground to football.

Soccer? Rugby?

Rugby in the United States would fit into an odd niche, an alternative to the American game, played by both men and women, and popular at some colleges. In the early decades of the twentieth century, it was most popular in northern California; the University of California, Berkeley, has the longest-running and best record of any college program. The gold medal–winning teams sent by the United States to the 1920 and 1924 Olympics were mostly made up of Californians. It is of course important to note that those competitions lacked the Anglo-Saxon rugby powers, and both finals were against France. Still, this was an achievement, especially in 1924. But rugby was dropped by the International Olympic Committee, and any momentum the sport might have had in the United States was lost. For the next three decades, rugby was an oddity, a game pursued in some regions, played by some schools and colleges, and still strong in northern California.

In the 1960s, it began to grow, and although it was mostly a club sport, it slowly solidified a base of support. By 2014, there were 32,000 registered college players, and rugby programs were at a great many colleges throughout the nation, although scarce in the South. By the mid-1970s, there was enough going on to form the United States of America Rugby Football Union and raise a national team, the Eagles.

The Eagles have qualified for six of seven Rugby World Cups. They finished 10th in 1987 and 16th in 2011, and are currently ranked 18th in the world. Of the squad in 2014, eight play for clubs in England, three in France, one in Japan, two in Australia, and one in Scotland. Attendance for home matches has reached 20,000 in recent years.

Then there's women's rugby.

Up to this point, this book has been entirely about male players, but since the 1970s that has changed. In fact, before World War II, there were successful women's soccer club teams in England; however, the world has changed dramatically on this particular axis, and in some ways the United States has led the charge.

In the United States, women's rugby got going in the 1960s, grew as a college club sport in the 1970s, and strengthened enough in the 1980s that in 1987, the United States of America Rugby Football Union formed the Lady Eagles. From the start, the American women have been a power in their sport, just as the American soccer women have been in theirs. The Eagles won the first official Women's Rugby World Cup in 1991, and were second in the next two editions, 1994 and 1998. In 2014, the U.S. women were eliminated in the group stage, with losses to Ireland and New Zealand. They went on to play in the fifth-place playoff but again ran up against the powerful New Zealand side, which crushed them, 55–5.

Then there's the saga of soccer in the latter decades of the twentieth century in the United States. After being virtually eliminated in the 1930s, hanging on in immigrant communities and a few strongholds, the association game began to make a comeback in the 1960s. In the 1970s, the North American Soccer League briefly won headlines as it brought an aging Pele to play for the Cosmos at Giants Stadium in New Jersey's Meadowlands. Other stars, like Franz Beckenbauer and George Best, would also play for the league.

Youth soccer became a national institution, with many kids having their first experience on a team game chasing number-three soccer balls across fields in California, Long Island, an almost anywhere in the United States.

Next came something unexpected, one of the twentieth century's most interesting surprises: the development of women's soccer and the American women's national team into media favorites, packing major stadiums for the 1999 Women's World Cup, held in the United States. More on that topic in the next chapter.

But before we go there, we must review the development of the last of the seven codes of football—Canadian football.

Canada took to rugby football early on. The Foot Ball Association of Canada, established in 1873, was rugby-oriented. The Canadian Rugby

Football Union was founded in 1880. There were teams from Quebec and Ontario at that point.

As Walter Camp and company altered the game in the United States, the Canadians looked south and adopted some of the changes as well. For some years, the Canadians seem to have been playing a game that was closer to rugby than the American style, but it wasn't rugby, either. In about 1900, there came further movement toward the American game. John Thrift Burnside, football captain at the University of Toronto, had come up with a set of rules, and they began to spread. The Burnside Rules were as follows:

1. Twelve players on a team instead of the rugby 15.
2. There was no scrum by this point, and now only six men could be on the line of scrimmage when the ball was put in play.
3. Play would be initiated by the snap back. The center would heel the ball back to the quarterback.
4. Three downs were allowed to make 10 yards of ground.

The Burnside rules were not accepted by every organization for several years, but Canadian football eventually took on its own style, close to that played in the United States, certainly much more distant from rugby, but still unique.

The Canadians did not adopt the forward pass until 1929. Touchdowns increased from five to six points in 1956.

From the beginning, the Canadians saw no reason to limit the playing field to the narrow one used by the Americans. The Canadian field is 110 yards long and 65 yards wide.

There are a number of other differences, mainly due to American changes in their game that the Canadians did not adopt.

The premier trophy has been the Grey Cup, donated by Lord Earl Grey in 1909. It started as an amateur trophy, but after professionalism took over in the late 1940s, the competition was dominated by professional clubs. The Canadian Football League (CFL) emerged from a welter of other organizations in 1958, and has been the primary professional Canadian league ever since. The league has never been anywhere near as profitable as the NFL and has struggled on occasion. The teams in Montreal, Toronto, and Hamilton in the east have been successful enough, but it has proved hard to keep a team in Ottawa. The western teams, the British Columbia Lions, Edmonton Eskimos, Calgary Stampeders, Saskatchewan Roughriders, and Winnipeg Bluebombers, have been stable, and some have renovated their stadiums or plan to build new ones. Still, the CFL exists in the media glare created by the NFL, and with a season that runs from late June to early November, with 18 games, it faces several significant challenges.

Recent studies have shown that the CFL remains the second most followed professional league in Canada, behind the National Hockey League. But it must share the football space with the NFL. In recent years, the CFL games have also been broadcast in the United States, in a deal with ESPN Networks. Throughout the decades of its existence, the CFL has been something of a feeder league for the larger NFL, with players from U.S. colleges playing in the CFL and hoping for a chance to move south again if noticed by a NFL club. There is, of course, a large gap in salaries between the two leagues, since the NFL enjoys unparalleled television funding. While the larger field in Canadian football aids speedy players capable of covering that surface, many players have played in both leagues despite the different styles of play.

13

ON TO THE MODERN WORLD

World War I truly changed the world. Many things vanished, empires fell, and republics arose in their stead. Britain and France defeated Germany with the help of the United States and assistance from the peoples of the British Empire. For the "white" dominions of that empire, the landscape of 1919 was very different from that of 1914. They had paid in blood to save the mother country from defeat; their relationship with Westminster would never be the same. For India, the "Jewel in the Crown," the expectation that the British would move forward with independence for the subcontinent was not to be met, and consequently the movement for independence would accelerate.

France had reclaimed Alsace and Lorraine. Germany had also been sundered from East Prussia by a Polish corridor to Danzig. The Austro-Hungarian Empire had gone, leaving both Austria and Hungary diminished, very much so in Hungary's case.

Other changes were also in the air. New York City had just slipped by London to become the world's biggest city, with 7.75 million people. The automobile was evicting horse-drawn traffic from U.S. roads and would soon do the same in Western Europe. The first flight across the Atlantic Ocean came in June 1919, from Newfoundland to Ireland, by English aviators Alcock and Brown in a Vickers Vimy World War I bomber, with the bomb bays replaced by extra fuel tanks.

England, Scotland, Ireland, and Wales had left the Federation Internationale de Football Association (FIFA) after demanding that Germany and Austria be kicked out.

The Olympics was starting to encroach on FIFA's territory, too, and in the 1920 Olympic Games, there were 14 national teams competing. In 1924, there were 22, including the United States and Uruguay, which won the gold.

Two Frenchmen, Jules Rimet, president, and Henri Delaunay, secretary, were preparing the riposte. They had been working on a plan since about 1920 for an international competition, open to all players, including professionals, and every nation within the ranks of FIFA. This neatly eclipsed the Olympic competition, which remained devoted to amateur athletes.

Uruguay, riding high at that point, offered to build a large new stadium in Montevideo for the 1930 tournament and pick up the tab for competing teams, including travel from Europe. This offer set a precedent that many have since regretted, but it solved Jules Rimet's problems, since financing his tournament was looking difficult in the European frame.

However, the Europeans decided not to compete. Uruguay was three weeks away by ship, and neither club professionals nor amateur players could face being away for more than two months. Rimet had to scramble to get France, Belgium, Romania, and Yugoslavia to go. Uruguay and Argentina cut a swathe through the competition to reach the final—a replay of the 1928 Olympic final, which had been won by Uruguay. Uruguay triumphed again, coming back from being down 2–0 at halftime to win, 3–2.

Europe did its best to ignore this, but in South America it was huge news and stimulated interest in the game all the way to high valleys in the Andes and remote clearings in the rain forest.

The Italians, who had tried to host the 1930 tournament, immediately went into high lobbying gear for the 1934 event. Mussolini's Italy was strong on pageantry and big events in big stadia; a FIFA World Cup would be a perfect gala for Il Duce and the Fascist Party.

England would, of course, be absent, having left FIFA again. But the Americans would be there, although they had to beat Mexico in Turin to get into the finals, which they did, 4–2, with their characteristic vigor. Still, the Americans had to play Italy in the opening game of the tournament, and the Azzuri were in strong form, annihilating them, 7–1. Italy squeaked by Spain and then Austria to reach the final against Czechoslovakia, which had defeated Germany in the other semifinal.

The final, in Rome, was attended by Mussolini, who had never uttered a single word about football and sat silent next to Jules Rimet throughout the regular 90 minutes and 30 more of extra time, before Italy managed to eke out a 2–1 win and take the trophy. It is said that Il Duce cracked a smile and even applauded.

The 1938 World Cup was played in France, but with the gathering storm to the east having an effect. On the eve of the competition, the Austrians had to announce that due to the Anschluss, Austria had ceased to exist and was now simply part of greater Nazi Germany. Hence, there was no Austrian team, either.

Adolf Hitler, like Mussolini, was not known for any interest in soccer, but he was a fanatical force in favor of Aryan prowess in sport in general. By 1938, he had just about recovered from the horror of seeing the African American Jesse Owens triumph in the 1936 Berlin Olympics. The mighty German team, complete with the best players from Austria, was knocked out by Switzerland, a team no one thought had the slightest chance at such a feat.

Brazil had come to France for the tournament and beaten Poland, 6–5, in the first round, with four goals coming from the "black diamond" Leonidas, their superstar forward.

Czechoslovakia proved a sterner test, requiring a second game, after a 1–1 draw, to be eliminated. And then came Italy, who edged out the Brazilians, 2–1, to meet Hungary in the final, where they won, 4–2, and lifted their second World Cup.

Twelve years later, after the dislocations and world-changing effects of World War II, FIFA put on the fourth edition of its World Cup tournament. This time, with most European countries still rebuilding from the war, the competition was set for Brazil, which was building the enormous Maracaña stadium for the final.

This time England showed up but quickly went home, having been beaten, 1–0, by an American team of part-timers and then 1–0 by Spain. This was just the first of a series of shocks that were to come for England, as they slowly realized that the decades in which the England team had unquestionably been the best in the world were over. In fact, England had been too isolated for too long, absorbed in its own league and ignoring tactical and training changes that other nations had adopted.

Brazil also came close to going out but managed to get past Yugoslavia. In the final round, a group competition of four teams, Brazil crushed Sweden, 7–1, and then Spain, 6–1. Thus, the last game became a final, between Brazil and Uruguay, with a packed Maracana expecting a victory for the men in yellow and blue. According to *The Simplest Game* by Paul Gardner, the governor of Rio de Janeiro implored the Brazilian team, "Fifty million Brazilians await your victory!" But it was not to be. A tense game followed, with Brazil scoring first but Uruguay scoring twice, which shocked the Maracana into silence and gave Uruguay its second World Cup trophy.

By this point most commentators had to admit that FIFA was onto something. The tournaments always seemed to produce some sort of drama and garner widespread attention in the soccer playing parts of the world.

In England in 1950, the Football League was starting its 62nd year; twelve of the 22 clubs that played in the First Division back then were in the Premier League as of the 2014–2015 season. The other eight were playing one or two tiers down and have been in the Premier League at some point in the past 16 years. In this sense English football has powerful stability, although it has also been through some ups and downs since 1950.

Crowds at this time were enormous, there not being many other diversions available and affordable on a Saturday afternoon for working folk. Crowds declined steadily throughout the 1950s, 1960s, and onward, and began to climb again after the Premier League was established in the early 1990s.

Elsewhere in Europe, there were football leagues everywhere, and following the lead of South America, where, in 1948, the Campeonato Sudamericano de Campeones had begun, a current of thinking in European football was promoting the idea of a pan-Europe club cup competition.

This idea was taken up by the Union of European Football Associations (UEFA), and in 1955, the European Cup was born. Real Madrid dominated the early years, winning five times in a row, led by Alfredo Di Stefano, their Argentinian star.

England's champion, Chelsea, was denied the chance to compete by the league's secretary, Alan Hardaker, who was known to be xenophobic and anti-European. In fact, Chelsea could have ignored Hardaker, an entrenched North of Englander who didn't like London, let alone anywhere with non-English languages as the standard, but it was known that Hardaker did not forgive slights, and so Chelsea stayed out.

Manchester United, the next English champion, defied Hardaker and entered the competition; they reached the semifinals that year and the next; however, the disaster at Munich on February 6, 1958, when eight team members were killed when their aircraft, caught by slush on the runway, failed to take off, cast a pall over United and the competition.

The European Cup carried on, through Benfica's two years of victories, to three years ruled by the Milanese giants, AC Milan and Internazionale.

In 1967, Glasgow Celtic became the first British club to win the trophy. The following year, Manchester United, with the astonishing George Best in the side, finally won the cup, 10 years after Munich.

Three dynasties unfolded during the 1970s. First came the Dutch, after Feyenoord won it all in 1970. Ajax of Amsterdam, playing the "total football" that caught the world's imagination at that time, won it for the next three years. Then came Franz Beckenbauer, Gerd Müller, Uli Hoeneß, and company, and Bayern Munich held the trophy for three years.

Then the era of English dominance finally dawned, with Liverpool winning twice, followed by Nottingham Forest, who won it twice, before Liverpool returned for their third trophy, beating Real Madrid, 1–0, in Paris. Aston Villa followed them, defeating Bayern, and then it was Liverpool again, this time winning a penalty shootout against Roma in Rome.

The next year's final, 1985, ended in disaster at Heysel Stadium in Belgium, where 39 Juventus fans died in a massive pile up after fighting broke out with Liverpool fans on the other side of a chain-link fence. Juventus won the game, and Liverpool and the other English clubs were banned from the competition for five years. In the aftermath of the tragedy, many questions remained unanswered, but the primary ones were directed toward the Belgian authorities, who had allowed tickets for the area next to the Liverpool fans to be put on general sale and snapped up by brokers, who fed them to Juventus fans. There was already bad blood on the Liverpool side regarding Italian teams following the dreadful events in Rome the previous year, when, after Liverpool had defeated Roma, gangs of Italian "Ultras" attacked Liverpool fans in the streets. Italian police looked the other way, and some Liverpool fans took shelter in the British Embassy. That the Belgian authorities in charge of the Juventus–Liverpool match at Heysel Stadium allowed the casual sale of the tickets that would prove fatal for the Juventus fans is something that has never been satisfactorily explained.

The cup went to new teams in the following years, including Steaua Bucuresti of Romania, Porto of Portugal, and PSV Eindhoven of the Netherlands. In 1989, AC Milan won the cup after 20 years and retained it the following year, beating Barcelona, 1–0.

The last edition of the cup was won by Barcelona's "dream team," coached by Johan Cruyff, the star of Ajax and the Netherlands 20 years earlier.

The European Cup was eventually changed to the European Champions League, with a new format, enlarging the competition, increasing the number of games, and raising more television revenue. This format continues today, and Barcelona is the current champion for 2015–2016, their 5th European top trophy.

The World Cup had, in the meantime, become the world's premier sporting event. The win by England in 1966 had driven English interest in the game to new heights. Then came the great tournament of 1970, held in Mexico. Brazil was to win this time, defeating Italy, 4–1, in the final. That Brazilian team, with Gérson, Rivellino, Carlos Alberto, Jairzinho, and the incomparable Pelé, set a new benchmark for the sport, winning their qualifying games and all six games in the finals. Brazil was permanently awarded the Jules Rimet Trophy, having won it three times. A new one would be used for the next tournament. The 1970 World Cup also set world television on fire. It was the first to be broadcast in color, and audiences everywhere responded, setting new records for viewership.

And it was to that football challenge, seen so clearly in that final game, that the teams led by Cruyff and Beckenbauer would respond. No team was likely to have the abundance of talent sported by Brazil in 1970, but a top-level team could now play the "total" game and switch any player to any position for a moment or so.

Many tactical schemes have come and gone since then, and today's top clubs and national sides play a variety of them to match different opponents. They may turn out in a 4–4–1–1 in a domestic league game on a Saturday and then 3–2–3–2 for a European Champions League game midweek. Top squads have to be large, with the best quality they can afford at each position twice over. Injuries are inevitable, and sometimes a team will field its third-string goalkeeper, second-string fullbacks, and a virtually unknown youngster in midfield, simply because by February, they have to.

However, by the 1990s, the way of the game was set, except for in the United States. The United States, as the world's leading economy, with a wealthy and glamorous "sportscape," was overwhelmingly attractive in ways that China and India were not. This led to the 1994 World Cup being played Stateside, which ended with yet another final between Italy and Brazil. This time it went to a penalty shootout, in which Roberto Baggio, one of Italy's greatest stars, missed the goal entirely and handed the cup to Brazil. That Italy would not have made it to the final without Baggio's play was lost in what became a defining moment for a great career. As the saying goes, "Football is a cruel game." The competition aroused considerable interest in the United States, briefly putting soccer back into the American sportscape.

To be sure, the American Major League Soccer (MLS) professional league was begun with the intention of piggybacking on the 1994 World Cup to get the best start possible. Close to completing its second decade, the league, which, uniquely in world soccer, is a single entity that owns every team, has seen its share of struggles. In early seasons, teams played in enormous, almost-empty American football stadiums. Two franchises folded in 2002. But the league has grown from the 10 teams that competed in 1996 to 20 in 2015, of which 17 are in the United States and three in Canada. The closed membership and lack of relegation and promotion are also unique in the soccer world.

The association game is now widely played in the United States at the youth and collegiate levels. It lacks the drawing power of American football at the college level and the tradition and innumerable links between the great college powers, Alabama, Oklahoma, Texas, Michigan, Southern California, Oregon, Ohio State, Notre Dame, and so forth, as well as their localities and, indeed, state political and social hierarchies. One only has to be in or near Norman, Oklahoma, on the day of a home game to feel the buzz, and it's the same for all the grand colleges with powerhouse football teams. That doesn't happen and will never be the case for college soccer (or rugby) teams.

But in the modern era this is not necessary. The sport does not depend on the college game the way the National Football League (NFL) depends on college football to train and groom its recruits. And bit by bit, MLS has inched its way into the American sportscape. It pulls in crowds that are, on average, a bit bigger than National Basketball Association (NBA) and National Hockey League (NHL) crowds. It has television coverage, but of course it does not have the national impact and interest maintained by the NBA and, to a lesser extent, the NHL. What it does have, however, is the World Cup tournament, which ignites nationwide interest every four years. In addition, and as a complicating factor, there's the current widespread television coverage in the United States of English and European soccer. This helps the sport by offering some of the highest-quality soccer there is, but it also tends to diminish the MLS teams, which, in terms of their transfer values—a crude but effective measure of a team in this sport—are nowhere near competitive with clubs in the English Premier League, or clubs in the Spanish or German leagues, for that matter.

Still, the Seattle Sounders draw an average crowd of 37,000 to their home games, which would place them in the top ranks for attendance in the Bundesliga or Premier League. Fans know they are supporting their team, their city, and the sport in general, and it's always fun to watch the team and cheer, sing, and take part in organized support. It seems likely that the MLS experiment will continue and, in time, solidify soccer's place in the American world of sports. At some point, the league may have to contemplate the relegation and promotion issue, but for now it is set up in the way of other American professional sports, with hermetic league divisions, conferences, and playoffs for the MLS Cup.

As detailed in the previous chapter, this book is mostly about the doings of men, inevitably because for most of football's history, it was men who played it.

There may have been women who ventured out to join in the wild Celtic games of "hurling" or *la soule* in the days of the druids. I suspect that they would not have done so. It would have been out of keeping with their culture. Again, women may well have joined in village-on-village games in the Dark Ages. That, I think, is more likely. And in the era of townball, the ladies certainly did join in, although not in the hug, but on the outskirts, ready to hide the ball or throw it if it came their way.

Nevertheless, their contribution was a minor one. And when country footeballe made its way to the elite schools in England, it went for a single gender, because those schools were boys-only institutions for some time. Furthermore, when upper-class girls began to go to their own elite schools, they played field hockey, not football, which was seen as far too rough-and-tumble and masculine.

But the Football Association (from 1863 onward) and the Rugby Union (from 1871 onward) were busy shaping sports that were less overtly violent and more about skill and speed. Both sports retained an edge—once you've been on the receiving end of a good sliding tackle in a soccer game, you understand this—but with the demise of hacking and increasing rules governing everything from holding and pushing to protecting goalkeepers from being knocked to the ground, the association game not only improved, but it also became attractive to some women. There were association football games between women's teams in the 1890s. An abortive effort at a game in Edinburgh in 1881 led to a riot by the crowd that spilled onto the field and ended the match.

The leading light of the Scottish team, Helen Graham Matthews, moved to England after women's football was banned in Scotland as a consequence of the disturbance. There she worked with Nettie Honeyball, who had played for the English ladies in the Edinburgh game, and they started the "Lady Footballers." In 1894, Honeyball founded the British Ladies Football Club, with Lady Florence Dixie, the daughter of the Marquess of Queensberry, as president. This appears to have been something of a suffragette project, with the intention of showing the world that women were actually "real, live" women, and not the protected, sheltered, and dominated creatures of the Victorian social model. Honeyball is quoted in the February 6, 1895, installment of the *Daily Sketch* as saying,

I founded the association late last year, with the fixed resolve of proving to the world that women are not the "ornamental and use-less" creatures men have pictured. I must confess, my convictions on all matters where the sexes are so widely divided are all on the side of emancipation, and I look forward to the time when ladies may sit in Parliament and have a voice in the direction of affairs, especially those which concern them most.

Of course, this pretty much horrified the Football Association (FA), but then again the concept of women having the vote horrified men in general at that time.

The British Lady Footballers managed to play a number of games against local female football teams. As this continued, they began to attract crowds, on occasion larger crowds than came out for local men's teams.

At this point it is imperative that I introduce the saga of the Dick, Kerr's Ladies FC. Dick, Kerr & Co. was a locomotive manufacturer that moved into the manufacture of electric trams, rails, and steam turbines. The company had factories in Preston, Lancashire, and Kilmarnock, Scotland. Preston, of course, is by now a familiar name to readers of this book, for it was one of a line of northern Lancashire towns in the valley of the River Ribble that took up association football early on and produced clubs, most of which still flourish today—Burnley, Blackburn Rovers, Blackpool, and Preston North End, names with great histories. Burnley is currently in the Premier League, and Blackburn Rovers is the only club outside of the London–Manchester axis of giants that has won the Premier League trophy.

During World War I, Dick, Kerr shifted some production to munitions, as well as electric locomotives. They hired many women to enter factory work, since the men had enlisted and gone off to trench warfare in France. The women at Dick, Kerr started playing football. In 1917, they had informal matches with the apprentices in the factory yard during lunch breaks. After beating the men in an informal game, the women formed a team under the management of Alfred Frankland, who worked in the offices. From the start, with both a novelty angle and the ability to play good football, the ladies drew decent crowds. On Christmas Day 1917, 10,000 onlookers gathered at the Deepdale stadium to see them beat Arundel Coulthard Factory, 4–0. It was the depth of the war, men's football had been put on hold after 1915, and the ladies had the field to themselves. They took advantage of the circumstances, playing a number of charity matches against similar women's factory teams and raising money for wounded soldiers. Players received 10 shillings a game from the company to cover expenses, equivalent to about £20 in today's money in terms of rail fares and sandwich prices. And one other notable detail: The ladies always wore toques with black and white stripes (woolen bobble hats) to match their black-and-white-striped shirts.

The war ended, but Dick, Kerr's Ladies FC continued playing. In 1920, they played a team of French women from Paris, led by the redoubtable Alice Milliat. Milliat was actively promoting women's sports in France and would go on to spur the Women's Olympic Games of 1922, after the men of the International Association of Athletics Federations refused to include women's track and field events in the 1924 Olympics. This is considered the first recognized women's international game in soccer. There were actually four matches in the set with the French women. Dick, Kerr's won the first two; drew 1–1 in Manchester; and lost 2–1 at Stamford Bridge, Chelsea's ground, in London.

The success of the tour by the French ladies aroused considerable interest in the press, so much so that a match on Boxing Day (December 26) at Goodison Park—Everton's home stadium—drew a mammoth crowd of 53,000. That crowd and the continued interest and good turnouts for the women's teams inspired yet another of the long line of petty and spiteful acts by male-controlled organizations upset by women's progress toward equality with men. The FA ruminated and then banned women's football from any stadium of a club belonging to the association.

In his book *Belles of the Ball*, David J. Williamson explains that the FA Consultative Committee stated that the "game of football is quite unsuitable for females and should not be encouraged." The committee tried to bolster this primary concern with others about the money being raised in charity matches, which it felt was being excessively absorbed in expenses. This seems to have been invented of whole cloth, by the way. The ladies played more than 800 matches and raised more than £180,000 for charity, which in today's money would be approximately £10 million. But the old boys needed some excuse, and against a backdrop of events regarding women's right to vote—women older than 30 and with property gained the right to vote in Britain in 1918, Dutch women got the vote in 1919, and American women headed to the polls for the first time in 1920—their primary complaint was seemingly not only stale, but also feeble.

Because the FA was, at this point, still adamantly opposed to the professionalism that had taken over the top tiers of the game, we can understand where that last objection came from; however, there was another sneaking fear, because the Dick, Kerr's Ladies team was capable of bringing in larger crowds for their games, often held earlier in the day, before a men's league fixture.

The ban by the FA would remain in place for 50 years, not falling away until 1971, and it had the effect of eventually stifling the women's game in England.

But the women of Dick, Kerr's Ladies FC were not finished yet. They continued to play on non-FA grounds and fields. And in 1922, they set off on a tour of Canada and the United States.

No sooner had they arrived in Canada than the Dominion Football Association ordered that no association teams in Canada would be allowed to play the women from Preston, because the Dominion Football Association objected to the idea of women playing football.

The Dick, Kerr's Ladies went south, to New Jersey, and played nine games in the United States, starting with one in Paterson, New Jersey. They drew crowds of between 4,000 and 10,000 for the games, and they played against men's teams, too. They came away with a 3–3–3 record.

Ed Farnsworth writes in his May 8, 2013, *Philly Soccer Page* article "First Women's Soccer Team in Philly, 1922," that the Paterson goalkeeper, Peter Renzuli, later recalled, "I played against them in 1922. We were national champions and we had a hell of a time beating them."

The Dick, Kerr firm turned into English Electric in 1918, and they parted ways with Alf Frankland. The team became Preston Ladies FC, and as such, it carried on until 1965, by which time the interest had faded and there were not enough young women keen to play football.

For a taste of how silly male-controlled soccer organizations became when confronted with women wanting to play the game, let's look at Germany's example. Today, the German women's national team is a powerful force, exhibiting the characteristics that make the men's team world champions: strength, skill, and organization. Along with the U.S. Women's National Team and Brazil's team, they dominate the national team competitions.

In 1955, however, the German Football Association (DFB) refused to let women's clubs in, although the women were already organized and playing soccer. They actually stated that women were too frail and likely to hurt themselves playing football. They also commented that "display of the body violates etiquette and decency."

Fifteen years later, the DFB allowed the women to join, but they were only to play soccer in warm weather. They were not to wear boots or shoes with studs, and they were to use a number-four ball and only play for 70 minutes.

The hidebound conservatism of the DFB finally came apart after 1981. The association had accepted an invitation to take part in an unofficial women's world championship, but West Germany (as it was then) did not have a national team. So, instead, they sent the women's club champions, Bergisch Gladbach 09, who won the tournament. After that, a national team was finally organized.

It took a few years, but by 1989, an effective national women's team was up and running. The European Championship of that year saw the first women's match shown live on German television, the semifinal against Italy, which went to penalty kicks. The Germans won the final, 4–1, over favored Norway.

At the first Women's World Cup in 1991, the German women reached the semifinal but ran into Michelle Akers and the U.S. women's team, who were unstoppable at that point, and lost, 2–5. Since then, however, the German women have won two World Cups, in 2003 and 2007, and eight European Championships, including the last six in a row. And, yes, they play with studs on their shoes and the full-size number-five ball, as does every other women's club and national team.

I should mention the U.S. team at this point, for they were ranked number one in the world in 2014, and have established a powerful tradition in the sport.

The key moment in the development of women's athletics and sports in the United States came with passage of Title IX, a portion of the Education Amendments of 1972, promoted by Senator Birch Bayh. In 2002, it was renamed the Patsy Mink Equal Opportunity in Education Act to honor its coauthor and sponsor in the House of Representatives. It made it illegal to discriminate against anyone in any program that receives federal financial assistance. There was resistance because it was clear that this would mean major changes to the way student sports would be run at the high school and college levels. Senator Bayh kept the effort on to retain the full weight of the legislation, and in 1975, the final regulations were published by the Department of Health, Education, and Welfare. There were legal challenges and intense opposition in some quarters, but the 1988 Civil Rights Restoration Act extended the coverage of Title IX to all programs of any educational institution that receives federal assistance, whether direct or indirect.

The Title IX legislation set off a surge in female participation in sports. In a survey from 2006, the number of participants was estimated to have increased by 900 percent. And women's basketball, volleyball, soccer, cross country, and softball have become major high school and college sports. Some of the opponents of Title IX point to a marked decline in some male sports, for example, wrestling, which have been dropped by many institutions as another consequence.

Title IX was not solely responsible for this, however. Since the 1970s, generational change has brought different attitudes toward sports and other activities; the old concept that denied athletic activity to young women—which ultimately came down to the concerns that, in some men's eyes, women were unsuited for aggressive exercise and competitive sports, especially contact sports like soccer—has become ridiculous. Such male attitudes linger, but their time is over, and were they forced to watch a soccer match between the German national women's team and the American equivalent, they would find no refuge for their outdated opinions.

In 1986, U.S. soccer authorities called on Anson Dorrance, coach of women's soccer at the University of North Carolina, to build a U.S. national team. Five years later, that team won the first Women's World Cup, winning all six of its games with 25 goals for and five against. Along the way they beat the leading powers in the sport: Sweden, Norway, and Germany.

Since this breakout onto the world stage, the U.S. Women's National Team has won four gold medals at the Olympics and a second World Cup, with the finale in front of 90,000 at the Rose Bowl, where they overcame a stubborn Chinese women's team, 5–4, on penalty kicks.

Along the way a number of U.S. women have become legends in the game, including, Michelle Akers, Kristine Lilly, Mia Hamm, Julie Foudy, Joy Fawcett, Tiffany Milbrett, and Brandi Chastain, and more recently, Abby Wambach and Alex Morgan.

This short report on the women's game must return to England and pick up that story. In 1971, UEFA, the European organization of football associations, applied pressure to the England FA to rescind the 50-year-old ban on women playing football on the grounds of its member clubs, and the FA finally gave way. Two years prior, representatives of

44 clubs had met in London to form the Women's Football Association (WFA). In 1971, they held a knockout cup competition, the Mitre Trophy, which turned into the FA Women's Cup. The WFA ran into some problems, primarily due to a lack of resources in the mid-1980s. In 1993, English women's football was transferred to the FA itself, and so 70 years after the initial ban, the FA found itself managing the women's game in England. And naturally, the English women were now well behind the curve established by the Germans, Americans, and the remarkable Norwegians and Swedes. (Norway is by far the most athletic small country in the world, and both Norwegian men and women have excelled at soccer.)

Once England got the ball rolling, as it were, they began to improve and have an impact on World Cups and the European Championships.

The first international match was against Scotland in 1972, under the WFA. Since 1993, England has reached the World Cup Finals on three occasions, in 1995, 2007, and 2011, and gone out each time at the quarterfinal stage. England reached the final of the UEFA European women's championship in 1984 and 2009.

By 2014, English women's football was nine tiers deep in terms of leagues. At the top was the FA Women's Super League (WSL), split into two divisions, with eight clubs in the top division and 10 in the second. This replaced the earlier setup of a women's Premier League at the top; that league is now the third tier and still plays a winter season. There is promotion and relegation between the two divisions of the WSL, but not yet with the other tiers in the system. In its first four seasons, the WSL Division One has seen Arsenal and Liverpool win twice each, Birmingham City win second twice and third once, Chelsea take second once, and Everton place third twice. Anyone familiar with English football will recognize these names, and I'd like note that it was at Everton's Goodison Park stadium, in 1921, that the Dick, Kerr's Ladies drew 53,000 spectators. Thus, a century after the women took up the game in a serious way, and despite 50 years of obstructionism, the women's game is alive and growing once more in English football.

The story is the same in rugby football. The seventh Women's Rugby World Cup was played in France in August 2014. The tournament featured 12 national teams, and most of the powers in men's global rugby were present for this competition—Australia, New Zealand,

South Africa, France, Ireland, Wales, and England. Also present were the United States, Canada, and Kazakhstan.

England arrived with a strong team and were the favorites to win the title. In the group stage, England and Canada cruised through their group until they met one another for a 13–13 draw. For England, the names Sarah Hunter and Emily Scarratt were already well known, but the two women now took their opportunity to shine. In the knockout stages, England romped against the Irish women in the semifinals. Canada edged France, 18–16, and set up a rematch with the English that went England's way, 21–9, with Emily Scarratt having an outstanding game. Canadian wing Magali Harvey was voted the IRB's (International Rugby Board) Women's Player of the Year and scored a memorable try against France.

At this juncture I should bring the story of rugby in general up to modern times. We last checked in on this code of football in about 1900, by which time the great split with rugby league had occurred and the outward spread of the game was in full flight.

There are a few strands of a complex tale that are worth surveying here. First, the English Rugby Union's commitment to amateurism had a decided effect on English rugby and the world game. The IRB only gave in to professionalism in 1995, and then only after the Southern Hemisphere powers, New Zealand, Australia, and South Africa, had begun allowing their players to be paid. A major part of this was a long resistance to the loss of purity in the sport, which also had social class implications. English rugby, centered on the stadium at Twickenham, became *the* upper-middle-class team sport. Throughout the twentieth century, the IRB and the English Union resisted change, for instance, not allowing substitutions for injuries until 1968. When rugby finally allowed professionalism, it unleashed a burst of growth everywhere. In the Southern Hemisphere, the Super 12 (later Super 15) club competition began, along with the Tri-Nations competition between New Zealand, South Africa, and Australia. Top players began to earn good money through the growth in the game that went with higher quality and increased television coverage. Stadiums became all-seaters with corporate luxury boxes, in the manner of other professional sports.

In Europe, clubs from the countries that compete in the Six Nations Championship—France, Scotland, Ireland, England, Wales, and Italy—played for the Heineken Cup from 1995 to 2013. That competition was replaced by the European Rugby Champions Cup, modeled on soccer's European Champions League, in 2014. The six nations provide 24 club teams, which also echoes the Super 15 in the Southern Hemisphere. The French club Toulouse won the Heineken trophy a record four times, signifying the strength in support for rugby in Southern France.

Another impetus to break the amateur hold on rugby was the beginning of the Rugby World Cup in 1987. Held jointly by New Zealand and Australia, it was well received, especially in the Southern Hemisphere. The eighth edition will be held in England in 2015, bringing the game home to where it began. Australia, New Zealand, and South Africa have won the tournament twice, England once. In 2015, 20 teams will compete.

The Rugby World Cup has become a television success, standing behind the FIFA World Cup, the Olympics, and the Tour de France in terms of overall tournament audience. The 2007 competition drew a cumulative world audience of 4 billion.

The challenges ahead for global rugby include growing the game in North America, where it lives between American and Canadian football and soccer, and encouraging growth in China and India. In China, the success of their women's Rugby 7 team is sparking greater interest. Rugby union is now widely played, but in terms of global competitions, it remains dominated by the core group of nations that were originally British colonies in the Southern Hemisphere or the six nations in Europe that play at a high standard.

Then there's rugby league.

Following the breakaway by the clubs in Northern England in 1895, the professional rugby game evolved away from the rugby union game in a series of small, incremental steps. Along the way, Australia and New Zealand developed rugby league clubs as well. And there it sat for much of the next 80 or so years.

Papua New Guinea became a hot spot for rugby league, but Wales did not. Fiji and Samoa eventually became sources for rugby league players, too. Rugby league became the leading type of football in New South Wales and Queensland, but the rest of Australia was Australian rules football territory. In Britain, the league game ruled a band of towns throughout the north, from Lancashire to Yorkshire, interspersed among the soccer strongholds. Wigan, St. Helens, Warrington, Leeds,

Bradford, Hull, and Castleford were the names associated with rugby league. But the game never managed to break out of these areas and never really succeeded in London or the south, although in 1932, Wigan played Leeds under floodlights in London.

In the 1930s, when the Rugby Union ejected France, again concerning the principle of amateurism versus professionalism, rugby league moved in quickly to put on a demonstration match. This took place in December 1933, at the Stade Pershing in Paris. Four months later, the French Rugby League was formed. Many French players switched to the league game, and rugby league became the game of choice in South West France; however, when the Germans defeated France in 1940 and occupied the northern part of the country, the Vichy government in the southern half banned rugby league and forced players and clubs to switch to rugby union. The club assets were seized by the state and never returned.

After the war, the state continued to favor union over league, and the French Rugby League had to call itself Jeu a Treize, the game of 13, instead.

Another problem was that the rules in different parts of the world had further evolved and were drifting apart. In 1948, the Rugby League International Federation was formed at the request of the French to bring things back to a common ground. That led to a World Cup, staged for the first time in 1954. But that competition has been intermittent and never quite taken hold in the world of rugby league, which still honors the "ashes" series between nations, based on the model in international cricket. In the 1960s, the league game moved onto television in Britain and Australia. More rule changes followed, for instance, limiting the number of tackles per possession, something similar to the "downs" in American football. It was set at six in 1971 and has remained at that level.

Throughout times of scandal and more expansion to found clubs in Western Australia, Queensland, and New Zealand, rugby league grew steadily. In 1997, two organizations merged to form the National Rugby League. That year also saw the first team from Aussie rules heartland, Melbourne Storm, enter the competition, and a few other clubs merged or folded.

The great change in rugby union, to allow professionalism, produced new pressures, as union clubs could offer big salaries to league players to switch codes. Some did, but after an initial flurry, things stabilized, and the two codes of rugby continue to operate, and even flourish, side by side. Rugby league has had successful world cups in recent times, in 2008 and in 2013. The last one was held in Europe, and the final was played at Old Trafford in front of 74,468 spectators. In 2014, the Four Nations competition was held in Australia and New Zealand, the fourth iteration of this competition. Australia, New Zealand, England, and Samoa were the contestants, and New Zealand edged out Australia, 22–18, in the final, after beating England, 16–14, to get there. This win confirmed New Zealand's current dominance of world rugby, with the All Blacks (uniform color and team name) being world champions in rugby union; the league team the Kiwis has established itself as the world's best—at least for now.

In November 2014, the All Blacks played the U.S. national team, the Eagles, in Chicago, winning 74–6, in a friendly matchup in front of 61,500 curious onlookers and dedicated rugby fans. It should be noted that of the Eagles' squad of 23, only 12 were professional players, and all of them play outside the United States.

And what about the United States? Rugby league has had a difficult history Stateside. Several efforts have been made to start up leagues, and California and the northeast are both rugby-friendly areas. But moving from an amateur club and league arrangement to a professional sport has proved difficult. Two rival organizations ran the sport as of 2014, the American National Rugby League (ANRL), with six teams spread between Philadelphia and Connecticut, and USA Rugby League, formed by seven other teams that left the ANRL in 2011. USA Rugby League has six clubs, spread between Washington, DC, and Boston. This organization is also making an effort to set up teams much farther afield, including Dallas and Los Angeles. Time will tell if such an enterprise can succeed in a country with such a complex and busy sportscape, dominated by American football.

As for that game, which we left percolating in the post–World War II era, the last three decades of the twentieth century were a time of astonishing growth, as the NFL soared to a preeminent position in the world of American sports and television. The formerly despised professional game has, by far, become the dominant force in the sport, although the college game continues to be a vital component. Indeed, there are states that do not have NFL teams, for instance. Alabama,

Oklahoma, and Nebraska, where mighty college teams rule the roost. Harvard and Yale still play, of course, but their days of being important in this game are long gone.

The NFL has gone from strength to strength, even while a slow-mounting crisis has begun to develop that may turn into a critical danger for the entire sport.

In a brief review like this, one cannot cover all the detail of what has occurred in American football since 1950, which would require a book of its own. There are some singular moments, however, that should be mentioned.

First, "The Game"—December 28, 1958. The 26th NFL championship game, which was played between the New York Giants and Baltimore Colts at Yankee Stadium in New York, was broadcast nationwide. Baltimore won a thrilling battle, 23–17, and set off the rise of the NFL as a national force. Before this game, NFL championships had been increasing in popularity but had yet to set off a national burst of interest. This game broke out of the previous audience for pro football.

Second, Super Bowl III—January 1969. Joe Namath led the New York Jets to an upset victory over the Baltimore Colts. The only championship won by the Jets franchise, this game scored low television ratings, but by then the term *Super Bowl* had been taken up by the media to replace the clunky "AFL–NFL Championship Game."

The American Football League (AFL), later the American Conference, was an upstart league begun in 1960. The first two matchups with the NFL champions, Vince Lombardi's Green Bay Packers, had shown unquestionable dominance by the NFL. The AFL was more of a passing offense league, and the NFL had more of a running game and was a solid-hitting league. Neither description was really true, but the NFL certainly had the stronger teams at this point. The Super Bowl of 1969 saw a strong Colts team arrive as heavy favorites. The Jets were not highly regarded, and Namath had actually thrown more interceptions than receptions in the season to that point. Yet, New York stymied the mighty Colts offense and took a 16–0 lead into the final quarter of the game. Baltimore could not score more than a single touchdown, and Namath ran off the field waving his index finger high, something that has since become a global symbol in sports.

While the game had relatively low television ratings, it sparked enormous postgame comment in the newspapers and on television and radio. From then onward, the Super Bowl was to rise to become a new unofficial "holiday"—albeit one that takes place on a Sunday. It also showed that the AFL teams had to be taken seriously, and they went on to win 11 of the first 15 Super Bowls.

Third, Super Bowl XVI—1982. The San Francisco 49ers beat the Cincinnati Bengals, 26–21, but it was the pregame singing of the national anthem by Diana Ross, the Motown Records superstar, that marked this moment. The Super Bowl had already become the leading television sports event in the United States, but this marked the beginning of the involvement of celebrities and pop music legends in the show. This has evolved into the mammoth halftime shows, featuring stars old and new in elaborate stagings of hit songs.

Fourth, Super Bowl XVII—1984. The Washington Redskins were swept aside by the Los Angeles Raiders, 38–9, but what everyone remembered afterward was the shockingly powerful television ad "1984," created by Ridley Scott (*Alien, Bladerunner*) for Apple computer's Macintosh debut. The ad was broadcast just once, but its iconic imagery of a young woman carrying a hammer and running through a dystopian future city, into a hall where a large Big Brother television face droned on to an audience of cyber-serfs, and then hurling the hammer into the screen, gave Macintosh computers undoubted cool props in the struggle with the IBM/Microsoft personal computer world. This ushered in the era of high-concept television ads using the Super Bowl's unmatched reach to launch products and create consumer interest. The "1984" ad was later described as the "greatest commercial of all time" by *TV Guide*. Super Bowl ads have become another important aspect of the event, with reviews of the ads sharing the limelight with accounts of the games.

The NFL has seen several dynasties rise and fall, for example, the Pittsburgh Steelers of the 1970s, the Dallas Cowboys of the 1990s, and the New England Patriots of the early 2000s. The game itself has grown more sophisticated and subtle, while also becoming faster and more dominated by the forward pass and the great, gifted quarterback. Names like Peyton Manning, Brett Favre, Troy Aikman, and John Elway have become etched into the American national consciousness in a way that few athletes from other sports can ever manage.

With an average attendance figure of 67,509, the NFL is far and away the world's leading professional football league. The total attendance of 17,282,225 for the season is also a world leader in football, with the English Premier League at 13,929,810 and the German Bundesliga at 13,310,000, well behind. For comparison sake, the National Rugby League in Australia averages 17,367 a game and a total attendance of just 3,490,776. The UEFA Champions League, soccer's top club tournament, drew 5,609,098 in 2012–2013, for an average of 44,873 a game.

The college football game also continues to be a strong, vibrant part of American culture. As noted, college teams are strongest in states without NFL teams, but many college teams draw enormous crowds to their home games. These include Michigan, Notre Dame, Ohio State, the University of Southern California, Florida, Florida State, Alabama, Auburn, Oklahoma, and the University of Texas.

However, with all this going for it, the American game is facing another great crisis, and one that may not have a reasonable resolution: head injuries and CTE, chronic traumatic encephalopathy. Thousands of former players have displayed conditions of dementia, depression, and general mental confusion as they've grown older. Suicides have attracted national headlines and attention.

The NFL spent 10 years or more trying to ignore the problem, which seems to be caused by the repetitive hits players take to the head, added to concussions. Many of the worst impacts are helmet to helmet, and since helmets have improved so much, players are more inclined to risk leading with their heads and absorbing that force. But by 2013, the issue was impossible to ignore, and in August 2013, the NFL agreed to a $765 million settlement with 4,500 former players. Some former players challenged that settlement, and the court gave its final approval of the deal in early 2015, with appeals possible. Examination of the settlement reveals many aspects that are less than generous toward the former players, with restrictions that seem, at the least, mean-spirited.

However the lawsuits in the NFL conclude, and many estimate that they will continue and increase as more players are diagnosed with CTE, it is the ripple effect that is more threatening to the sport. California has passed a law barring middle school and high school teams from full contact in practice for more than three hours a week during the season, with no contact during the off-season. This may be but the first falling leaf of autumn for the game. New York imposed new protocols on high school coaches (in all sports) with regard to concussions incurred in games or practices. But this is a slippery slope, not only because school districts now have to ensure that coaches and trainers evaluate any head injury and make the correct decisions, but also because the issue is now fully described and understood, so there is increased legal liability. And this increased liability leads a lit fuse to the insurance industry. At some point, if there are many claims in this area, health insurers and liability insurers will refuse coverage. Without liability coverage, school districts, youth clubs, and even colleges would have to abandon the sport. If something like this happens, the NFL would also be doomed, because the supply of new athletes will cease.

With a sport so deeply entwined with American nationhood, this prospect is culturally appalling to many. But Pop Warner football, the leading youth league organization, saw a 9.5-percent drop in participation between 2010 and 2012. Since Pop Warner youth football is estimated to be where between 60 and 70 percent of NFL players begin to play, this is a chilling development for the sport and the league.

The sport is already responding with efforts to take head-to-head impacts out of the game. The Seattle Seahawks, the 2014 Super Bowl champions, have been training their players to make tackles in the rugby style, wrapping their arms around the target, putting their own heads on the side away from the ground, and avoiding helmet-to-helmet impact. A proposal being looked at in the youth football world would pull linemen to their feet and have them start each play standing up, reducing the number of head-to-head impacts. Another suggestion involves going back to a time before hard helmets were introduced (1939). Without helmets to give a false sense of protection, players would change their approach to tackling and blocking, potentially making safer choices. Others recoil, as the iconic rows of helmets, the bright-colored plastic bearing the famous logos of great teams, are now woven into the game. To some, this would be tantamount to cultural sacrilege.

On a brighter note, the NFL, which has tried to expand into Europe by running a now-defunct European Football League, is said to be once again seriously thinking about international expansion, this time with an actual NFL franchise. London and Mexico City are at the top of the list of possible locations. Occasional exhibition games in London have sold out Wembley Stadium, and it's quite possible that a London NFL franchise might sell out every home game, especially if it's a successful team; however, there is also the thought that having just one club in Europe would not work and that there would need to be a revived franchise in Germany as well. During the period when the NFL supported a European league, the Rhine franchise had the best continuing support, in large part because of the proximity of U.S. military bases.

It is important to consider that the American game has been widely exported via television and is played at an amateur level in several European countries, but it remains a niche sport, far less significant than rugby or soccer. The problem with establishing footholds for the NFL on non-American soil is clearly the lack of local participation. The structures that produce players for the NFL do not exist in Britain or Germany, or really anywhere else, although there are a handful of German and British players in the NFL's ranks. For now we can only wait and see.

The other giant in the world of football, FIFA, also has a crisis approaching, but unlike the existential threat faced by the NFL, the problem for FIFA is entirely of its own creation. At root it comes from the structure of the organization, which now has 209 members. Like the United Nations General Assembly, FIFA gives one vote to each member, equating Trinidad and Tobago with Italy or Malta with Brazil. This matters when votes are taken on elected officers and committee members. As many critics of FIFA contend, this has led to institutionalized corruption throughout the years.

The selection of Russia for the 2018 World Cup, followed by Qatar for the 2022 event brought FIFA's selection process for the World Cup under serious scrutiny by other important actors. Some of whom, like the FBI in the USA, were already investigating FIFA officials over an alleged $10 Million in bribes paid to secure the World Cup for South Africa in 2010. The FBI had already swooped on Chuck Blazer, an American and a senior FIFA official, who had failed to pay taxes for 18 years despite having millions pass through his bank account. Blazer agreed to cooperate in 2011 and that lit a fuse that exploded in May 2015. That blast saw the arrest of 7 FIFA officials in Zurich, Switzerland, followed by indictments of another seven. Sepp Blatter the much criticized and allegedly corrupted president of FIFA, who had boasted of being like "a mountain goat that never makes a fatal misstep" then resigned, five days after being re-elected on the back of his massive support from African and Asian countries.

The World Cups in Russia and Qatar are under investigation at the time of writing by Swiss authorities. It is quite possible that one or both will be cancelled and the competitions moved to other countries. Both the Russian and Qatari World Cup bids were allegedly accompanied by bribes, in the Qatari case a sum of $5 Million has been mentioned. Indeed, some observers noted that accepting a bid for the World Cup from Qatar, a nation that has a minimal presence in the sport, no stadiums, and a culture inimical to drinking beer was the moment when FIFA let all pretenses fall away to reveal the corruption in the process.

While Russia plays Association Football, has a league, stadiums and a culture that might support a World Cup, Qatar is an arid peninsula jutting into the Persian Gulf, that, at the time of the bidding, had no stadiums and very little in the way of a football-playing culture. Under its strict Islamic culture, a single bar in a very expensive hotel used by foreigners is allowed to dispense alcoholic beverages.

The World Cup is a summer event, played after the major European league seasons are over. But in Qatar, temperatures in July can reach 105°F/40°C on a daily basis. The climate is described as a subtropical dry, hot desert. A hot wind, called the Shamal, blows from March through August. Asking some of the world's most highly paid athletes, to play up to seven games in such conditions is one thing, requiring the services of those athletes from the giant clubs that they play for— Barcelona, Chelsea, Real Madrid, Bayern Munich, Manchester United, Juventus, Milan AC, etc.—is another.

In the summer of 2015, all of this seemed in flux. The Qatar World Cup, and the Russian one, too, may be played somewhere else, Putting the hundreds of deaths of immigrant construction workers in Qatar into a peculiar kind of historical ignominy. Relations with Russia, already poor in 2015, could be guaranteed to sink into something considerably worse if the 2018 competition was pulled away. But, if massive bribery is revealed by the investigation, such a result would be inevitable.

This all raises the question of how to reform FIFA. The "one nation one vote" rule will not be surrendered willingly by the small countries that have profited from it. But without some major change in that rule, the situation is unlikely to change significantly. Suggestions have been mooted that voting "weight" should be given to the number of players registered to play in amateur and professional leagues in a country, as well as to the size and crowd totals of the professional leagues. Such weighting would put Germany, England, Spain, Italy and France in control, with Brazil, Argentina, Mexico and other latin american nations in contention. The USA would surely be there, too, courtesy of its extensive youth soccer programs as well as Major League Soccer. However, a FIFA reorganized on those line is likely to be resisted to the end by the rest of the organization's 209 members.

The future, therefore is unclear. An unreformed FIFA could simply lead to the Europeans, South Americans and North Americans walking out and starting their own World Cup competition. The Australians and New Zealanders would likely join them. Japan and Korea, both with strong leagues and many amateur players would feel the pressure to do so, too. The remains of FIFA would sink into insignificance. It may take such a threat to bring about any reform at all. One crucial factor will be the attitude of the corporate sponsors. From soft drinks giants to banks to automobiles to sports clothing, these companies will want a cleaned up competition, failing to get it, they are likely to remove themselves and their money.

Ultimately, some major change is likely following the stunning events of May 2015, and with luck and diplomacy, perhaps FIFA can be reformed satisfactorily and the corrupt practices of the past forty years or so done away with. However, at the time of writing, there is no clear solution visible and a considerable amount of legal action, further arrests, trials and sentencing lies ahead. We will just have to see how it all develops.

However this plays out, the crisis has shaken confidence in FIFA and exposed massive corruption within the organization. If it goes spectacularly badly, it could even lead to some kind of breakaway movement by the Europeans, urged by the leading clubs, who, after all, are the ones who pay the players and provide the backbone for the global game. It may ultimately be for the good of the game, if it leads to a serious reform of the organization, most probably including some "weighting" of voting power determined by such things as size of nation, financial status of professional leagues, ranking of national team, and so on.

Again, this is an area with no clear solution visible in 2015, and we will just have to see how it develops.

☼ ☼ ☼

And so we come to the end of this story. From the colorful hand balls of ancient Egypt, to the Greek games of *episkyros* and *pheninda*, and on to the Romans, with their formidable empire and legions who loved to play *harpastum*, football has made its way through the ages, kicked and carried, bruised and battered, muddy and triumphant, and rolled right up to us. The druids had a role to play in it, as did the Celtic peoples of Britannia and Brittany. The Anglo-Saxons stuck a foot in, as well as the Danes and Normans. For a long time, perhaps 400 years, it persisted as a simple, cheerfully violent game in the English and Irish countryside. It went off to school, where it was eventually refined and codified. Then it was exported and, in one shape or another, dispersed throughout the world to grow into the seven codes we know today, grouped in four families: First, the association "soccer" game, with its indoor varieties; second, the rugby and rugby league pairing; third, Australian rules and Gaelic, long-kicking and running games; and fourth, the North American varieties, American and Canadian, with lines of scrimmage, forward passes, helmets, and blocking—all different but stemming from the same root.

What wonder would light up in the eyes of Julius Caesar, a keen *harpastum* player, were he to get a seat at the 50-yard line for Michigan's next game with Ohio State? Or for Oliver Cromwell, country footeballe player, to enter Manchester United's "theatre of dreams" at Old Trafford for a game against rival Liverpool? While they would have to adjust to vast elements of modernity—plastics, electric lights, and modern clothing—I imagine that with Caesar's keen appreciation of military-style balance, the cut and thrust of the game would soon come to the fore in his thinking while watching it unfold. Cromwell, too, would likely get the more fluid strategies set before his eyes and probably enjoy the crunch as young men clash in the air over a corner kick. Perhaps even the Sky Jaguar King of the Mayans or the Emperor Wudi of the Han would get it and come to their feet with a roar of approval at a great goal, try, or touchdown pass. That's the secret of these games, the fire that football lights for all of us.

BIBLIOGRAPHY

Adam (of Eynsham). *Life of St. Hugh of Lincoln*. Oxford, UK: Clarendon, 1985.

Anglicus, Galfridus (Geoffrey the Grammarian). *Promptorium parvulorum* (*Storehouse for Children*). 1440; reprint, Boston: Adamant Media, 2001.

Armitage, Jill. *Derby: A History*. Stroud, UK: Amberley, 2014.

Ash, Geoffrey. *From Caesar to Arthur*. London: Collins, 1960.

"Ashbourne Royal Shrovetide Football." *Ashbourne-town.com*, 2015.http://www.ashbourne-town.com/events/football.htm(accessed February 10, 2015).

Bell's Life in London, and Sporting Chronicle. Microfilm. London. W. I. Clement Green Library, Media-Microtext Collection (MFILM N.S. 3623).

Bernstein, Mark. *Football: The Ivy League Origins of an American Obsession*. Philadelphia: University of Pennsylvania Press, 2001.

Bindoff, S. T. *Tudor England*. Harmondsworth, Middlesex, UK: Pelican Books, 1950.

Boxer, C. R. *The Dutch Seaborne Empire*. New York: Knopf, 1965.

Brands, H. W. *The Reckless Decade: America in the 1890s*. Chicago: University of Chicago Press, 1995.

———, ed. *The Selected Letters of Theodore Roosevelt*. Lanham, MD: Rowman & Littlefield, 2006.

Brennan, Patrick. "The British Ladies Football Club." *Donmouth.co.uk*, January, 22, 2015. http://donmouth.co.uk/womens_football/blfc.html (accessed February 10, 2015).

Brinker, Helmut. "The Cradle of Football." *FIFA.com*, October 19, 2004. http://www.fifa.com/newscentre/news/newsid=94490/ (accessed February 10, 2015).

Butler, Bryon. *The Football League, 1888–1988*. London: McDonald Queen Anne Press, 1988.

Butler, Samuel. *The Life and Letters of Dr. Samuel Butler*. London: John Murray, 1896.

Caesar, Julius, and Aulus Hirtius. *Commentarii de Bello Gallico*. Trans. W. A. McDevitte. Project Gutenberg Release #10657.

Cannadine, David. *The Decline and Fall of the British Aristocracy*. New York: Vintage, 1999.

Carew, Richard. *Survey of Cornwall*. Published from the original manuscript by Francis Lord de Dunstanville. J. Faulder New Bond Street and Bees and Curtis, Plymouth. London, 1811; reprint, Rare Books Club, 2012.

Castleden, Rodney. *Minoans: Life in Bronze Age Crete*. New York: Routledge, 1990.

———. *Myceneans*. New York: Routledge, 2005.

Catholic Encyclopaedia. "Shrovetide." http://www.newadvent.org/cathen/13763a.htm

Catton, Bruce. *The Civil War*. New York: American Heritage Books, 2004.

Clark, Gregory. *A Farewell to Alms: A Brief Economic History of the World*. Princeton, NJ: Princeton University Press, 2007.

Cobban, Alfred. *A History of Modern France*. New York: Penguin, 1961.

Coe, Michael D. *The Maya*. London: Thames & Hudson, 1966.

Cooper, Jeremy. *A Fool's Game: The Ancient Tradition of the Haxey Hood*. Haxey, Lincolnshire, UK: Lord & Boggins, 1993.

Court, W. H. B. *A Concise Economic History of Britain*. Cambridge, UK: Cambridge University Press, 1965.

Creasy, Edward S. *Decisive Battles of the World*. Lincoln, NE: Lamb Publishing, 1899.

Cunliffe, Barry. *The Ancient Celts*. New York: Penguin, 1999.

Dardess, John W. *Ming China, 1368–1644: A Concise History of a Resilient Empire*. Lanham, MD: Rowman & Littlefield, 2011.

Donnelly, James S., Jr. *The Great Irish Potato Famine*. Mount Pleasant, SC: History Press 2008.

Drouin, Shawn. *A Beginner's Guide to Harrow Football*, Vol. 1. Costa Mesa, CA: MicJames, 2014.

"Eliot against Basketball; Harvard President Says Rowing and Tennis Are the Only Clean Sports." *New York Times*, November 28 1905. http://query.nytimes.com/gst/abstract. html?res=9C03E1DE1331E733A2575BC2A9679D946797D6CF (accessed March 2, 2015).

Elliott, J. H. *Imperial Spain, 1469–1716*. Harmondsworth, Middlesex, UK: Pelican, 1963.

Elyot, Sir Thomas. *The Book Named the Governour*. Ed. S. E. Lehmburg. 1531; reprint, New York: Dutton, 1963.

Farnsworth, Ed. "First Women's Soccer Team in Philly, 1922." *Philly Soccer Page*, May 8, 2013. http://www.phillysoccerpage.net/2013/05/08/first-womens-soccer-team-in-philly-1922/ (accessed March 2, 2015).

Feiling, Keith. *A History of England: From the Coming of the English to 1918*. London Macmillan, 1950.

Fischer, David Hackett. *Albion's Seed: Four British Folkways in America*. New York: Oxford University Press, 1989.

Fisher, H. A. L. *A History of Europe*. London: Edward Arnold & Co., 1936.

Fitzstephen, William. *A Description of London*. Transcript Henry Thomas Riley, Ed. Liber Custumarum. *Rolls Series* 12, vol. 2 (1860): 2–15.

Foster, R. F. *The Oxford History of Ireland*. Oxford, UK: Oxford University Press, 2001.

Fraser, Antonia. *Cromwell*. New York: Grove Press, 2001.

Gardner, Paul. *The Simplest Game: The Intelligent Fan's Guide to the World of Soccer*. New York: Macmillan, 1976.

Gomme, A. B. *The Traditional Games of England, Scotland, and Ireland*. London: Thames & Hudson, 1984.

Goodman, Nigel. *The Pitkin Guide to Eton College*. London: Pitkin Unichrome Ltd., 1993.

Grant, Michael. *The Rise of the Greeks*. New York: Charles Scribner's Sons, 1987.

Grimal, Nicholas. *A History of Ancient Egypt*. Oxford, UK: Blackwell, 1992.

Guillame, Alfred. *Islam*. Harmondsworth, Middlesex, UK: Pelican, 1954.

Hassall, W. O. *They Saw It Happen: An Anthology of Eyewitness Accounts of Events in British History, 55 BC–1485 AD*. Oxford, UK: Basil Blackwell, 1957.

Haywood, John. *The New Atlas of World History: Global Events at a Glance*. Princeton, NJ: Princeton University Press, 2011.

Heath, James. *Flagellum, or, the Life and Death, Birth and Burial of Oliver Cromwell, the Late Usurper Faithfully Described, with an Exact Account of His Policies and Successes, Not Heretofore Published or Discovered*. 1663; reprint, Charleston, SC: BiblioBazaar, 2011.

Herodotus. *The History*. Trans. Aubrey de Selincourt. New York: Penguin, 1954.

Homer. *The Iliad and The Odyssey*. Trans. Robert Fagles. New York: Viking, 1996.

Hughes, Thomas. *Tom Brown's Schooldays*. New York: Hurst & Co., 1895.

Huizinga, Johan. *The Waning of the Middle Ages: A Study of the Forms of Life, Thought, and Art in France and the Netherlands in the XIVth and XVth Centuries*. New York: Doubleday Anchor, 1954.

Iakovidis, S. E. *Mycenae Epidaurus: Argos-Tisyns-Nauplion.* Athens, Greece: Ekdotike Athenon, 1978.

Jacob, James R. *The Scientific Revolution: Aspirations and Achievements, 1500–1700.* Atlantic Highlands, NJ: Humanities Press International, 1998.

James, Edward. *The Franks.* Oxford, UK: Basil Blackwell, 1991.

Keay, John. *China: A History.* New York: Basic, 2009.

———. *India: A History.* New York: Basic, 2000.

Knox, Father Ronald. *The Miracles of King Henry VI.* New York: Cambridge University Press Archive, 1923.

Lewis, Mark Edward. *The Early Chinese Empires: Qin and Han.* Cambridge, MA: Belknap Press, 2007.

Lichfield, Patrick. *The Illustrated History of Harrow School.* London: Michael Joseph, 1988.

Lysons, Daniel, and Samuel Lysons. *Magna Britannia: The County Palatine of Cheshire.* London: T. Cadell, 1810.

Macquoid, Katharine, Sarah Gadsden, and Thomas Robert Macquoid. *Through Brittany.* 1877; reprint, Charleston, SC: Nabu, 2010.

Malcolmson, Robert W. *Popular Recreations in English Society, 1700–1850.* Cambridge, UK: Cambridge University Press, 1973.

Massie, Robert K. *Dreadnought: Britain, Germany, and the Coming of the Great War.* New York: Random House, 1991.

McEvedy, Colin. *The Penguin Atlas of Ancient History.* New York: Penguin, 1967.

———. *The Penguin Atlas of Mediaeval History.* New York: Penguin, 1969.

———. *The Penguin Atlas of Modern History.* New York: Penguin, 1973.

McPherson, James. *Battle Cry of Freedom: The Civil War Era.* New York: Oxford University Press, 1988.

Miles, Clement A. *Christmas Customs and Traditions: Their History and Significance.* New York: Dover Publications, 2011.

Murray, Bill. *The World's Game: A History of Soccer.* Champaign: University of Illinois Press, 1998.

Neale, J. E. *Queen Elizabeth I.* Harmondsworth, Middlesex, UK: Pelican, 1961.

"Nettie J. Honeyball: The British Ladies Football Club." *Daily Sketch,* February 6, 1895.

Ormerod, George, Daniel King, William Smith, William Webb, and Sir Peter Leycester. *The History of the County Palatine and City of Chester: Compiled from Original Evidences in Public Offices, the Harleian and Cottonian Mss., Parochial Registers, Private Muniments, Unpublished Ms Collections of Successive Cheshire Antiquarians, and a Personal Survey of Every Township in the Count, Incorporated with a Republication of King's Vale Royal and Leycester's Cheshire Antiquities,* Vol. 1. Ed. Thomas Helsby. 1819; reprint, New York: Routledge, 1882.

Owen, Francis. *The Germanic People: Their Origin, Expansion, and Culture.* 1960; reprint, New York: Dorset, 1990.

Owen, Sir George. *The Description of Pembrokeshire, 1603.* Ed. H. Owen. *Cymmrodorion Society Research Series* 1 (1892): 270–82.

Paludan, Ann. *Chronicle of the Chinese Emperors.* London: Thames & Hudson, 1998.

Parker, H. M. D. *The Roman Legions.* New York: Dorset, 1992.

Parker, Matthew. *The Sugar Barons: Family, Corruption, Empire, and War in the West Indies.* London: Hutchinson, 2011.

Parry, J. H. *The Spanish Seaborne Empire.* London: Hutchinson, 1966.

Piggot, Stuart. *The Druids.* London: Thames & Hudson, 1968.

Pincombe, Mike, and Cathy Shrank, eds. *The Oxford Handbook of Tudor Literature, 1485–1603.* Oxford, UK: Oxford University Press, 2009.

Pont, Sally. *Fields of Honor: The Golden Age of College Football and the Men Who Created It.* New York: Harcourt, 2001.

"Recording the History of Rugby Football." *RugbyFootballHistory.com.* http://www.rugbyfootballhistory.com (accessed February 10, 2015).

Riordan, James. *Sport and Physical Education in China.* London: Sport Press, 1999.

Robinson, Cyril E. *History of Rome.* Vester Skerninge, Denmark: Apollo, 1965.

Ross, Ann. *Everyday Life of the Pagan Celts*. New York: G. P. Putnam's Sons, 1970.

Schele, Linda, and David Freidel. *A Forest of Kings: The Untold Story of the Ancient Maya*. New York: William Morrow, 1990.

Sheard, Kenneth, and Eric Dunning. *Barbarians, Gentlemen, and Players: A Sociological Study of the Development of Football*. New York: Routledge, 2005.

Shearman, Montague. *Athletics and Football*. London: Longmans, Green, and Co., 1887.

Stenton, Doris Mary. *English Society in the Early Middle Ages*. Harmondsworth, Middlesex, UK: Pelican, 1951.

Strutt, Joseph. *The Sports and Pastimes of the People of England*. 1801; reprint, Whitefish, MT: Kessinger Publishing, 2007.

Sweet, Waldo E. *Sport and Recreation in Ancient Greece*. New York: Oxford University Press, 1987.

Tate, W. E. *The Enclosure Movement*. New York: Walker, 1967.

Thompson, E. P. *The Making of the English Working Class*. New York: Pantheon, 1964.

Thomson, David. *Europe since Napoleon*. New York: Knopf, 1957.

Thornbury, George Walter, and Edward Valford. *Old and New London: A Narrative of Its History, Its People, and Its Places*. New York: Cassell, Peter, and Galpin, 1872.

Trollope, T. A.. *A Summer in Brittany*. Ed. Frances Trollope. London: H. Colburn, 1840.

Tuathaigh, Gearard O. *Ireland before the Famine, 1798–1848*. Dublin, Ireland: Gill & Macmillan, 2007.

Wallerstein, Immanuel. *Historical Capitalism*. London: Verso, 1983.

Watterson, John Sayle. *College Football: History, Spectacle, Controversy*. Baltimore, MD: Johns Hopkins University Press, 2000.

Webster, Graham, and Donald R. Dudley. *The Roman Conquest of Britain*. London: Pan Books, 1965.

Williamson, David J. *Belles of the Ball: The Early History of Women's Soccer*. Devon, UK: R&D Associates, 1991.

Willughby, Francis. *Francis Willughby's Book of Games: A Seventeenth-Century Treatise on Sports, Games, and Pastimes*. Burlington, VT; Ashgate, 2003.

Wood, Michael. *In Search of the Dark Ages*. New York: Facts on File, 1987.

INDEX

ABOUT THE AUTHOR

Christopher Rowley is best known as a science fiction and fantasy author (*The War for Eternity, Starhammer, Bazil Broketail, Pleasure Model*, etc.). He lives in the Hudson Valley, New York, with his wife Anitra.

He has also nurtured a keen interest in "football" from an early age.

Born to an English father and an American mother, he started out in the United States, reached the point where baseball cards became fascinating, and then moved to England, where cricket replaced baseball. Due to parental wanderings—England, Canada, and England again—he was aware by age 12 that "football" meant several different things.

Indeed, the first professional football match he saw was the 1956 FA Cup Final, in which Manchester City defeated Birmingham City, 3–1. The next professional football game he saw involved the Hamilton Tiger Cats and the Montreal Alouettes in the Canadian Football League. Having learned the rudiments of soccer, he now learned the basics of the Canadian style of football.

Then, in 1958, while living in Montreal, he saw the championship game for the National Football League in the United States, courtesy of Channel 5 in Plattsburgh, New York. A young eye, honed on the ways of Canadian football, immediately noted the differences in the American game, especially the narrowness of the field of play.

Back in England in the 1960s, Rowley encountered school rugby, and, of course, soccer, both as player and observer. He witnessed the artistry of George Best, one of the greatest soccer players of all time; saw England win the World Cup; and had close brushes with the violent world of London's warring soccer tribes. Running down Cold Blow Lane with the fans of Millwall FC in pursuit is an experience not easily forgotten.

In New York in the late 1970s, he began watching the New York Giants and Jets on television, as tickets were not available, and saw a good coach elevate the Giants, year by year, into a Super Bowl champion. His wife hails from Oklahoma, which inevitably drew him into the world of college football and its rivalries. At the same time, Rowley managed to get into Giants Stadium to see the New York Cosmos overpower weak opponents with the likes of Pele and Franz Beckenbauer in their ranks.

In the 1980s, living in New York City, he watched one World Cup entirely on Spanish-language television and then saw FIFA's global tournament slowly work its way into the American consciousness. Soccer and, to a lesser extent, rugby were visible on playing fields throughout Long Island and New Jersey, and at some point it was sure to break out culturally into the national consciousness. Next came the 1994 World Cup, hosted in the United States, and the game began to do just that. The 1999 Women's World Cup added another layer to the cake, although Rowley was not surprised by the quality of play. He'd become aware of the U.S. Women's National Team in the early 1990s and was already familiar with the team of Akers, Foudy, Chastain, Hamm, Lilly, and the rest.

At the same time, satellite television sprouted new channels, bringing Australian rules football, European soccer, and even rugby, both union and league, into Rowley's living room. He watched much of the 2003 Rugby World Cup, which ended with England's nail-biting victory over Australia, and marveled at both the technology involved and the improvement in that game since it had become fully professional.

This input, along with comments from Americans concerning the nature and origins of "football," spurred a search for a book on the subject. How did "football" begin and where? At that time there was no concise, single-volume book on the topic. This set off the research that has resulted in this book, which endeavors to show how it all began, how it almost didn't survive, how it mutated into different forms, and how it spread throughout the world.